'I buy this piece of ground here'

AN ITALIAN MARKET-GARDENER COMMUNITY
IN ADELAIDE, 1920s–1970s

'I buy this piece of ground here'

AN ITALIAN MARKET-GARDENER COMMUNITY IN ADELAIDE, 1920s–1970s

MADELEINE REGAN

ANU PRESS

BIOGRAPHY SERIES

For

Johnny Marchioro (1940–2023), dear friend, market gardener and mentor who lives in these pages

Katherine (Kass) Healy (1955–2023), dear friend, poet and reading companion who encouraged my writing

ANU PRESS

Published by ANU Press
The Australian National University
Canberra ACT 2600, Australia
Email: anupress@anu.edu.au

Available to download for free at press.anu.edu.au

ISBN (print): 9781760466695
ISBN (online): 9781760466701

WorldCat (print): 1484386745
WorldCat (online): 1484387531

DOI: 10.22459/IBPGH.2025

This title is published under a Creative Commons Attribution-NonCommercial-NoDerivatives 4.0 International (CC BY-NC-ND 4.0) licence.

The full licence terms are available at creativecommons.org/licenses/by-nc-nd/4.0/legalcode

Cover design and layout by ANU Press. Cover photograph: Costantina and Giovanni Santin, Valetta Road, Lockleys, mid 1940s. Photo supplied by Christine Rebellato nee Mattiazzo.

The Biography Series is an initiative of the National Centre of Biography at The Australian National University, ncb.anu.edu.au.

This book is published under the aegis of the Biography editorial board of ANU Press.

This edition © 2025 ANU Press

Contents

List of illustrations	ix
Acknowledgements	xv
1. Building a group biography	1
2. Beginnings in Adelaide	29
3. Attachment to land	67
4. Family life and labour	97
5. Life within the community	129
6. Community in times of crisis	171
7. Pathways: The 1.5 and second generations	197
8. Transforming the *paese*	227
9. Conclusion: Continuity of the *paese*	259
Bibliography	281
Index	297

List of illustrations

Maps

Map 1.1: Johnny Marchioro's mud map drawn in 2007	5
Map 1.2: Map of the western and south-western suburbs of Adelaide, early to mid-1930s	11
Map 2.1: The provinces of the Veneto region	32
Map 3.1: Map drawn by Lino Ballestrin showing Veneto and other market gardeners in the Lockleys area, 1940s–50s	78
Map 8.1: Detail of street directory marked with names of some Veneto market gardeners	234

Plates

Plate 1.1: Adrian Tonellato, Frogmore Road, c. 1951	1
Plate 1.2: Angelo Innocente testing alcohol content for his wine, Lockleys, March 2010	3
Plate 1.3: Pine half-case belonging to Giancarlo (Johnny) and Eleonora Marchioro	4
Plate 1.4: Veneto market gardeners' exhibition, Findon, South Australia, August 2011	14
Plate 1.5: Angelina and Vittorio Marchioro, c. 1937	17
Plate 1.6: Ermenegilda Simeoni listens to her oral history interview, Riese Pio X, Italy, October 2018	21
Plate 2.1: Bruna Zampin at far right with, from left, Angelina Marchioro, Amelia Zampin nee Shaw (Bruna's mother), Maria Ballestrin and Angelina Compostella, Adelaide, c. 1955	30

Plate 2.2: Veneto families and *paesani*, Lockleys, mid-1940s   33

Plate 2.3: The Rossetto family, Bigolino, Italy, c. 1918   35

Plate 2.4: Vittorio Marchioro's landing papers, December 1927, which include
the name and address of his brother Francesco   41

Plate 2.5: Isidoro Ballestrin's Italian passport, 1927   44

Plate 2.6: Isidoro Ballestrin's work registration card, issued four months after
his arrival in Adelaide   45

Plate 2.7: Attilio and Serafina De Pieri and other workers, Caruso mica mine,
Central Australia, 1941   46

Plate 2.8: Aerial photo of the Lockleys area, late 1950s   49

Plate 2.9: Margherita and Francesco Marchioro with their first two daughters,
Lina and Mary, Adelaide, c. 1927   53

Plate 2.10: Giovanni Santin pours drinks for his own and others' children who
had recently arrived from Italy, at Lockleys, December 1935   54

Plate 2.11: The Ballestrin family: Cesira and Giuseppe, with children Norma
and Lino, Adelaide, c. 1943–44   56

Plate 2.12: The formal photo of Lina Bordin's proxy marriage, Bigolino,
Italy, 1930   59

Plate 2.13: Angelina and Vittorio Marchioro's official wedding photo,
Adelaide, 1938   61

Plate 2.14: Amelia Zampin nee Shaw and Silvano Zampin, Adelaide,
mid-1930s   63

Plate 2.15: The marriage of Eugenio Zalunardo and Luigia Ballestrin,
Adelaide, 1943   65

Plate 3.1: Lino Tonellato, Adelaide, 2014   68

Plate 3.2: Angelina and Secondo Tonellato outside the house where the
Tonellato family grew up, in Caselle di Altivole, Italy, 1962   70

Plate 3.3: Aerial photo showing the approximate location of the Veneto
market gardens, 1935   73

Plate 3.4: Gelindo, Lina and Romeo Rossetto, Lockleys, c. 1932   75

Plate 3.5: The Tonellato *vagòn*, Lockleys, 1935   76

Plate 3.6: Gelindo Rossetto's letter to the attorney-general requesting early
consideration of his application to buy land for his market garden,
13 August 1942   83

LIST OF ILLUSTRATIONS

Plate 3.7: Gelindo Rossetto at the Spotted Tiger mica mine, Northern Territory, 1930s — 87

Plate 3.8: The Ballestrin families preparing celery for sale at market, Flinders Park, late 1950s — 93

Plate 3.9: The Zampin family, Lockleys, c. 1954 — 95

Plate 4.1: Giancarlo (Johnny) Marchioro and his father, Vittorio, tending tomatoes in a glasshouse, Bolivar, 1976 — 98

Plate 4.2: Romildo Santin, Valetta Road, early 1940s — 100

Plate 4.3: Luigina Zalunardo nee Ballestrin with Noemi and Maria Gina Ballestrin nee Andreazza with Dolfina, c. 1947, take time off from the market gardens to care for their babies — 105

Plate 4.4: The Ballestrin family: Narcisio, Lina, Maria, Jimmy and, in front, Silvano and Norina, Flinders Park, c. 1959 — 107

Plate 4.5: The marriage of Vito Santin and Anna Mattiazzo, Adelaide, 1949 — 110

Plate 4.6: Mary, Connie and Lina Marchioro, Adelaide, c. 1946 — 113

Plate 4.7: Norma Ballestrin on the family property, Hartley Road, c. 1956 — 114

Plate 4.8: An independent young woman with her Zundap scooter: Maria Rosa Tormena, Adelaide, c. 1953 — 118

Plate 4.9: The marriage of Arturo Semola and Sandra Zampin, Lockleys, 1966 — 124

Plate 4.10: A group of young Veneto men in front of the Santin house, 1962 — 126

Plate 5.1: Assunta Tonellato and her uncle Secondo Tonellato, Frogmore Road, c. 1952 — 130

Plate 5.2: Emilio Mattiazzo in his butcher's shop, City of Adelaide, 1940s — 134

Plate 5.3: The baptism of Louis Ballestrin, Hartley Road, c. 1951 — 136

Plate 5.4: A group of Veneto women with Irene Destro, Frogmore Road, c. 1946 — 137

Plate 5.5: Baptism of Peter Zampin, Adelaide, c. 1953 — 139

Plate 5.6: Pietro and Alberto Berno, Valetta Road, early 1960s — 143

Plate 5.7: Group of Veneto families, St Kilda, early 1950s — 146

Plate 5.8: Confirmation party for Robert Berno and John Torresan, Berno packing shed, Lockleys, 1959 — 147

Plate 5.9: Veneto group the day after Anna Mattiazzo and Vito Santin's wedding, Lockleys, 1949 — 149

Plate 5.10: Maria Berno and daughter Lucy with cousins Diana and Marisa Berno, Glenelg Beach, Adelaide, c. 1962 — 150

Plate 5.11: Ermenegildo Ballestrin unloading grapes for making wine, Flinders Park, late 1950s — 153

Plate 5.12: Peter Rebellato and his father-in-law, Oscar Mattiazzo, deboning stockfish for *baccalà*, West Lakes, Adelaide, 2009 — 155

Plate 5.13: Maria and Narciso Ballestrin and their daughter Norina are farewelled on their first return visit to Italy by friends and family among the crowds at Outer Harbour, Adelaide, 1965 — 159

Plate 5.14: Veneto market-gardener family picnic, Morialta Falls, Adelaide, early 1950s — 168

Plate 6.1: The Tormena family: Johnny and Maria Rosa, at back, with Severina and Galliano, Adelaide, 1940s — 172

Plate 6.2: Excerpt from 'Report from Commonwealth Attorney-General's Department in Recommendation for Ministerial Warrant for Restriction or Detention under Regulations 25 & 26 of National Security (General) Regulations' — 177

Plate 6.3: Lina and Gelindo Rossetto with three of their children, from left, Aldo, Romeo and Lena, Adelaide, c. 1937 — 181

Plate 6.4: Angelina (holding Romano), Vittorio and Johnny Marchioro, Frogmore Road, late 1942 — 184

Plate 6.5: Letter written by Antonio Ballestrin to explain his reasons for not serving with the Civil Aliens Corps in 1944 — 187

Plate 6.6: Report by a military official in Adelaide of an interview with Walter Reid about Giosue Zoanetti, 4 May 1943 — 191

Plate 7.1: Romano Marchioro, Lake Eppalock, Victoria, 2013 — 198

Plate 7.2: Three generations of the Santin family, Bolivar, 1985: Alan and his father, Romildo, and Aaron, son of Dean Santin, and Dean Santin — 204

Plate 7.3: Costantina Santin and grandson Alan, Frogmore Road, c. 1961 — 206

Plate 7.4: Vittorio Marchioro on his lettuce block, Lockleys, mid-1960s — 210

Plate 7.5: The Tonellato family, Adelaide, c. 1947. Back: Lui, Orlando, Rosina, Lino and Albert. Front: Secondo, Assunta and Elisabetta — 212

Plate 7.6: Three generations of the Tonellato family, Frogmore Road, 1962 — 213

Plate 7.7: The Piovesan brothers, Nillo, Bruno and Dino, Adelaide, c. 1945 — 216

LIST OF ILLUSTRATIONS

Plate 7.8: Noemi, Renato and Eugenio Zalunardo and Amalia Bernardi, Grange Road, c. 1965 — 219

Plate 7.9: Italia and Lui Tonellato with children Luciana and Adrian, Frogmore Road, 1962 — 220

Plate 7.10: Johnny Marchioro tending tomatoes in his backyard, Nailsworth, Adelaide, March 2023 — 224

Plate 8.1: Berno siblings: Diana, Remo and Robert, Valetta Road, c. 1964 — 228

Plate 8.2: Sunday afternoon *bocce* group, Santin market garden, Frogmore Road, 1962 — 239

Plate 8.3: Silvano Zampin tending tomatoes, Findon, late 1970s — 243

Plate 8.4: The Mazzarolo family: Lina, Sonia, Maria and Arsenio, Frogmore Road, c. 1972 — 248

Plate 8.5: Amelia and Silvano Zampin celebrate their fiftieth wedding anniversary at the Veneto Club, Beverley, 1981 — 253

Plate 8.6: Example of a family biography page on the Veneto Market Gardeners 1927 website — 256

Plate 9.1: Giuseppe Chiumento and his wife, Monica Urbani, Malo, Italy, 2018 — 260

Plate 9.2: Children of the Ballestrin, Marchioro, Piovesan and Tonellato families in front of the Tonellato truck, Frogmore Road, c. 1946–47 — 264

Plate 9.3: Group of Veneto families on one of the market gardens, early 1950s — 265

Plate 9.4: Baptism of Remo Berno, Adelaide, 1953 — 266

Plate 9.5: Representatives of first-generation market-gardener families at a gathering, Seaton, South Australia, 22 October 2022 — 268

Plate 9.6: Members of the Ballestrin family: Jacqueline and Simon Ballestrin with Ariana, Louis Ballestrin, Michelle Ballestrin and Fay Ballestrin with Archie Ballestrin-Egan, Castelfranco Veneto, Italy, 2017 — 270

Plate 9.7: Vito Rebuli and Antonietta Danieli, Monte Grappa War Memorial, province of Treviso, Italy, 1962 — 272

Plate 9.8: Marriage of Teresa Zampin and Lui Mazzarolo, Adelaide, 1965 — 274

Plate 9.9: Amanda Rossetto making a presentation at a Veneto market-gardener families and friends gathering, Seaton, South Australia, 22 October 2022 — 277

Plate 9.10: The names of Veneto market gardeners in the *paese* at Lockleys as featured in the design of a commemorative tea towel, 2019 — 278

Acknowledgements

This book is the result of 17 years of exploration and research, and I am thankful to the many people who have been part of my endeavour to record the history of the Veneto market-gardener community at Lockleys. It began with the market gardeners, and I acknowledge all the women and men in Adelaide and the Veneto region of Italy who generously agreed to be interviewed and provide family photos for the Veneto market gardeners' oral history project. I have learned so much about market gardening and the experience of migration in their families and I am so pleased to have made good friends in the Veneto community.

My friend Aida Innocente introduced me to the first contacts in the Veneto community of market gardeners in Adelaide in 2007 and I appreciate her continued interest. I am grateful to Johnny and Eleonora Marchioro for welcoming me into their lives and the world of market gardening and introducing me to narrators whose stories are recorded in this book. I have valued their friendship and continued enthusiasm for the research and the discoveries.

Thank you to Viv Szekeres, former director of the Migration Museum in Adelaide, who recommended that I speak with June Edwards, then archivist at the State Library of South Australia, in 2007. June encouraged me to record interviews and document an unknown history of migration and settlement in Adelaide's western suburbs. I am grateful for the assistance with oral history recordings of staff at the State Library of South Australia over so many years: archivists June Edwards, Tonia Bradstreet, Enid Woodley and Sally Stephenson and audio engineers Silver Moon, Peter Kolomitsev and Andrea Hensing-Matto.

The book began life beyond the community as my PhD thesis at Flinders University. I thank Diana Glenn and Daniela Cosmini for guidance with early research. Christine Winter and Prudence Flowers gave me the confidence to work with the historical themes and interviews with members of market-gardener families to produce my thesis and I am grateful for their supervision and encouragement to publish the book. I thank also the examiners of my thesis, Professor Frank Bongiorno and Professor Lorenzo Veracini, for suggesting that I publish it. I am so appreciative for the encouragement and support my brother, Anthony Regan gave me.

When Ian Halkett asked me in 2015 if I would be interested in having him as a mentor and reader of my thesis, neither of us foresaw the enormous and sustained commitment he made in reading all my work and providing me with new ways of thinking and writing. I appreciate the enduring assistance from Michael Campbell, friend and technological expert, who helped with technical issues and the formatting of photos. I am grateful to Duncan Campbell who produced the audio clips at the beginning of each chapter. I thank the many friends and relatives who have supported me and shown interest in the evolution of the oral history project to book. Thank you to readers Alex Bennett, Geoff Gray, Ian Halkett, Kass Healy, Anthony Regan and Jane Swift.

Thank you to the people who have assisted with research at the National Archives of Australia. I am grateful to relatives of Veneto friends I have made in Adelaide who helped me in the parish archives and municipal record offices in the Veneto region in 2018. Thank you, in particular, to Giuliano Berdusco and also to Irene Zampin who helped with interviews.

I have appreciated the guidance and advice given by Melanie Nolan, the support of the staff at ANU Press, and thank you to Jan Borrie for copyediting and indexing. I am grateful to Alex Bennett, my dearest companion, for all the ways he has generously assisted and shared in the development of the project and enabled me to complete this history.

1
Building a group biography

So, a lot of them, whoever helped, helped each other, started working in the market garden and some of them decided why not? This sounds alright … And it was a very small community then, everybody knew each other and became friends because even in Italy where they come from, it was all very close as well.

—Adrian Tonellato, 2016[1]

Plate 1.1: Adrian Tonellato, Frogmore Road, c. 1951
Source: Photo supplied by Assunta Giovannini nee Tonellato.

---

1   Adrian Tonellato interviewed by Madeleine Regan, Transcript, J.D. Somerville Oral History Collection, State Library of South Australia, Adelaide, OH 872/35, 30 January 2016: 54.

'I BUY THIS PIECE OF GROUND HERE'

The history of a small, disparate group of migrants from the north-east of Italy who arrived in Australia in the late 1920s begins with a box. The simple pine box, known as a half-case, was the artefact that led me to research a cohort of Veneto migrants who became market gardeners on the western plains of Adelaide in the interwar years. The half-case, used by market gardeners to transport and sell their tomatoes at the market, was critical to the commercial sustainability of the migrant community.

The half-case is a compelling material object and a symbol for the group biography of 19 Italians. Seventeen single men and a married couple with an infant arrived without resources, plans or prospects and, within 10 years, had established a self-reliant community in the peri-agricultural area between the city and the sea. They had migrated from eight villages in two different provinces in the Veneto region and not all had known each other before migration. However, they had in common their origins as *contadini* (peasant farmers) and shared the experience of poverty and the devastation of their villages during World War I. After their arrival in Adelaide, they confronted the uncertainty and unemployment that characterised the Great Depression. Yet, during the 1930s, the *veneti* gradually recognised the opportunity to lease agricultural land 8 kilometres west of Adelaide City, within comfortable reach of the wholesale fruit and vegetable market. They drew on their shared skills as peasant farmers to live and work in the market gardens and create a community that was like a small *paese* (village), which sustained their families and subsequent Veneto arrivals for more than five decades.

I was drawn to explore the biography of the small community through a deep interest in, and curiosity about, Italian migrants and market gardens in the western suburbs of Adelaide. An opportunity to develop an understanding of the community and the context of market gardening was made through a connection to an elderly Italian man, Angelo Innocente, the father of a friend, Aida, who had manufactured pine half-cases for vegetable growers. Angelo and his wife, Elsa, collected the pine from a mill about 60 kilometres from Adelaide and processed it at the small factory near their home, making up to 1,000 boxes a day. At the end of each working day, Angelo delivered the half-cases to market gardeners in the western suburbs and the agricultural area north of Adelaide.

Plate 1.2: Angelo Innocente testing alcohol content for his wine, Lockleys, March 2010

Source: Madeleine Regan.

Angelo Innocente migrated to Australia in 1950 from a small village in the province of Treviso and was part of the wider Veneto community in Adelaide that included the first generation of Veneto market gardeners. I was interested in his role in supplying half-cases to cohorts of Italian, Bulgarian and Greek market gardeners in the Adelaide metropolitan area who contributed to commercial food production until the use of pine was superseded by new materials.

In 2007 I encountered the box again when I met Johnny and Eleonora Marchioro, who were commercial market gardeners at Bolivar, about 20 kilometres north of Adelaide.[2] The Innocente and Marchioro families had been close neighbours, and a godparent relationship strengthened the bonds when Aida Innocente was born in 1956. Johnny had grown up and worked in his parents' market garden at Lockleys, which is now a suburb of Adelaide. In 1965 he married Eleonora Ottanelli and they moved to Bolivar and worked together to establish their own market garden. Johnny's

---

2   Johnny Marchioro is formally known as Giancarlo Marchioro.

father had migrated from the Veneto between the wars and developed market gardens adjoining other Veneto families in the 1930s in a locality that the community named Lockleys. From the 1950s, most Veneto market gardeners bought the boxes manufactured by the Innocente family to sell tomatoes and celery at the market. The Marchioro family has retained a few half-cases as material reminders of, and symbolic links to, Johnny and Eleonora, who carried on the market-gardening tradition of the first generation and embodied the *contadino* heritage. The half-case is a tangible object that signifies the belonging and continuity of a migrant family's cultural practice as market gardeners.[3]

Plate 1.3: Pine half-case belonging to Giancarlo (Johnny) and Eleonora Marchioro
Source: Alex Bennett.

---

3   See Ilaria Vanni Accarigi, 'Transcultural Objects, Transcultural Homes', in *Reimagining Home in the 21st Century*, eds Justine Lloyd and Ellie Vasta (Cheltenham: Edward Elgar Publishing, 2017), 192–206, at 193–94.

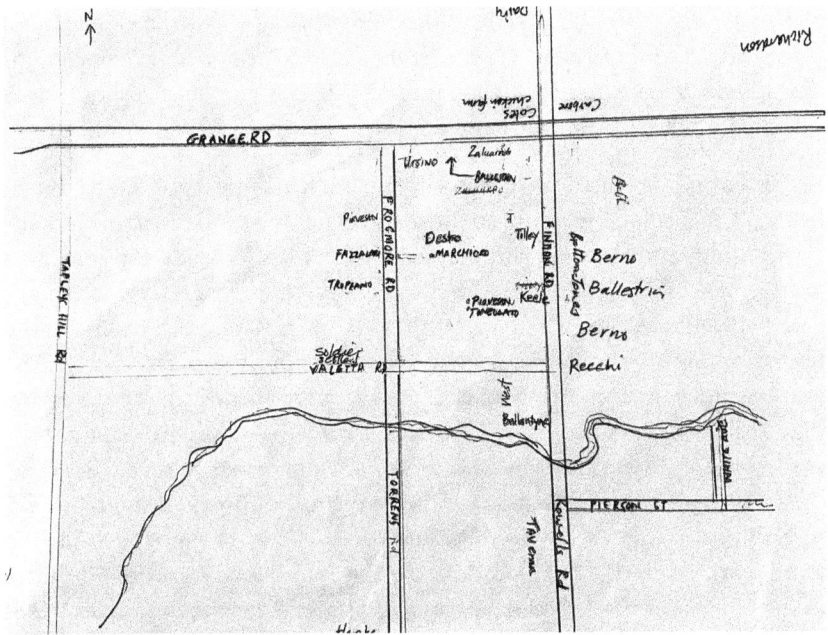

Map 1.1: Johnny Marchioro's mud map drawn in 2007

Note: Names of market gardeners including Anglo-Australian families are identified on the map as well as the locations of farms, roads and the River Torrens.

Source: Johnny Marchioro

A second object that drew me into the history of the Veneto market gardeners was a mud map drawn by Johnny Marchioro in 2007 as he told me about growing up on the market gardens at Frogmore Road. To illustrate the neighbourhood, Johnny identified Italian (and some Anglo-Australian) families who worked market gardens in the western suburbs close to the River Torrens—the most reliable source of water on the Adelaide Plains—and who lived on their properties within a radius of about 3 kilometres.

Through the map I learned about a place in the western suburbs that was new to me because, by 2007, the area had long been a densely populated inner suburb with no evidence of the previous intensive agricultural activity. Johnny also described the first-generation community of Veneto market gardeners who had made a living on the land and shared a heritage that linked back to the traditions of the Veneto region. Between the wars, the market gardeners in the Lockleys area were a blend of people with different origins who worked and lived on their properties of variable dimensions. The group included Italian families from different regions, returned World War I servicemen who had been granted soldier-settler blocks, other Anglo-Australians who had orchards and a few dairy farmers.

As I followed my interest in interviewing Angelo Innocente, I was drawn in the first instance to learn about his experience of manufacturing half-cases and his connections with market gardeners in Adelaide and imagined it as a one-off opportunity. I was aware of the first generation of Italians who had migrated to Australia after the war and began reading some of the migration histories to gain a context for this period.[4] However, I realised a new possibility after meeting Johnny and Eleonora and hearing from Johnny that he had maintained close friendships with the sons and daughters of market-gardener families whose fathers had migrated from the Veneto in the 1920s. I became conscious of a more complex history of migrants and market gardening in the western suburbs of Adelaide through the mud map that identified families, the locations of their farms, roads and other features in the context of the 1930s, 1940s and 1950s. It led me to examine a wider context of Australian migration history and consider the literature about Italian migration before World War II and issues relating to the experience of Italian communities.

Historiography

The migration and settlement of southern European migrants after World War II have been the primary focus of Australian migration history rather than interwar arrival and settlement. Early demographic research analysed the arrival and settlement of southern Europeans between the wars and provided context for the development of Italian communities in different parts of Australia.[5] The limitations of the early literature on migration between the wars became obvious when I realised that it comprised essentially

---

4 For examples of general historical perspectives of Italian migration to Australia, see: Robert D. Pascoe, *Buongiorno Australia: Our Italian Heritage* (Melbourne: Greenhouse Publications, 1987); Julia Church, *Per l'Australia: The Story of Italian Migration* (Melbourne: Miegunyah Press, 2005). For a text focused on the migration of Italians to South Australia, see: Desmond O'Connor, *No Need to be Afraid: Italian Settlers in South Australia between 1839 and the Second World War* (Adelaide: Wakefield Press, 1996).

5 Charles A. Price, *Southern Europeans in Australia* (Melbourne: Oxford University Press, 1963); Wilfrid David Borrie, *Italians and Germans in Australia: A Study of Assimilation* (Melbourne: Cheshire, 1954). An earlier text provided a sharply racist study of Italians (and other non-British groups) within the context of the White Australia policy: Jens Lyng, *Non-Britishers in Australia: Influence on Population and Progress* (Melbourne: Melbourne University Press, 1935 [1927]).

census and other official records rather than accounts of the settlement and development of communities and the experience of migration that were more relevant for my study.[6] However, Price was influential in articulating issues related to chain migration and understanding how migrants from southern Europe, including Italians, chose to settle in Australia and develop close settlements before the war.[7] Other early studies into the concentration of migrant groups, including Italians who settled in certain areas of Australia, were helpful for their examination of the relationship between chain migration and population clusters.[8]

The analysis of the post-Federation period—including the racist environment that was intensified by the Depression, the development of fascism, the crisis of World War II and the shadow cast on Italians by their designation as 'enemy aliens'—provides a background for recognising the experience of Italian migrants before the period of mass migration and the development of multiculturalism. Through Cresciani's scholarship, I gained an understanding of the history of Italian migration and settlement in Australia and the correlation with modern Italian history.[9] Other Italian diaspora accounts taken from a sociological perspective address issues related to identity, intergenerational transmission of ethnicity and what it means to be Italian Australian. For example, Marino's focus on Calabrian families in Adelaide examines differences between three generations and the formation of their distinctive identities.[10]

---

6   This is a point also made by Simone Marino, 'Thrown into the World: The Shift between Pavlova and Pasta in the Ethnic Identity of Australians Originating from Italy', *Journal of Sociology* 57, no. 2 (2021): 231–48, doi.org/10.1177/1440783319888283, at 235.
7   Price, *Southern Europeans in Australia*, 107–12; Charles A. Price, 'Southern Europeans in Australia: Problems of Assimilation', *International Migration Review* 2, no. 3 (1968): 3–26, doi.org/10.1177/019791836800200301.
8   Frank Lancaster Jones, 'The Territorial Composition of Italian Emigration to Australia, 1876 to 1962', *International Migration* 2, no. 2 (1964): 247–65, doi.org/10.1111/j.1468-2435.1964.tb00632.x; Frank Lancaster Jones, 'Ethnic Concentration and Assimilation: An Australian Case Study', *Social Forces* 45, no. 3 (1967): 412–23, doi.org/10.2307/2575200.
9   Gianfranco Cresciani, *The Italians in Australia* (Cambridge, UK: Cambridge University Press, 2003).
10 Simone Marino, *Intergenerational Ethnic Identity Construction and Transmission among Italian-Australians: Absence, Ambivalence and Revival* (Cham, Switzerland: Palgrave Macmillan, 2020), doi.org/10.1007/978-3-030-48145-2; Marino, 'Thrown into the World'.

The complexity of migration history in Australia must consider the dispossession of Aboriginal and Torres Strait Islander peoples of their land and their fatal interactions with Anglo-Celtic settlers, southern Europeans and other migrants. The racist practices legitimised by the White Australia policy followed in the shadow of earlier controls on the Indigenous population. These complexities persist today and are addressed by various scholars.[11] Ricatti focuses on the issue of racism in Australia in the context of Italian migration. He cites the internal Italian racism that manifests as a discrimination between northern and southern Italian people and asserts that migration history in Australia and the experience of Italian migrants must be examined in the context of a settler-colonial nation.[12]

In terms of the settlement of Italians in South Australia, O'Connor's text provides a context for understanding the experience from the foundations of the colony up to World War II.[13] Another study that was useful in relation to the context of Italian migrants in Adelaide examines the residential and commercial locations of Italian communities in the postwar years, many of which had existed before World War II.[14]

Accounts of Italian regional or provincial communities that had migrated to South Australia from the nineteenth century included first-person accounts and provided a perspective of change in those settlements. The earliest study

---

11 Francesco Ricatti, *Italians in Australia: History, Memory, Identity* (Cham, Switzerland: Springer International, 2018), doi.org/10.1007/978-3-319-78873-9; Francesco Ricatti, 'The Emotion of Truth and the Racial Uncanny: Aborigines and Sicilians in Australia', *Cultural Studies Review* 19, no. 2 (2013): 125–49, doi.org/10.5130/csr.v19i2.2839; Helen Andreoni, 'Olive or White? The Colour of Italians in Australia', *Journal of Australian Studies* 27, no. 7 (2003): 81–92, doi.org/10.1080/14443050309387853; Catherine Dewhirst, 'Collaborating on Whiteness: Representing Italians in Early White Australia', *Journal of Australian Studies* 32, no. 1 (2008): 33–49, doi.org/10.1080/14443050801993800; Joseph Pugliese, 'Migrant Heritage in an Indigenous Context: For a Decolonizing Migrant Historiography', *Journal of Intercultural Studies* 23, no. 1 (2002): 5–18, doi.org/10.1080/07256860220122368, at 6–18; Anna Haebich, *Spinning the Dream: Assimilation in Australia 1950–1970* (Fremantle: Fremantle Press, 2008).
12 Ricatti, *Italians in Australia*, 66–71. See also Ruth Balint and Zora Simic, 'Histories of Migrants and Refugees in Australia', *Australian Historical Studies* 49, no. 3 (2018): 378–409, doi.org/10.1080/1031461X.2018.1479438, at 378–86; Anna Green, 'Intergenerational Family History and Historical Consciousness', in *Contemplating Historical Consciousness: Notes from the Field*, eds Anna Clark and Carla L. Peck (New York: Berghahn Books, 2019), 200–11, doi.org/10.2307/j.ctvw04bhk.19, at 208–9; Lorenzo Veracini, 'On Settlerness', *Borderlands* 10, no. 1 (2011): 1–17; Jayne Persian and Karen Agutter, 'European Post-War Migrants and Indigenous Australians: A History in Fragments', *History Australia* 18, no. 1 (2021): 112–29, doi.org/10.1080/14490854.2021.1878912.
13 O'Connor, *No Need to be Afraid*.
14 See Angela A. Alessi, 'Reimagining Italian Spaces: *La Fiamma* as a Lens to Explore the Development of the Italian Community in Adelaide, South Australia, between 1947 and 1963', in *Voices of Challenge in Australia's Migrant and Minority Press*, eds Catherine Dewhirst and Richard Scully (Cham, Switzerland: Palgrave Macmillan, 2021), 107–25, doi.org/10.1007/978-3-030-67330-7_6.

of a regional group in South Australia explores the development of the fisher community from Molfetta in the region of Puglia and considers the issue of assimilation of families in the city of Port Pirie over time with a comparison of settlers from northern Italy.[15] The value of this study is the focus on an Italian community that developed over time through a single occupation, which was useful in terms of comparing the Port Pirie fishers with the Veneto market gardeners to understand the influence of occupation on the formation of an Italian community between the wars. Chronological narratives of settlement and detailed histories of Italian communities from single villages commissioned by provincial organisations offer detailed histories of settlement in South Australia.[16] These studies reference the small numbers who migrated before World War II; however, the main focus is on the narratives of much larger post–World War II Italian communities in Adelaide.

Studies that cover the presence of Veneto migrants in Australia include a general history and microhistories that examine distinctive geographical settlements. The general approach is illustrated by Baldassar and Pesman, who examine the experience of emigration as a way of being in the lives of Veneto people and trace their history and experience of settlement in various parts of Australia before 1940.[17]

Local studies of the settlement of Veneto migrants in the interwar years in states other than South Australia explain that chain migration was a factor in the clustered rural settlements of *veneti*.[18] Veneto groups in

---

15 J.E. Bromley, 'The Italians of Port Pirie' (MA thesis, The Australian National University, Canberra, 1955).

16 See, for example, Daniela Cosmini-Rose and Desmond O'Connor, *Caulonia in the Heart: The Settlement in Australia of Migrants from a Southern Italian Town* (Adelaide: Lythrum Press, 2008); Don Longo, ed., *Terra Lasci, Terra Trovi: From Molinara to Adelaide—The History of a Southern Italian Community in South Australia 1927–2007* (Adelaide: Molinara Social and Sports Club Inc. and Lythrum Press, 2010); Antonio Mercurio and Angela Scarino, *We Left: Narratives of the Sangiorgesi in South Australia = E Partimmo: Narrazioni die Sangiorgesi del Sud Australia* (Adelaide: San Giorgio la Molara Community Centre, 2004); Michael Peter Corrieri, *Italians of Port Pirie: A Social History* (Port Pirie: Our Lady of Martyrs, Port Pirie Italian Community, 1992).

17 Loretta Baldassar and Ros Pesman, *From Paesani to Global Italians: Veneto Migrants in Australia* (Perth: University of Western Australia Press, 2005). Rosoli argues that migration was a common feature in the lives of the *veneti*, who accounted for nearly 12 per cent of all Italian emigrants between the 1870s and the 1970s (in Baldassar and Pesman, p. 22).

18 See Annamaria Davine, *Vegnimo da Conco Ma Simo Veneti: A Study of the Immigration and Settlement of the Veneti in Central and West Gippsland 1925–1970* (Melbourne: Italian Australian Institute, La Trobe University, 2006); Diana Ruzzene Grollo, *Cooper's Creek Gippsland: The Trevisani* (Melbourne: Mure, 2004); Rina Huber, *From Pasta to Pavlova: A Comparative Study of Italian Settlers in Sydney and Griffith* (Brisbane: University of Queensland Press, 1977); Lesley Jenkins, *Power of the Land: A Social History of Italian Settlement in Lismore* (Mullumbimby: L. Jenkins, 1993).

Victoria and New South Wales settled in rural regions generally through chain migration and worked in a range of occupations including as wage-earners. In contrast, the Veneto market gardeners in Adelaide formed their distinctive community mostly through post-migration relationships. There are few studies of Veneto migrants in South Australia, however, the analysis of Veneto clubs and associations in South Australia before and after World War II gives an insight into the cultural and entrepreneurial inclinations of *veneti* from the period between the wars.[19] The Veneto Club Inc., Adelaide, was established in 1974 and has published three books that record the genesis, formation and operations of the club.[20]

I considered the importance of 'place' and 'belonging' in the context of migration in Australia and the ways that migrants, and Italian migrants in particular, create a sense of belonging through place.[21] For example, Pascoe discusses the importance of placemaking and the development of community for Italians and argues that the opportunity to set themselves up in a particular place creates the possibilities for establishing their identity in Australia.[22]

In contrast to the groups who settled in the same location through chain migration, not all of those in the Veneto cohort were known to each other and they made the choice post-arrival to follow one-by-one to the area where they could cultivate the land with the companionship of others from the Veneto.

---

19   Desmond O'Connor, 'Club e Associazioni dei Veneti nel South Australia [Clubs and Associations of the Venetians in South Australia]', in *Veneti d'Australia*, eds Luciano Segafreddo and Ilma Martinuzzi O'Brien (Ravenna, Italy: Angelo Longo Editore, 2005), 177–87.
20   Veneto Club Adelaide Inc., *In 84 Domeniche nasce il Veneto Club: Ricordi, Appunti e Riflessioni sugli Eventi dal 1971 al 1974* [*The Veneto Club was Born in 84 Sundays: Memories, Notes and Reflections on Events from 1971 to 1974*]; *Veneto Club 25th Anniversary, 1974–1999* (Adelaide: Veneto Club Adelaide Inc., n.d.); Veneto Club with assistance from Madeleine Regan, *History of the Veneto Club Inc., Adelaide 1974-2024*, Veneto Club Inc., Adelaide, Openbook Howden Print and Design, Adelaide, 2024.
21   Robert Pascoe, 'Place and Community: The Construction of an Italo-Australian Space', in *Australia's Italians: Culture and Community in a Changing Society*, eds Stephen Castles, Caroline Alcorso, Gaetano Rando, and Ellie Vasta (Sydney: Allen & Unwin, 1992), 85–97. For discussion of 'emplacement' as a physical and emotional state that involves the processes of belonging as they adapt to their new country, see Ricatti, *Italians in Australia*, 37–39.
22   Pascoe, 'Place and Community'.

1. BUILDING A GROUP BIOGRAPHY

Map 1.2: Map of the western and south-western suburbs of Adelaide, early to mid-1930s

Note: The approximate location of the Veneto market gardens, then known as St James Park, is highlighted, 8 kilometres west of the City of Adelaide.

Source: City of Charles Sturt, reproduced with permission.

I was influenced by a question asked by Canadian oral historian Alexander Freund about the use of oral history to understand the experience of migration: 'Why not ask immigrants and their descendants themselves if we want to find [out] about their experience of migration, settlement and integration?'[23] Learning about the group of first-generation market gardeners led me to document the history of the Veneto families and community through oral history interviews.[24] After beginning the interviews, I soon became aware of my position as an outsider.[25] My early attempts were tentative because, as a fifth-generation Irish-Australian woman, I did not have the experience of what it meant to be an Italian Australian and I was considerably younger than most of the 'narrators', several of whom were born in the 1920s.[26] At the time, I did not know much about market gardens and the history of primary production in South Australia. While I felt the limitations of being an outsider, I also understood the advantages of not being a community member, which included being detached from personalities and context and the opportunity to learn from narratives rather than taking knowledge for granted as an insider.

---

23   Alexander Freund, *Oral History and Ethnic History*, Immigration and Ethnicity in Canada Series Booklet No. 32 (Ottawa: Canadian Historical Association, 2014), 24.
24   Sixty-five oral history interviews and more than 140 hours of recordings of interviews for the Italian market-gardener project have been deposited in a series in the J.D. Somerville Oral History Collection in the State Library of South Australia (OH 872) since 2008. They include recordings by two other interviewers. The library's 'Conditions of Use Form for Oral History Interviews' specifies joint ownership of the copyright with the person who is interviewed and with the library. This includes the right to use the interview in different circumstances. In allowing the interview to be made available to the public, the narrator can place restrictions on its use.
25   An issue examined by several oral historians—see, for example: Paul Thompson and Joanna Bornat, *The Voice of the Past: Oral History*, 4th edn (Oxford: Oxford University Press, 2017), 211–12; Amy Tooth Murphy, 'Listening In, Listening Out: Intersubjectivity and the Impact of Insider and Outsider Status in Oral History Interviews', *Oral History* 48, no. 1 (2020): 35–44; Louise Ryan, 'Inside and Outside of What or Where? Researching Migration through Multi-Positionalities', *Forum, Qualitative Social Research* 16, no. 2 (2015).
26   I use the word 'narrators' to describe the people interviewed for this project in preference to 'interviewees'. 'Narrator' assigns more authority and agency to the person telling their story in an oral history interview.

Early steps: Documenting the history of the market gardeners

My early aims were 'documentary in intent', which Linda Shopes contends is a starting point in a community oral history project.[27] However, she encourages oral historians to go beyond and explore the significance of what narrators recall about the events or historical periods that they recount in their interviews. Through the combination of oral histories, archival materials from Australia and Italy and published records of the interwar years, the group biography bridges intimate and national histories of migration.[28]

Like Shopes, other oral history scholars argue for critical engagement when undertaking a community project and defining its purpose. This approach includes considering the selection of a range of narrators and the imperative to address the context of historical periods related to the narrators' accounts. They caution against compiling a simple celebratory document about the past using oral history interviews.[29] I asked narrators to remember the past through their experiences of being a member of a Veneto family who had commenced working market gardens in the period between the wars. The initial focus of the project was on gathering recollections of the place and the physical environment at Lockleys in which the Veneto group lived and worked. The scope of the project expanded when I formed a 'reference group' with Johnny Marchioro and two other narrators whose fathers were first-generation market gardeners.[30] They suggested new candidates for interviews, and we discussed the themes that arose from the interviews and reflected on the information in the narratives, which resulted in an

---

27 Linda Shopes, '"Insights and Oversights": Reflections on the Documentary Traditions and the Theoretical Turn in Oral History', *The Oral History Review* 41, no. 2 (2014): 257–68, doi.org/10.1093/ohr/ohu035, at 260.
28 Anna Clark, 'Private Lives, Public History: Navigating Australian Historical Consciousness', in *Contemplating Historical Consciousness: Notes from the Field*, eds Anna Clark and Carla L. Peck (New York: Berghahn Books, 2019), 113–24, doi.org/10.2307/j.ctvw04bhk.13.
29 See, for example, Lynn Abrams, *Oral History Theory* (London: Routledge, 2010), doi.org/10.4324/9780203849033, 153–74; Joanna Bornat, 'Two Oral Histories: Valuing Our Difference', *The Oral History Review* 21, no. 1 (1993), 73–95, doi.org/10.1093/ohr/21.1.73; Thompson and Bornat, *The Voice of the Past*, 21–22, 286–97; Alistair Thomson, 'Oral History and Community History in Britain: Persona and Critical Reflections on Twenty-Five Years of Continuity and Change', *Oral History* 36, no. 1 (2008): 95–104; Linda Shopes, 'Oral History and the Study of Communities: Problems, Paradoxes and Possibilities', *The Journal of American History* 89, no. 2 (2002): 588–98, doi.org/10.2307/3092177.
30 The group, including the wives of the narrators, evolved over several years. The three men assisted with public presentations about the history of the Veneto market-gardener community.

exhibition in 2011 that we organised with support from the local council and a grant from Multicultural SA. The collaboration progressed and became a community oral history project that continued to develop far beyond the formal research phase.[31]

Plate 1.4: Veneto market gardeners' exhibition, Findon, South Australia, August 2011
Note: Seated, from left to right: Angelo Innocente, Mary Tonellato nee Zoanetti, Guido Rebuli, Aldo Rossetto and Nina Quaresima nee Fazzalari.
Source: Di Kidd.

In the reference group, we began to generate a form of historical consciousness about the Veneto market gardeners and the community at Lockleys. Anna Green identifies three elements of orientation in intergenerational family projects that build historical consciousness: temporal, moral and place or physical environment.[32] The interviews incorporated the element of time—the evidence of continuity and change over the years in the market gardens

---

31   See Michael Frisch, *A Shared Authority: Essays on the Craft and Meaning of Oral and Public History* (Albany: State University of New York, 1990); Linda Shopes, 'Oral History and the Study of Communities'; Thompson and Bornat, *The Voice of the Past*, 360–72; Abrams, *Oral History Theory*, 158–59; Katherine Fobear, 'Do You Understand? Unsettling Authority in Feminist Oral History', *Journal of Feminist Scholarship* 10, no. 10 (2016): 61–77, at 74–75.
32   Green, 'Intergenerational Family History and Historical Consciousness'.

at Lockleys. The issue of morality was addressed in questions about the observance of the Catholic faith and *contadino* values of hard work and compliance with family structures. All narrators recalled the place and the physical environment through their accounts of work on the family market garden. In the group biography, a fourth dimension of orientation has been added because narrators spoke about Lockleys as more than a physical place that was emotionally significant.[33] They attributed to Lockleys the meaning of a community, a network of *paesani* (villagers) that had enduring significance over three generations. There are limitations to intergenerational oral history projects that are evident in the group biography of the Veneto market gardeners because it was not viable to have an even spread of narrators representing each generation.

Three generations of voices

I learned about three distinct generations in the Veneto market-gardener community. Those in the first generation were aged between 17 and 41 years when they arrived in Australia. Some were married and had left their wives and children in Italy until they gathered sufficient resources to bring them to Adelaide.[34] Others married after arrival and one man in the first generation remained single. A second level, the '1.5 generation', was new to me because I had previously understood that the Veneto migrants had formed two generations: those who were born in Italy and those born in Adelaide. The 1.5 generation describes children up to the age of late adolescence who migrated in the company of their parents.[35] Sons and daughters born in Australia to parents in the first generation or in the 1.5 generation form the second generation. The voices of the narrators are differentiated and communicate experience in distinct periods in the three generations from the late 1920s to the present.

In an oral history study of a group of first-generation Campanian migrants who settled in Adelaide after World War II, participants were able to provide pre-migration and post-migration accounts of their lives.

---

33 ibid., 208.
34 It was a common migration practice for lone men to arrive first; the wives and children followed them and then elderly parents often joined the family unit. See Price, *Southern Europeans in Australia*, 112–13.
35 Ruben G. Rumbaut, 'Ages, Life Stages, and Generational Cohorts: Decomposing the Immigrant First and Second Generations in the United States', *International Migration Review* 38, no. 3 (2004): 1160–205, doi.org/10.1111/j.1747-7379.2004.tb00232.x.

Recording first-generation narratives of migration provides benefits for understanding the circumstances of life in villages in Italy in contrast with settlement in Australia and evidence of 'the multiple and complex ways that transnational migration reconfigures an individual's sense of belonging, family networking, formation of social bonds and enactment of community cultural traditions'.[36] Documentation of observations, reflection and emotion in the life before migration and the experience of settlement are particular to the first generation.

For me, it was too late to meet any of the first generation as they had already died, so I recorded memories of family life through their children, in both the 1.5 and the second generations.[37] However, the unexpected discovery of interviews recorded in 1984 with a first-generation couple, Vittorio and Angelina Marchioro, was a beneficial addition to the spoken history of the community.[38] Listening to the two Marchioro interviews provides a basis for understanding the experience of Italian migrants between the wars, the role of parents and the imperative of building a future for their children in Australia.

Vittorio and Angelina were in their seventies when interviewed, and they reflected on the hardship, or *la miseria*, they endured in Italy, living in poor farming households that had been disrupted by World War I, where it was common to send even young children away to employment to contribute to the family economy. The respective accounts of their early existence in Australia illustrate the desperation of poverty for Vittorio, who was without regular work for several years before he partnered with his brother and sister-in-law to lease land for market gardens at Lockleys. Angelina Marchioro's memories of her first years as a proxy bride when she knew no one else in Adelaide reflect the loneliness and sorrow of leaving her family to marry an unknown man in Australia and begin a new life.

---

36   Diana Glenn, 'Writing Campanian Lives: Considerations of Transnational Identity and Belonging', *Forum Italicum* 47, no. 1 (2013): 150–66, doi.org/10.1177/0014585813478924, at 151.
37   Between 2017 and 2024, 20 narrators—a mix of 1.5 and second generations—died.
38   Vittorio and Angelina Marchioro recorded interviews in 1984 with Michael Tsounis for the Migrant Oral History Project (Social History Museums), deposited in the J.D. Somerville Collection, State Library of South Australia, Adelaide, OH 12/1. I coincidentally discovered the interviews when I was well into my research.

Plate 1.5: Angelina and Vittorio Marchioro, c. 1937

Note: The images were taken separately — Angelina in Malo, Italy, and Vittorio in Adelaide — before their proxy marriage.

Source: Photo supplied by Johnny Marchioro.

In their interviews, Vittorio and Angelina assert their happiness as elderly migrants, settled comfortably in Australia 50 years after arrival, and their appreciation of the security and wellbeing of their two sons, daughters-in-law and grandchildren residing in Adelaide. They also express contentment in being among *paesani* and living on the land they had bought for their market garden more than three decades previously. Angelina explained her sense of equilibrium: 'We got Italian people all around from there down the street, my house is in the middle of the garden.'[39] At the end of the interview, Angelina summarised their lives in Adelaide: 'Everything going better and better.'[40]

Marino's study of Calabrian-Australians living in Adelaide extends to three generations: those who arrived as migrants after World War II, their children and their grandchildren, who were born in Adelaide.[41] Marino analyses the differences in perceptions of the ethnicity of the three generations, contrasting the challenges for the first cohort with the experiences of their children, who feel they live a conflicted life between two worlds: the family and the environment beyond, like school. This finding reflects

---

39 Angelina Marchioro interviewed by Madeleine Regan, Transcript, J.D. Somerville Oral History Collection, State Library of South Australia, Adelaide, OH 12, 13 March 1984: 11.
40 ibid., 18.
41 Marino, *Intergenerational Ethnic Identity Construction*.

that of an early study of second-generation Italian Australians by Vasta, who emphasised that the formation of identity can be complex because of competing influences from family and the world beyond the culture of the home.[42] Further, the category of the second generation is often a 'subjective' definition because of multiple identities that individuals may embody as a result of family migration and, in Australia, the influence of multiculturalism.[43] Those in the second generation are the recipients of the family enculturation of ethnicity even as they negotiate the environment of school, peer group and working life.[44] In his study, Marino reports a marked distinction with the grandchildren, the third generation, who have been shaped by different interactions and a more inclusive experience of schooling that could be linked to a more multicultural context. The third generation experiences a positive feeling of ethnicity expressed as pride in their sense of being Calabrian-Italian in Australia.[45]

The voices of the 1.5 generation are neglected in most migration studies because this cohort is not considered to have agency in the decision to migrate and their authority to speak is therefore not so valued. Yet, the 1.5 generation bridges the experiences of a child in a migrant family in the home of origin with the experiences as an adult in the new country.[46] In this study, the voices of the elderly 1.5-generation narrators nuance the experience of migration because they speak of their origins and some provide memories of their childhood in fascist Italy. They also reflect on their coming of age during World War II in Adelaide when Italy and Australia were enemies, and the narrators describe their working lives as adults—most of them as market gardeners. Echoing the research of Rumbaut, I found that the experiences of most of the 1.5 generation were closer to those of the

---

42   Ellie Vasta, 'The Second Generation', in *Australia's Italians: Culture and Community in a Changing Society*, eds Stephen Castles, Caroline Alcorso, Gaetano Rando, and Ellie Vasta (Sydney: Allen & Unwin, 1992), 155–56. For a study of gender and development of sexuality in a group of second-generation Italian Australian young people in Perth, see also Loretta Baldassar, 'Marias and Marriage: Ethnicity, Gender and Sexuality among Italo-Australian Youth in Perth', *Journal of Sociology* 35, no. 1 (1999): 1–22, doi.org/10.1177/144078339903500101, at 1–20.
43   Zlatko Skrbis, Loretta Baldassar, and Scott Poynting, 'Introduction—Negotiating Belonging: Migration and Generations', *Journal of Intercultural Studies* 28, no. 3 (2007): 261–69, doi.org/10.1080/07256860701429691, at 262–63.
44   Emanuela Sala and Loretta Baldassar, 'Time to Revisit the Family in Italian-Australian Studies: Charting a Way Forward', *Flinders University Languages Group Online Review* 5, no. 2 (2017): 6–7.
45   Marino, *Intergenerational Ethnic Identity Construction*, 103–40.
46   The experience of the child migrant 'being in between "two cultures"' is captured in a study in which the author reflects on the loss of what and who was left behind in England when her parents settled their family in Adelaide in the late 1960s. There is emphasis on the child's lack of agency in the family's decision to migrate. See Annmarie Reid, 'Ella's Clippy Mat: Progging the Memories of Migrants from England's North East' (PhD diss., University of South Australia, Adelaide, 2015), 362–63.

first generation than of the cohort born in Australia because of their direct link to, and memories of, the home country.[47] In the Veneto families, sons and daughters in the 1.5 generation assisted their parents in the market gardens before they married, bought their own properties and maintained market gardening as a livelihood in the same locality.[48] The configuration of the 1.5 generation living close to their parents reflects the intimacy of generations who shared households in the Veneto region.

A span of 26 years explains the differences in experience and memories within the second generation. Some who were born in the late 1920s or during the 1930s had memories of their parents when the market-gardener community was young. For example, Lina Rismondo nee Marchioro, born in Adelaide in 1927—the year that 15 of the Veneto market gardeners arrived—could remember lone men who met socially at the place where Angelo Piovesan and Secondo Tonellato were neighbours on Frogmore Road. Lina was six or seven years old when she witnessed early social gatherings, and her memories evoke the practice of Veneto traditions and customs that provided comfort for the new migrants. She recalled the frequent occasions that drew the men together when her mother was the only woman in that small cluster of *veneti*:

> At least twice a week the men would go there of a night-time and Mum would be roasting some chestnuts and the men would be singing, and that was lovely. I can still hear them singing … and I know there was seven … and there was another, Mr Atto Rossetto, he used to come from the city to come down and spend the evening with these men, you know, they were all bachelors, and they all knew each other … Oh, the singing was beautiful. I can still hear them singing. I feel as though I can remember them all standing out with their arms around each other's shoulders, you know, singing away [laughs] … [M]y mother was the only woman.[49]

Lina's memory of the early group of Veneto men singing songs from their childhood and her mother's role in creating the intimate domestic activities provides an insight into the nostalgia of those men, who nurtured strong emotional bonds to their origins and the families they had left behind. The image of roasting chestnuts is a transnational marker of a food tradition

---

47 See Rumbaut ('Ages, Life Stages, and Generational Cohorts', 1167), who refined the category of adolescents aged between 13 and 17 years as a '1.25 generation'.
48 This was also the case for most of the 1.5-generation women who worked with their husbands on the market gardens.
49 Adelina Rismondo nee Marchioro interviewed by Madeleine Regan, Transcript, J.D. Somerville Oral History Collection, State Library of South Australia, Adelaide, OH 872/9, 9 June 2010: 8–9.

and an example of domestic material culture brought to Australia by the first generation. It is possible to appreciate the group of men savouring the familiar sensory experience of the smell and taste of roasted chestnuts and associating it with their memories of the Veneto and the comfort of sharing seasonal food in the company of family.[50] When Lina refers to 'bachelors', she includes the lone men who had arrived without wives. Later in the interview, she gives details of the men who had been married in Italy and those who married after settling in Adelaide.

On the other hand, those second-generation narrators who grew up in the 1950s and 1960s recalled a community that had existed for more than 20 years, with established patterns of working life and social interactions. By the time the second generation formed memories, the *paesani*— the people in the close network of *veneti* at Lockleys—had established themselves as market gardeners, lived through the war years in Adelaide and incorporated a younger generation of Veneto migrants who arrived in Australia after the war.

Memory and connections to the first generation

Contrasting the themes in the interviews recorded with the two members of the first generation with those of the 1.5- and second-generation narrators, I was alerted to the emotional reframing of intergenerational memory. Children of the first generation were familiar with the experiences of their parents as disadvantaged migrants and the progression to successful small business owners, and some transmitted the memories of challenges their parents faced. It was helpful to understand the concept of inherited memory within families developed by memory studies scholar Marianne Hirsch. Her research refers to memories formed by the children of those who survived the Holocaust and who 'remembered' through the stories their parents told the images or behaviours that originated beyond their own experience and that became 'postmemory'.[51]

---

50   Olivia Hamilton, 'Senses of Home', in *Reimagining Home in the 21st Century*, eds Justine Lloyd and Ellie Vasta (Cheltenham: Edward Elgar Publishing, 2017), 179–91, doi.org/10.4337/9781786432933. 00021, at 183–84.
51   Marianne Hirsch, *The Generation of Postmemory: Writing and Visual Culture after the Holocaust* (New York: Columbia University Press, 2012); Marianne Hirsch, 'The Generation of Postmemory', *Poetics Today* 29, no. 1 (2008): 103–28, doi.org/10.1215/03335372-2007-019.

In the context of 'postmemory', the second generation undertakes the role of transmitting memory as an intergenerational task. The descendants of the first generation of the Veneto market gardeners, the 1.5- and second-generation narrators, recall their childhood and convey a strong connection to the circumstances of their parents' lives. They also recall the experience of their fathers and mothers, who endured the fragmentation of family through migration, the early years of marginalisation and hardship in the Depression and the challenges of establishing themselves in a new country.

Plate 1.6: Ermenegilda Simeoni listens to her oral history interview, Riese Pio X, Italy, October 2018
Source: Madeleine Regan.

The voices of the first, 1.5 and second generations bring together individual memories and create a communal account of the experience of migration and settlement of the market-gardener families at Lockleys. They articulate the experiences of their families working their new land, bartering for glasshouses, selling vegetables at the market, celebrating in packing sheds and establishing a stable community within an often politically hostile and economically challenging new world. These experiences of family and community life created emotional responses in the narrators. There is nostalgia for some in recalling the origins of the first generation, emotional connections to other families, the rituals of working the market gardens and the celebrations and structures that held the community together as a *paese* at Lockleys. The descriptions of the 1.5 and second generations reflect the post-settlement experience: work and community within the identity of the family—an area of Italian Australian and migration research studies that has been under-researched.[52]

Narrators often express nostalgia for a lost life and regret that the first-generation men and women are no longer alive and the community they had known no longer exists.[53] The past is idealised and the *paese* is associated with security, order and the companionship of *paesani* or people who came from the same or similar villages in the Veneto and shared the *contadino* heritage. The image of home with links between place, family and community conveys 'a sense of belonging … an apparently comforting bounded enclosure'.[54] It was this sense of belonging that the Veneto market gardeners created in their families on their respective landholdings and within their close-knit community at Lockleys. Marino identifies the same experience of belonging created by Italian regional groups in Adelaide because of their social and economic needs. He asserts that they built

---

52 See Sala and Baldassar, 'Time to Revisit the Family in Italian-Australian Studies'; Alexandra Dellios, '"It Was Just You and Your Child": Single Migrant Mothers, Generational Storytelling and Australia's Migrant Heritage', *Memory Studies* 13, no. 4 (2018): 586–600, doi.org/10.1177/1750698017750000.
53 For discussion of memory and imagination, see Michael Janover, 'Nostalgias', *Critical Horizons* 1, no. 1 (2000): 113–33, doi.org/10.1163/156851600510453. For nostalgia and the experience of Italian migrants, see Robert Orsi, 'The Fault of Memory: "Southern Italy" in the Imagination of Immigrants and the Lives of their Children in Italian Harlem, 1920–1945', *Journal of Family History* 15, no. 1 (1990): 133–47, doi.org/10.1177/036319909001500108; and Anne-Marie Fortier, 'Re-Membering Places and the Performance of Belonging(s)', *Theory, Culture & Society* 16, no. 2 (1999): 41–64, doi.org/10.1177/02632769922050548.
54 Doreen Massey, 'A Place Called Home', in *The Doreen Massey Reader*, eds Brett Christophers, Rebecca Lave, Jamie Peck, and Marion Werner (Newcastle upon Tyne: Agenda Publishing Limited, 2018), 1701–172.

'a sense of "common place", where *paesani* have continued to live closely with one another, drawing imagined boundaries through the maintenance of their social relations'.⁵⁵

A bridge between the past and the present

After gathering 27 interviews with the 1.5- and second-generation narrators, and knowing that oral history recordings often end up sitting on archive shelves, I looked for additional ways to broaden access to the project for a larger audience.⁵⁶ In 2014, I received funding to create a website to incorporate the sound files of the growing number of interviews, transcripts, family photos, maps and other documents that represent family and community memories of the market gardens.⁵⁷ The website has become a link between the past and the present for the descendants of the Veneto market gardeners. In place of the physical market gardens, there is a virtual point of reference where the descendants can access an archive of memories in recordings of oral history interviews and images of working and cultural lives and the *paese* created by the community at Lockleys.

The website facilitates the expression of a strong emotional attachment to the place where the community had its origins in Adelaide. It transmits the history of the Veneto families as migrants, market gardeners and memory-makers. Second-generation family members are the main contributors to the website, seeing it as a valuable way to share family and community histories, and community members report listening to interviews recorded by other narrators and looking at other features, especially the family photographs.

Building a group biography

My approach to examining the Veneto market gardeners at Lockleys is through a fine-grained group biography that examines family and community life. Barbara Caine argues that group or collective biographies are useful means of focusing on a cohort such as an ethnic group whose lives

---
55 Marino, *Intergenerational Ethnic Identity Construction*, 9.
56 Luisa Del Giudice, 'Italian-American Oral History and Its Digitized Sites', *Italian American Review* 3, no. 2 (2013): 154–65, doi.org/10.5406/italamerrevi.3.2.0154.
57 I received a Cultural Heritage Grant from the City of Charles Sturt for the design and implementation of the website, which was launched in May 2014. See: www.venetimarketgardeners1927.net.

are on the margins of previous historical writing.[58] Group biography enables an examination of the dynamics of race, gender and class within a given period. The documentation of the Veneto community, the market gardens and the *paese* provides evidence of family lives, changes in the physical work involved in market gardening, the significance of land, the impact of World War II on individual families and the formation of a community that developed bonds as proxy relationships for the families left behind in the Veneto region.

The formation of a migrant community

The group biography incorporates the pre-migration and post-migration circumstances of the Veneto market-gardener families. This book explores the regional identity of a group of Veneto migrants who shared a single occupation as market gardeners, lived close to each other and developed a *paese* between the wars. The Veneto market-gardener community is distinctive because it was not formed through chain migration, which was the usual pattern of migration and settlement of Italians and other southern Europeans in Australia from the nineteenth century.[59] The Veneto group formed their *paese* with the social and emotional benefits of a small, harmonious community and did not establish an institutional, organisational centre. There was no Italian church, community hall, Italian shop or *osteria* (neighbourhood bar) in Lockleys in the 1940s and 1950s. The families formed their own network and maintained their self-reliance without having to relinquish their identity to Anglo-Australian culture.

The history of the Veneto group departs from other Italian migration studies in Australia in its close examination of a distinct community whose members remained market gardeners in the same location in Adelaide from the interwar years to more than five decades later. This book documents the Veneto market-gardener community from their arrival in Australia in the late 1920s to the sale of the market gardens in the 1960s and 1970s. The following eight chapters form a chronology that reveals the experience of the community over that period. Chapter 2 describes the circumstances in the early years after the Veneto migrants arrived in Australia and outlines the trajectory of the men, from transient working lives in the Depression to their

---

58 Barbara Caine, *Biography and History*, 2nd edn (London: Red Globe Press, 2019), 2–3.
59 For a definition and depiction of types of chain migration, see Price, *Southern Europeans in Australia*, 107–12; Lancaster Jones, 'Ethnic Concentration and Assimilation'.

role as market gardeners. It provides an overview of the strategies they used to achieve stability through reunions with wives and children or taking the step to marry and form nuclear family households. Chapter 3 explores the ways that the Veneto market gardeners adapted the *contadino* imperative to occupy and cultivate land and begin the process of establishing themselves and achieving *sistemazione* (the process of settling and establishing themselves in a new country). This included taking opportunities to negotiate the land-tenure system in South Australia and eventually becoming landowners, in the 1950s.

In Chapters 4 and 5, the focus is the cohesion of the market-gardener community and the desire to maintain the boundaries of the *paese* at Lockleys. Chapter 4 explores the creation of the family labour unit, changes in gendered roles and the separate positions of the 1.5 and second generations in the structures of the market gardens. Chapter 5 examines the everyday lives of the Veneto market gardeners and the significance of proxy family relationships that assisted intergenerational connections for the second generation. It also examines interactions outside the *paese*, including the influence of the Catholic Church.

Both Chapter 6 and Chapter 7 examine changes that tested the community. Chapter 6 investigates the impact of the war years and the imposition of regulations after Italians became 'enemy aliens'. It describes some of the challenges the community confronted and acknowledges the strength and sense of belonging held in the *paese*. In Chapter 7, the differences between the first, 1.5 and second generations are explored in relation to the *contadino* heritage. The discontinuity is most obvious among the second generation, who took pathways away from the market gardens.

Chapter 8 develops the theme of change and explores the transformations that occurred in the *paese* of the Veneto market gardeners. The gardens were imbued with significance because of the strong network of *paesani* established by the first generation. The connections continued into the 1.5 and second generations and a virtual dimension of the *paese* has been formed through the existence of the website.

Chapter 9 considers the distinctive aspects of the Veneto market-gardener *paese* and illustrates the ways in which the second and third generations have held the market gardens as the heart of the history of the Veneto community even after nine decades. The continuity extends to descendants who live in Italy and maintain connections to the market gardens and the community through virtual means.

Images from family photograph albums in the following chapters convey a sense of intimacy in the portraits of individuals and groups and in the activities that were part of the daily lives of the market-gardener households. The photographs capture the presence of generations in the *paese* and offer a material record of the existence of the market-gardener community.

Framing the history of the Veneto market gardeners

Oral history interviews with descendants of the first-generation Veneto market gardeners illuminate the experience of families who faced the Depression, fascism, World War II and the racialised environment of the White Australia policy era. The Veneto families encountered postwar adjustments when large numbers of non-British migrants, including Italians escaping war-affected Italy, arrived and were welcomed in the *paese*. The first generation endured practices of assimilation in the implementation of Australian immigration policies.[60] They also witnessed and participated in the hopeful new direction of multiculturalism and its more inclusive environment that offered migrant groups greater visibility through the formation and government support of 'ethnic' associations. Withstanding discrimination and marginalisation in the first decades after settlement at Lockleys, the community prospered and created a sense of belonging and identity on, and through, their market gardens.

Attachment to the land is an important thread in the group biography of the community of Veneto market gardeners and their descendants. The narrators ascribe three meanings to the association of the market gardens with the formation of a new kind of community or new form of *paese*. First, the market gardens represent the land that became the economic foundation for the families and their place of permanent settlement. The second meaning relates to their identity as cultivators of the land, which connected the first generation of Veneto men and women to their *contadino* heritage in the Veneto, where, for most, it was impossible to own land because of historical structural impediments to proprietorship. The third

---

60 Paul Sendziuk and Robert Foster, *A History of South Australia* (Cambridge: Cambridge University Press, 2018), doi.org/10.1017/9781139196352, 152–53; Gwenda Tavan, 'The Dismantling of the White Australia Policy: Elite Conspiracy or Will of the Australian People', *Australian Journal of Political Science* 39, no. 1 (2004): 109–25, doi.org/10.1080/1036114042000205678.

meaning provided by the narrators enables them to reconstruct the market gardens as a space that transcended the physical and became an emotional and social site of attachment.

A new strand of migration history

The pine box and mud map that prompted my research are symbolic and material features threaded throughout the following chapters. The half-case symbolises the shared occupation of the Veneto market gardeners and their use of land. The mud map contextualises the location of the physical and relational *paese* at Lockleys. The individual and collective biographies of the Veneto families are woven into the narrative through the quotations from oral histories. The website features in the group biography as a transnational archive that preserves and develops the continuity of the community's history.

The market gardens enabled the self-contained community to build a new identity and their attachment to the land represented an economic and emotional anchor for their settlement and flourishing in Australia. The group biography of a homogeneous, family engaged migrant group demonstrates the initiative, unity and vision that can enable an immigrant community to flourish and integrate into Australian society over three generations. This intergenerational history of market gardeners at the fringe of urban space raises new questions in migration history in Australia about the role of place in adjustment processes, resilience and belonging.

2
Beginnings in Adelaide

Well, they were a pretty poor family and I think like everybody else, just wanted to make a new life and some of them migrated and hoped for the best when they got here. But conditions weren't the best. They had to take any job that was available at the time because I think it was around the Depression time, so they just took what work they could.

—Bruna Semola nee Zampin, 2016[1]

Bruna Semola nee Zampin confirms that her father, who arrived in Adelaide as a 17-year-old in 1928, was from a poor Veneto family—the second son to migrate to Australia. However, she acknowledges the 'new life' was not better than the old one. After arrival in Adelaide, the first generation faced the challenges of the Depression, unemployment, racism and the uncertainty of existence in Australia, competing for what little work was available in the late 1920s and early 1930s. Within 12 years, they were confronted with the impact of their classification as 'enemy aliens' during World War II.

---

1 Bruna Semola nee Zampin interviewed by Madeleine Regan, Transcript, J.D. Somerville Collection, State Library of South Australia, Adelaide, OH 872/39, 8 November 2016: 3–4.

Plate 2.1: Bruna Zampin at far right with, from left, Angelina Marchioro, Amelia Zampin nee Shaw (Bruna's mother), Maria Ballestrin and Angelina Compostella, Adelaide, c. 1955
Source: Photo supplied by Zampin family.

The restrictions of Australia's immigration policy, with its focus on homogeneity, impeded acceptance of non-British 'aliens' in the difficult economic period during which Silvano Zampin and other *veneti* struggled to exist in the early years.[2] They were forced to find work in rural locations in South Australia, Victoria and Queensland. The early migrants endured separation from family and home in Italy and tolerated the impact of the Depression in Australia alone, without resources, including the English language.

The first generation arrived without education or skills that might have made it possible to occupy jobs in industry or trades or even in the catering roles that many Greek migrants accepted between the wars.[3] The Veneto migrants had no safety net in terms of income, accommodation or emotional support. They made the transition from an ordered life in an intergenerational household as *contadini* (peasant farmers) in the Veneto region to the peripatetic life of labourers in their first years in Australia.

---

2   See Gwenda Tavan, *The Long, Slow Death of White Australia* (Melbourne: Scribe Publications, 2005). For discussion of Italian migrants in South Australia in the 1920s, see O'Connor, *No Need to be Afraid*, 93–108.
3   See Price, *Southern Europeans in Australia*, 159–62.

The first generation of the Veneto market gardeners were intent on achieving *sistemazione*, the process of settling and establishing themselves in a new country. As individuals, they wanted to find a measure of security before they could establish their families. *Sistemazione* was a primary goal for Italian migrants in adult life and provided the motivation to become independent through marriage, own a home and raise a family.[4]

From the Veneto to Lockleys

The first generation of the Veneto market gardeners—the 19 adults who arrived in Adelaide—comprised two main groups: married men who had left wives and children in Italy and single men. Among the cohort was a young married couple with an infant. For all but one man, who did not marry, the key strategies of *sistemazione* included earning an income and finding stable accommodation. The men who arrived alone realised that family reunion or marriage were foundations for remaining permanently in Australia.

The Veneto market gardeners were not a homogeneous group of Italian migrants. They originated from villages in eight different *comuni* (municipal areas) in the Veneto.[5] The two most distant were about 50 kilometres apart—a considerable distance in the days of travel by horse and cart. In addition to the various locations of origin, the differences in age and marital status of the cohort on arrival indicate the diversity of their life experiences, although all were from *contadino* families who had worked the land for generations. In her study of contemporary migrant families in market-gardening businesses in outer Sydney, Sarah James explains that networks develop through their shared occupation as market gardeners despite not having a 'pre-migration' relationship.[6]

---

4 See Loretta Baldassar, *Visits Home: Migration Experiences between Italy and Australia* (Melbourne: Melbourne University Press, 2001), 40–42, 160–67, 183–84; Ricatti, *Italians in Australia*, 36–37.
5 In the province of Treviso, the *comuni* were Altivole, Castelcucco, Ponzano Veneto, Riese, Vallà and Valdobbiadene. In the province of Vicenza, the *comuni* were Malo and Monte di Malo.
6 Sarah James, *Farming on the Fringe: Peri-Urban Agriculture, Cultural Diversity and Sustainability in Sydney* (Cham, Switzerland: Springer, 2016), doi.org/10.1007/978-3-319-32235-3, 162.

'I BUY THIS PIECE OF GROUND HERE'

Map 2.1: The provinces of the Veneto region

Note: Most of the Veneto market gardeners came from the province of Treviso and three originated in Vicenza.

Source: Wikimedia Commons (commons.wikimedia.org/wiki/File:Map_of_region_of_ Veneto,_Italy,_with_provinces-it.svg).

The migration and settlement patterns of the Veneto cohort diverge from the model of chain migration documented in many histories of migrants. The *veneti* did not follow the practice in which relatives or friends from the same village were 'called' by one of their own who had met with some success in the new country. In that model, settled migrants assisted the newcomers on arrival, often living in concentrated settlements based on kinship and employment. Between the wars, some 93 per cent of southern Europeans arrived through chain migration.[7] It was a feature of Veneto migration and settlement patterns in other parts of Australia.[8]

---

7   Price, *Southern Europeans in Australia*, 107–39, 278–89.
8   See Baldassar and Pesman, *From Paesani to Global Italians*, 33–37; Davine, *Vegnimo da Conco Ma Simo Veneti*, 51–54.

While they did not arrive through chain migration, this small cohort of Veneto migrants developed a geographically and socially contained community. One second-generation narrator explained the kinship ties that linked people in the community as 'relatives'. Lina Campagnaro nee Ballestrin spoke first about her parents and their close ties with other Veneto market-gardener families. She also referred to the continuity of the connections in her generation—a phenomenon that has been part of the family culture.[9] The godparent relationship is considered as close as a blood relative:

> Oh, everyone around the area would have been their friends, the Ballestrins, the Piovesans, the Marchioros, the Zampins, the Tonellatos, the Bernos, everyone around that area were friends and then they were all related in some way with being godparents to their families … But you know what? We still do the same, we still interact because I have got lots of Veneti friends … And we're all related, godmother, godfather and so forth.[10]

Plate 2.2: Veneto families and *paesani*, Lockleys, mid-1940s
Source: Photo supplied by Christine Rebellato nee Mattiazzo.

---

9   The custom of godparents as 'a family alliance' in successive generations is noted by Simone Marino and Giancarlo Chiro, 'Family Alliances and "Comparatico" among a Group of Calabrian-Australian Families Living in Adelaide, South Australia', *Journal of Anthropological Research* 70, no. 1 (2014): 107–30, doi.org/10.3998/jar.0521004.0070.105, at 147.
10 Lina Campagnaro nee Ballestrin interviewed by Madeleine Regan, J.D. Somerville Oral History Collection, State Library of South Australia, Adelaide, OH 872/28, 13 March 2014: 7, 19.

'I BUY THIS PIECE OF GROUND HERE'

Limits of land and migration

All 19 Veneto adults who arrived in Adelaide in the late 1920s were members of *contadino* families. Some had inherited land but most had been raised in intergenerational family households in a semi-feudal contractual arrangement called the *mezzadria*. This Latin-derived term explains an agrarian, feudal-like economy in which the *padrone* (proprietor) provided accommodation and owned the land but it was cultivated by the *contadino*.[11] The *padrone* received half of all annual production including crops, livestock and other foodstuffs. In either case, landholdings were small in the Veneto, with rare opportunities to expand the family economy. In his interview, Lino Tonellato, who arrived in Australia as a child, remembered the challenge for his mother, Elisabetta, to manage the land and support and feed herself and five children for eight years after her husband, Secondo, emigrated to Australia in 1927:

> I remember going down there and help her to weed the corns and … then they used to make bread with it, that's all. That's the only bread we had out of corn … Oh yeah, there was poverty alright, yeah … [T]hat's why we couldn't eat *polenta*. Do you know what that is? We like it now, but it took us thirty years before we'd start eating it [laughs].[12]

Some families on inherited properties had barely enough to support members in a multigenerational household because the land was continually carved up by successive generations.[13] The inadequate means of living, poverty and lack of resources were factors in the decision taken by individual family members to emigrate, hoping for a life better than mere subsistence.

Healthy, young men in Veneto households often gained seasonal employment in neighbouring countries such as France, Switzerland and Germany and added to the family economy. For the Veneto people, this was 'an inherited and accepted way of life'.[14] In addition to the seasonal emigration to nearby countries, Veneto men had also emigrated before

---

11   Huber, *From Pasta to Pavlova*, 20–21. See Remo Berno, 'The Mezzadria System', *Veneto Market Gardeners 1927 Blog*, 15 September 2019, venetimarketgardeners1927.net/the-mezzadria-system/.
12   Lino Tonellato interviewed by Madeleine Regan, Transcript, J.D. Somerville Oral History Collection, State Library of South Australia, Adelaide, OH 872/10, 16 July 2010: 14–15. Polenta was made from corn or maize, which was a staple crop in the Veneto.
13   Price, *Southern Europeans in Australia*, 27–28; Davine, *Vegnimo da Conco Ma Simo Veneti*, 35.
14   Baldassar and Pesman, *From Paesani to Global Italians*, 20–25.

World War I to the Americas, Africa and Australia. Donna Gabaccia estimates that before World War I approximately 9 million people born in Italy were living in other countries including in Europe.[15] Several narrators referred to male relatives who had migrated to other countries to find work between the wars. For example, in Dino Piovesan's family, apart from his father and uncle, who had migrated to Australia, other uncles went to Belgium and Venezuela.[16] Lino Tonellato asserts that 'most of the young people left'.[17] Lino's grandparents died at a young age and left the family in poor circumstances. All but one of their children emigrated before World War II; Lino's father and his youngest sister migrated to Australia and another aunt and two uncles went to Canada.

Plate 2.3: The Rossetto family, Bigolino, Italy, c. 1918
Note: Eight of the nine siblings migrated as adults between the wars.
Source: Photo supplied by Maria Rosa Tormena.

---

15   Donna R. Gabaccia, 'Italian Diaspora', in *Encyclopedia of Diasporas*, eds M. Ember, C.R. Ember, and I. Skoggard (Boston: Springer, 2005), 143–52, doi.org/10.1007/978-0-387-29904-4_15.
16   Dino Piovesan interviewed by Madeleine Regan, Transcript, J.D. Somerville Oral History Collection, State Library of South Australia, Adelaide, OH 872/17, 23 September 2011: 2.
17   Lino Tonellato, OH 872/10, 16 July 2010: 17.

Most southern European migrants in Australia were young single men who were fit and able to travel and negotiate prospects for employment. Until 1939, fewer than 10 per cent of southern European migrant men were accompanied by wives or children.[18] Those in the Veneto group who were married had left behind children—some of them so young they had no memories of their father before migration. When Secondo Tonellato migrated in 1927, his wife, Elisabetta, was pregnant with their fifth child.

Another way of augmenting the family income in the Veneto region was a gendered form of 'out' employment that involved daughters being sent away to become domestic servants in wealthy households. Lina Rossetto nee Bordin gave an account of her experience working in domestic service from the age of 12, looking after a small child and attending to all household cleaning and laundering.[19] Daughters were less independent than sons in the patriarchal family structure; sons had some autonomy about undertaking seasonal work. In the tradition of outwork, Veneto families accepted the absence of members of the household and the compensation was the supplementary income and fewer members at the table.

While the limitations of land and poverty were among the reasons for the Veneto market gardeners migrating in the late 1920s, political circumstances also caused problems for some families. Political unrest impacted the daily life of Italians in both urban and country areas between 1919 and 1920 in the aftermath of World War I. Strikes by industrial and agricultural workers increased during these two years and led to protests and unrest in what was called *biennio rosso* or the 'two red years'.[20] Groups of armed men (*squadristi*) perpetrated violence and, in this way, fascist influence spread during the 1920s.[21] With Benito Mussolini's march on Rome in 1922, the hold of fascism strengthened and expanded and, consequently, some Italians left the country as 'political refugees'.[22] Most narrators did not refer to fascism as a reason for their parents' migration but it had become part of the political, social and economic context of late-1920s Italy.

---

18   Price, *Southern Europeans in Australia*, 104.
19   Marietta Rossetto, *La Pioggia nelle Scarpe: Aneddoti di una protagonista = Rain in These Shoes: Anecdotal Memoirs of Adelina Rossetto* (Adelaide: VIA Magenta, 1995), 61–62.
20   Danilo Breschi, 'Genealogia E Fenomenologia Do Fascismo: Entre a história E a interpretação [Geneaology and Phenomenology of Fascism: Between History and Interpretation]', *Locus: Revista de História* 28, no. 2 (2022): 41–63, doi.org/10.34019/2594-8296.2022.v28.37466.
21   John Foot, 'A Microhistory of Fascist Violence; Squadristi, Victims and Perpetrators', *Journal of Modern Italian Studies* 27, no. 4 (2022): 528–49, doi.org/10.1080/1354571X.2022.2045454; Alessandro Saluppo, 'Paramilitary Violence and Fascism: Imaginaries and Practices of Squadrismo, 1919–1925', *Contemporary European History* 29, no. 3 (2020): 289–308, doi.org/10.1017/S0960777319000390.
22   Baldassar and Pesman, *From Paesani to Global Italians*, 46.

Albert Tonellato recalled being told about the impact of fascism on his extended family and the fear that existed because local groups of violent fascists imposed control on communities. Albert communicated the complexity and distress of life in a small village and relationships divided by the political regime:

> [My father] could see what was going on. Because of my mother's brother … the two brothers—they were against the Fascists, and one of the Fascists was a friend of his. He said, 'You'd better take off, go somewhere else, or else they're going to kill you.' They used to go and pick them up. The Fascists, they was going to go and pick him up … and he said, 'You'd better take off', he said, 'Before the truck pulls up.' And they went—from the Veneto region, they went to France, walked through the mountains.[23]

Migration, legislation and sponsorship

The migration and settlement narratives of the first generation of Veneto market gardeners in the late 1920s are considered in the political context of both Italy and Australia. Selective migration policies were developed and amended as governments changed.[24] During the 1920s, Italian migration to Australia increased because of the quota system introduced by the United States, which severely reduced the number of Italian migrants accepted there. In Australia, there was a threefold expansion of Italian migrants between 1921 and 1933 and an even greater increase in South Australia, which increased racial tensions as competition for employment heightened.[25] In Italy, the fascist government had restricted emigration as part of its nationalist campaign in the late 1920s,[26] yet it was during this period that the Veneto cohort of market gardeners arrived in Australia.

The White Australia policy, enacted in 1901 to maintain a homogeneous British society, determined the climate for the reception of Italians who arrived in the 1920s.[27] At that time, several requirements were imposed by

---

23 Albert Tonellato interviewed by Madeleine Regan, Transcript, J.D. Somerville Oral History Collection, State Library of South Australia, Adelaide, OH 872/4, 3 October 2008: 27–28.
24 Michele Langfield, '"White Aliens": The Control of European Immigration to Australia 1920–30', *Journal of Intercultural Studies* 12, no. 2 (1991): 1–14, doi.org/10.1080/07256868.1991.9963375.
25 O'Connor, *No Need to be Afraid*, 93–98.
26 Philip Cannistraro and Gianfausto Rosoli, 'Fascist Emigration Policy in the 1920s: An Interpretive Framework', *International Migration Review* 13, no. 4 (1979): 673–92, doi.org/10.1177/01979183790 1300404.
27 Stephen Castles and Mark J. Miller, *The Age of Migration: International Population Movements in the Modern World*, 3rd edn (Basingstoke: Macmillan, 1993), 50–53.

the Australian Government. Intending Italian migrants had to be nominated by an Australian resident, who was obliged to provide accommodation and employment to relieve the state of the responsibility for the material support of the immigrant population. Migrants were required to pay a considerable landing fee if they did not have a sponsor and Italian passports were restricted to dependent relatives. In 1928, by which time the 19 *veneti* had arrived, an annual national quota of 3,000 migrants from Italy was introduced.[28]

Although the narrators were unable to provide information about the cost of their parents' migration, it seems it was common for Italian men to borrow money for the voyage or for whole families to contribute to the expenses. The costs were considerable for families who lived on the margins of poverty in the Veneto. In 1924, passage from Italy to Australia cost £37 at a time when a man's average annual wage in Australia was £94/3/0.[29] Most in the Veneto group arrived with £10, although the exception was Giovanni Santin, the eldest of the cohort at 41, who arrived with £20— undoubtedly the result of having worked in Canada for nine years. These meagre financial resources did not bridge the difficult economic conditions the migrants faced in South Australia in the late 1920s.

The 17 lone men who arrived in Adelaide in the 1920s conformed to the common pattern of Italian migration in which a man arrived without a spouse.[30] Unaccompanied men were more likely to take work opportunities anywhere they could find them. Wives emigrated later or the men married in Australia after establishing a firm financial base. Francesco and Margherita Marchioro, the sole married couple to migrate, were advantaged because Margherita's brother, who owned a concrete business, sponsored them and provided employment and assistance with boarding house accommodation after their arrival in 1926.

Leaving security

When members of Veneto families travelled for seasonal work to neighbouring European countries, they returned to the stability of the intergenerational household. The long sea journey from Italy and

---

28   J.S. McDonald, 'Migration from Italy to Australia with Special Reference to Selected Groups' (PhD diss., The Australian National University, Canberra, 1958).
29   O'Connor, *No Need to be Afraid*, 3; Australian Bureau of Statistics (ABS), *Official Year Book of the Commonwealth of Australia*, No. 18 (Canberra: ABS 1925), 570.
30   Borrie, *Italians and Germans in Australia*, 52–56; Price, *Southern Europeans in Australia*, 104–13.

disembarkation in Australia broke this pattern. For these people, the voyage, the physical and emotional separation from family and their arrival in a foreign land with a different language were unfamiliar challenges. Author Tony De Bolfo, whose grandfather migrated from Italy with two brothers in 1927, examined the records of 110 passengers who disembarked from the *Re d'Italia* in Melbourne in November 1927.[31] He recorded oral history interviews with surviving passengers in the late 1990s. In the following excerpt, one passenger provides an image of the privations of the 46-day journey from Italy:

> The voyage was very, very bad; the food was awful and I was sick the whole time. As everything was rationed for the long and arduous journey we were fed a lot of soup but hardly any pasta, which was awful, and as the ship was loaded with heavy cargo there were almost no individual cabins and my sleeping quarters comprised a very large room of thirty people or more.[32]

Ampelio Acquasaliente (Salent) from the Veneto province of Vicenza recalled his desolation when he arrived in Melbourne and his sponsor was not present to meet him because he had travelled to New South Wales to seek work after nominating Ampelio. It was 14 years before they met each other, by which time Ampelio had worked in Melbourne, Sydney and Queensland. The challenge for some migrants was to navigate the new country alone without support from a sponsor, government or trade union. The Australian Labor Party did not support the level of 'alien' migration in 1927 and was concerned about the increasing numbers of southern Europeans whose sponsors, if unable to offer wages, provided food in return for work. The argument was that the migrants would lower the industrial conditions that unions had fought to establish.[33] While some Veneto groups who settled in other parts of Australia had the support of *paesani* (people who came from the same village) through chain migration and were provided with work and accommodation, most Veneto market gardeners did not experience that security.[34]

---

31   Tony De Bolfo, *In Search of Kings: What Became of the Passengers of the 'Re d'Italia'* (Melbourne: HarperCollins, 2004).
32   Ampelio Acquasaliente (Salent), in ibid., 33–36.
33   'Question: Migration Commission—Mentally Affected Migrants', 50-5, in Australia, House of Representatives, Debates, 15 November 1927, historichansard.net/hofreps/1927/19271115_REPS_10_116/.
34   Annamaria Davine, 'Pioneer Veneti in Gippsland and Their Role in the Development of an Italian Farming Community', *Italian Historical Society Journal* 10, no. 2 (2002); Baldassar and Pesman, *From Paesani to Global Italians*, 33–35.

'I BUY THIS PIECE OF GROUND HERE'

Negotiating the first years

The contrast of the safety net provided by the family household in the Veneto region with the instability and risk of a forced itinerant existence could not have been more complete. The sponsorship system may have provided a proxy safeguard for new arrivals and given them more security had the economic conditions not been so difficult in Australia in the late 1920s. While a mix of 'friends' and relatives were identified as sponsors on landing documents, it is difficult to understand how the arrangements advantaged the first generation of the Veneto men. The sponsors lived in the City of Adelaide in boarding houses, many of which were owned by *veneti* who had arrived in previous years.[35]

The boarding house addresses suggest that sponsors were not market gardeners and were therefore unable to offer work. Providing the name of a sponsor did little more than satisfy an administrative requirement. After arrival, the Veneto cohort likely became part of the network formed through the boarding houses. Yet, without work, the new migrants had to leave their sponsors to pursue any opportunity that arose. Even kin could not protect them from the dire economic situation, as illustrated by the experience of Vittorio Marchioro, who was sponsored by his older brother Francesco in 1927.

Vittorio's survival was tenuous because he was forced to move interstate alone to find work:

> Oral Historian [OH]: But for three years you had no steady work?
>
> VM: No money at all, nothing, nothing.
>
> OH: What did you write back home?
>
> VM: Oh, crying here ... Because you know, left, no friend, girlfriend, came here, no work, no nothing.
>
> OH: Did you meet, were there other Italian people here?
>
> VM: Plenty Italians, nobody work.[36]

---

35   O'Connor, 'Clubs and Associations of the Venetians in South Australia', 179.
36   Vittorio Marchioro interviewed by Michael Tsounis, Transcript, J.D. Somerville Oral History Collection, State Library of South Australia, Adelaide, OH 12/1, 13 March 1984: 8.

2. BEGINNINGS IN ADELAIDE

S.A. 6491 Applicant for Naturalization.
PERSONAL STATEMENT AND DECLARATION. 17-12-27

Name of Ship.	Class Travelled.	Date of Arrival.	Port of Landing.
ORAMA	III	12.12.27	Adelaide

1. Surname *MARCHIORO* 2. Christian name *VITTORIO*
   (In BLOCK Letters.)
3. Place of Birth—Town *Malo* Country *Italy* 4. Date of birth *23/12/1906*
5. Nationality *Italian* 6. Race *White*
7. Particulars of passport or permit held—
   (a) Number *6462* (d) Where issued *Vicenza*
   (b) Date of issue *14/11/1927* (e) If visaed by a British Consul, state place and date of
   (c) By whom issued *Police Auth.* visa— *none*
8. Married or single *single*
9. If accompanied by wife and/or children under the age of 16 years, give particulars of each—
   Name. Sex. Age. Birthplace.
   Wife...............
   Children—(1)...........
   (2)...........
   (3)...........
10. Last permanent address abroad *Malo - Vicenza - Italy*
11. Occupation or profession *Farmer* 12. Intended occupation in Australia *Farmer*
13. Personal description—Height *5-4* Hair *Brown* Eyes *Brown* Marks *none*
    (Extract from Passport.)
14. (a) Do you intend to settle in Australia? *yes*
    (b) If temporary business visit, state intended duration...
    (c) If tourist visit, state intended duration...
15. If you have {(a) relatives / (b) friends} in Australia, give names and addresses of two—
    Name. Address.
    (a) Relatives—(1) *Brother*
    (2) *Marchioro Francesco 285 Hindley St. Adelaide*
    (b) If no relative, (1)
    but *friend* (2)
16. Proposed permanent address in Australia *as above*
    (If not known, state temporary address).
17. What amount of money your own bona fide property can you produce? (If more than £100, state £100.) £ *10*
    If less than £40, state whether maintenance or employment has been guaranteed by any resident of Australia; and, if so, give name and address of such person *as above*
18. Are you, and any dependants accompanying you, in sound mental and physical health? *yes*
    If not, state disability...
19. Have you had any training? (a) Navy........ (b) Army *yes* (c) Air Force........
    In what country *Italy*
20. Are you a Reservist? *yes* If so, state in what unit *Inf*
21. Have you previously resided in Australia? *no* If so, state period of residence *no*
    date of leaving Australia *no* port of departure *no*

I hereby declare that I understand the above questions, and that the answers given by me to the questions are true and correct. I undertake that while in Australia I will faithfully observe and obey the laws of Australia.

Correctness of signature and particulars herein acknowledged
by the declarant............... Signature *Marchioro Vittorio*
before me at...............
this...............19...... Date.........19

Officer of Customs. (SEE OTHER SIDE.)

Plate 2.4: Vittorio Marchioro's landing papers, December 1927, which include the name and address of his brother Francesco
Source: National Archives of Australia (D4880, 'Italian, Marchioro, V.').

The repetition of 'nothing' and the acknowledgement of his tearful desperation communicate the deprivation and hardship that Vittorio endured as a 21-year-old. Vittorio had initially worked in a terrazzo and concrete business with his brother-in-law but employment opportunities in Adelaide were unstable and he travelled to Rushworth in Victoria, about 200 kilometres north of Melbourne, where he felled timber in difficult conditions that he recalled vividly in his interview.[37] The work was physically demanding; he endured isolation, the privations of restricted access to food and poor accommodation, and recalled with a sense of irony that his employer was a fellow Italian.

Vittorio may have recognised his boss in the role of a *padrone* in the semi-feudal system of rural Italy who demanded rights to the production of crops in a structure that maintained inequality. He earned £5 for six months' work when, in 1930, the average Australian weekly wage was £5/1/5 for adult men.[38] Vittorio returned to Adelaide in the early 1930s and gradually made an income from labouring work before the opportunity to lease land for a market garden at Lockleys with his brother and sister-in-law offered a more secure future.

Enduring the Depression years

Vittorio's experience was consistent with that of the thousands of men who were without regular work during the Depression in Australia. Not speaking English and with no knowledge of Anglo-Australian culture, migrants were even more disadvantaged than most. The scale of unemployment among newly arrived migrants is recorded in a memoir by Giovanni Amadio, who arrived in Adelaide from Italy in 1927. He stayed in a boarding house with 47 other Italians, 'all of whom, to my great disappointment were out of work'.[39] In South Australia, nearly one-third of the potential workforce was unemployed by 1930, and the situation did not improve until 1935— a longer period than in other states and territories.[40] Italians were unwelcome whether they looked for work in the city or in rural areas. Attempts to find work in the country were noted in South Australian newspapers with provocative headlines such as 'Country Invaded: Italians Seek Work'.[41]

---

37   ibid., 9–10.
38   '"Real" Wages Show an Increase', *Sydney Morning Herald*, 26 January 1932: 7.
39   Joe Amadio, *An Immigrant's Story* (Adelaide: Self-Published, 1997), 5.
40   Ray Broomhill, *Unemployed Workers: A Social History of the Great Depression in Adelaide* (Brisbane: University of Queensland Press, 1978), 11–29.
41   *News*, [Adelaide], 2 January 1928: 1.

Most of the Veneto migrants became wage labourers after arrival, which was a model of work that differed from their experience of belonging to a peasant farmer household and economy in their home region. Short-term employment included labouring on farms, building rural roads or working for farmers in a relationship familiar to the *veneti* who had worked on the land for *padroni* (bosses). Using a snapshot of Eugenio Zalunardo's life, it is possible to track his mobility in his first 10 years in the country. Arriving in Adelaide at 22 years of age in 1927, Eugenio spent more than seven years in rural South Australia, mostly working as a farmhand. He worked for four years on Kangaroo Island, two years on the Eyre Peninsula, which was more than a day's travel from Adelaide, and 14 months at Halidon, 140 kilometres east of Adelaide, working for a Veneto man who had a contract to build roads. When he applied for naturalisation in 1933, Eugenio was unemployed and living in a boarding house in the City of Adelaide. By 1937, he had leased land on Grange Road, St James Park, for his market garden, close to other *veneti* who were also settling there during the second half of the 1930s.[42]

Learning about the experiences of the first generation

Most sons and daughters of the first generation born in Australia recollect their everyday lives on the market gardens and in the Veneto community although they have limited knowledge of the early experiences of their parents in Australia. Francesco (also known as Frankie) Ballestrin holds the memory of his father's difficult first years after arrival: 'I didn't witness it, but that's what I was told by my parents, anyway, by my Dad.'[43] He demonstrates that extraordinary or distressing events can become imprinted through emotions— a conclusion made by Hirsch in what she observes as the 'trans-generational transmission of traumatic knowledge and experience'.[44] The experience of Francesco's father, Isidoro Ballestrin, provides an impression of the impact of the Depression on a young Italian migrant.

---

42   Department of Immigration, Central Office, A446, Correspondence files, annual single number series with block allocations [Main correspondence files series of the agency], 01 Jan 1926 – 1955/50846, Application for Naturalisation—Zalunardo Eugenio born 18 February 1905, 1933–1955, National Archives of Australia, Canberra [hereinafter NAA].
43   Francesco Ballestrin interviewed by Madeleine Regan, Transcript, J.D. Somerville Oral History Collection, State Library of South Australia, Adelaide, OH 872/7, 5 January 2009: 46.
44   Hirsch, 'The Generation of Postmemory', 106.

'I BUY THIS PIECE OF GROUND HERE'

The 23-year-old Isidoro undertook work near Finke, in a remote desert country about 1,500 kilometres north-west of Adelaide. With another Italian man, he laboured on a pastoral lease, living in tents. Francesco describes the extreme situation his father was in:

> In the beginning there wasn't any work at all … My father, Isidoro, went up north, up at Finke, up that area, sinking wells and building fences for the farmers, and actually the chappie that he went with—I don't know who he was—but he hung [sic] himself. And Dad panicked and he got lost, no water, and the blackfellas found him, the Aboriginals, what you want to call them—at that time they used to call them 'blackfellas'—and they gradually got him back to life again because he was almost gone. And then he come down here and I don't know what he did after that, I don't know what he picked up after that. But I know he kept saying … that it was really horrendous.[45]

Plate 2.5: Isidoro Ballestrin's Italian passport, 1927
Source: NAA (A435 1947/2/2012, 'Ballestrin Isidoro — born 15 May 1905 — Italian').

---

45 Francesco Ballestrin, OH 872/7, 12 December 2008: 1–2.

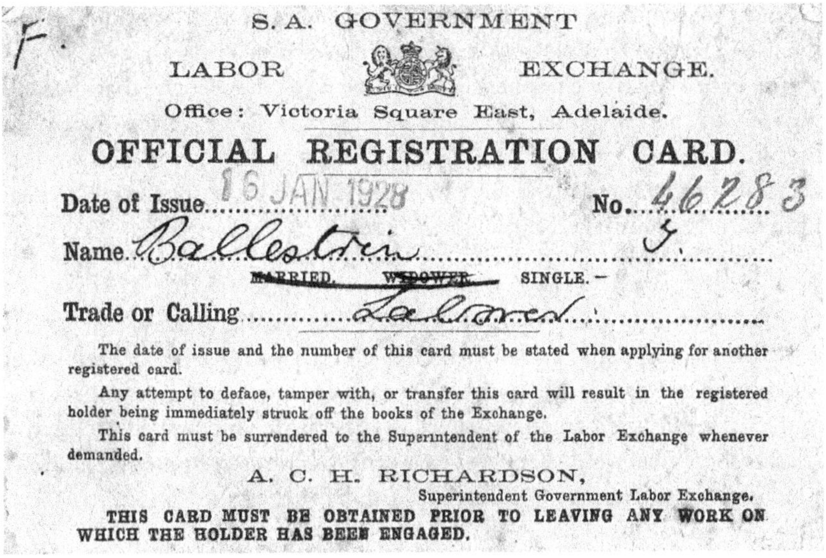

F.

S.A. GOVERNMENT

LABOR EXCHANGE.

Office: Victoria Square East, Adelaide.

OFFICIAL REGISTRATION CARD.

Date of Issue 16 JAN 1928 No. 46283

Name Ballestrin I.

~~MARRIED.~~ ~~WIDOWER.~~ SINGLE. –

Trade or Calling Labourer

The date of issue and the number of this card must be stated when applying for another registered card.

Any attempt to deface, tamper with, or transfer this card will result in the registered holder being immediately struck off the books of the Exchange.

This card must be surrendered to the Superintendent of the Labor Exchange whenever demanded.

A. C. H. RICHARDSON,
Superintendent Government Labor Exchange.

THIS CARD MUST BE OBTAINED PRIOR TO LEAVING ANY WORK ON WHICH THE HOLDER HAS BEEN ENGAGED.

Plate 2.6: Isidoro Ballestrin's work registration card, issued four months after his arrival in Adelaide

Source: Card supplied by Francesco Ballestrin.

The reference to Aboriginal people as saviours is unusual in the collection of oral histories as Francesco is the only narrator to mention such an encounter with Indigenous people. The scene provides a counterpoint to the image of urban Aboriginal people, especially in the Depression years, when they were the most vulnerable group in Australia, together with itinerant labourers and newly arrived migrants, on the margins of society. At 71 years of age, Francesco remembered what he was told and, in reconstructing this episode, he imagined his father's near-death experience as a young man and his salvation at the hands of Aboriginal people—a dramatic chapter of his family's migration history.

Francesco's report of his father's interaction with Aboriginal people endures as 'a fragment' of what Persian and Agutter discuss in relation to the views of European postwar migrants towards marginal groups in Australia. An account like Francesco's stands out because it forms a fragment of history that does not reflect the general contemporary attitude towards Indigenous people.[46] It also is distinctive in this project because other narrators did not refer to their Veneto parents or grandparents encountering Aboriginal

46 Persian and Agutter, 'European Post-War Migrants and Indigenous Australians', 112.

people.⁴⁷ A second-generation woman expressed surprise after reading about the use of land in the Lockleys market garden area in a blog that was posted on the Veneto market gardeners' website, which acknowledged that the land the Veneto market gardeners occupied along the River Torrens had been first inhabited by the Kaurna people for thousands of years. The woman had not considered that the land had been owned by people in precolonial history and appropriated by colonial settlers.

In another context, Veneto men and women who lived and worked in the mica mines in the Northern Territory before and after World War II provided photographic evidence of close contact with Aboriginal groups in the mining camps. Oral histories were recorded for a project about Italians in the mica camps. Women who lived in the camps remembered productive relationships that were characterised by 'mutual respect and co-operation', which were not common in Central Australia at the time.⁴⁸

Plate 2.7: Attilio and Serafina De Pieri and other workers, Caruso mica mine, Central Australia, 1941
Source: Photo supplied by Adelina Pavan nee De Pieri.

---

47   This absence is consistent with Ricatti's observation that First Nations peoples are almost completely invisible in most histories of Italian migration. Ricatti, *Italians in Australia*, 67.
48   David Frederick Hugo, 'Mica Mining at Harts Ranges, Central Australia, 1880s–1960: A Study of Ethnicity and the Impact of Isolation' (PhD diss., Northern Territory University, Darwin, 1995), 290.

As noted by scholars, acknowledgement of First Nations people and their sovereignty has been consistently overlooked in the narratives of migrants.[49] Ricatti asserts that this absence or 'silence' in the literature about relationships between Aboriginal people and Italians 'is a significant aspect of the complex and unresolved question about the racial and colonial role played by migrants in Australia'.[50] Ricatti argues that migration is a challenging experience because the migrant has conflicting encounters with what is unfamiliar and a sense of nostalgia for what was familiar. However, Italian settlement must be considered in the context of dispossession and colonialism mixed with racism.[51] This complexity is also examined in the context of multicultural Australia where the dispossession experienced by Aboriginal people and the problems of colonial settlement are subsumed by a focus on 'the racialised hierarchy of Australian whiteness'.[52]

The second generation interviewed for this project narrated their parents' experiences and generally did not consider the question of Indigenous sovereignty. By the time the first generation leased their land in the Lockleys area in the 1930s, Indigenous people had long been supplanted by colonial-settler farmers and there would have been few opportunities to meet Aboriginal people in the Italians' circumscribed lives as market gardeners mixing almost exclusively within their own community. Especially in the first years, the first-generation Veneto group was challenged by the unfamiliar in many contexts and, as the experience of Francesco's father demonstrated, they were driven, as members of a marginal group, to survive and maintain their focus on settlement at a time of national economic crisis.

Electing to stay in Australia

The impact of the Depression contributed to the high percentage of Italian migrants who re-migrated. Large numbers of Italians left Australia in the late 1920s and early 1930s and returned to live in Italy. It was estimated that more than one-third of the 12,000 Italians who migrated in the interwar

---

49   Ricatti, 'The Emotion of Truth and the Racial Uncanny'; Ricatti, *Italians in Australia*, 53–74; Pugliese, 'Migrant Heritage in an Indigenous Context'.
50   Ricatti, 'The Emotion of Truth and the Racial Uncanny', 126.
51   ibid., 130.
52   Susan Schech and Jane Haggis, 'Migrancy, Multiculturalism and Whiteness: Re-charting Core Identities in Australia', *Communal/Plural* 9, no. 2 (2001): 143–59, doi.org/10.1080/13207870120081460, at 153.

period had returned to Italy by 1940.⁵³ However, those who remained persisted in their ambition to settle in Australia and endured negative public opinion about Italian migrants. Some Italian men made short trips to Italy to choose wives, reunite with family or sell land and returned to Australia intending to remain permanently. Four of the Veneto cohort visited Italy for brief periods within seven years of arrival and returned to Australia— a demonstration of their commitment to achieving *sistemazione*. Adeodato Rossetto returned to Italy for six months in 1931 and resettled in Adelaide. He had arrived in South Australia in 1927 with two brothers and a brother-in-law, and the reason for returning to Italy cited in his application for naturalisation in 1933 was ill health.⁵⁴ Three other men who returned to their home village to find spouses in 1934 resumed life, with their respective wives, in Adelaide after eight months.

Finding stability in the *paese* at Lockleys

The Veneto market gardeners (and narrators) applied the name 'Lockleys' to the area where they established the market gardens and developed their community. Although the suburb of Lockleys was on the southern side of the River Torrens, there is a tradition of also referring to the locality north of the river where the market gardeners settled as Lockleys. It is not a correct geographical location.⁵⁵ Flinders Park and St James Park were the names of the two suburbs when the Veneto market-gardener families settled there. One possible reason for using the name 'Lockleys' was because the nearest post office was located there. The post office, for the *veneti*, was important as the point of distribution of mail to their families in Italy at a time when the post was the most common form of contact between families in Italy and Australia.⁵⁶

---

53 Baldassar and Pesman, *From Paesani to Global Italians*, 26.
54 Department of the Interior, [1], Correspondence files, annual single number series [Main correspondence series of the agency], 01 Jan 1890 – 31 Dec 1069, 1934/857, Adeodata [Adeodato] Rossetto—Naturalisation 1933–1934, NAA.
55 Surprisingly, some official documents identified the area where market gardens hugged both sides of the River Torrens as Lockleys—for example, in descriptions of the locality in security reports during the war. In NAA files related to applications for purchase of property, both 'Lockleys' and 'Findon' were used to identify the area of the market gardens where the Veneto community lived. Today, it seems quite a fluid naming.
56 An elderly second-generation narrator confirmed that the postman delivered mail that was issued from the Lockleys Post Office. He recalled that the Veneto families associated the physical location of the post office with the area from which the mail was delivered, so it became known as 'Lockleys'. Lino Ballestrin, Personal communication, 17 August 2023.

2. BEGINNINGS IN ADELAIDE

Plate 2.8: Aerial photo of the Lockleys area, late 1950s

Notes: The location of the Veneto market-gardener properties is highlighted. The River Torrens, seen at the bottom of the photo, was an important feature of the area.

Source: City of Charles Sturt, reproduced with permission.

Oscar Mattiazzo, a 1.5-generation relative of a market-gardener family, clarified the enduring identification of the locality:

> We called it Lockleys because that's the area we refer to, although it's Flinders Park and Findon and all that type of thing. There wasn't so many houses there, a lot of gardens, and a lot of empty spaces, many

49

> empty spaces, and it wasn't until, let me see, until 1960 that things started really to develop in Lockleys, and market gardens were being cut up for blocks of land and all that type of thing, until today.⁵⁷

The tendency to assign names to identify the meaning of a place that has a large population of Italians can create a sense of belonging to a locality.⁵⁸ The use of a special name evokes an identity that assists people in creating their own history of a place.⁵⁹ The Veneto migrants had other geographical markers such as roads that indicated clusters of market gardens. Narrators also pinpointed the locations of Frogmore Road, Valetta Road and River Road (or Findon Road as it is today). These markers communicate a sense of local knowledge, familiarity, proprietorship and an identity associated with the longevity of the Veneto community in the area. Some narrators referred to the River Torrens as a significant feature of the area—both as a source of water for those who lived beside it and as a boundary at the southern margins of the Veneto market gardens.

During the 1930s, 17 of the 19 Veneto migrants, including the married woman, became market gardeners in the Lockleys area within about 3 kilometres of one another. Although the narrators did not know the reason for their parents' convergence on land at Lockleys, the two Berno brothers provide a clue. They had worked as labourers for an Anglo-Australian who owned farmland near the River Torrens. As plots in the area became available for lease, they may have communicated these opportunities to other Veneto men in the city boarding houses. The chance to lease land enabled the Veneto market gardeners to reclaim a sense of order and control over their everyday lives and facilitated the continuity of their *contadino* identity in Australia.

At first, the Veneto men lived alone in various basic forms of accommodation on their land. Living alone but setting up a home for a nuclear family was another unfamiliar aspect of life for people who had always lived and worked in large intergenerational households. In Adelaide, the sense of isolation, separation from family and ordered domestic life, mixed with uncertainty about the future, provided impetus for attaining the goal of *sistemazione*.

---

57   Oscar Mattiazzo interviewed by Madeleine Regan, Transcript, J.D. Somerville Oral History Collection, State Library of South Australia, Adelaide, OH 872/13, 6 June 2012: 169.
58   Pascoe, 'Place and Community', 93–96.
59   Doreen Massey, 'Places and Their Pasts', *History Workshop Journal* 39, no. 1 (1995): 182–92, doi.org/10.1093/hwj/39.1.182.

Stability through marriage and family

Those who experienced the challenges of migration and desired permanent settlement generally sought stability through the institutional structures of marriage and raising a family—'a family migration strategy'.[60] Although most Italian male migrants arrived alone, they reunited with wives after some years or married after they had achieved the stability required to form a family and attain *sistemazione* in Australia. The first-generation Veneto market gardeners carried an image of the household in which all labour was provided by family members.

The experience of the peasant household was dependent on the number of members, 'family composition and its labour force'.[61] The marriage of young family members had an impact on labour, domestic arrangements, interactions between men and women and relationships between generations.[62] However, Veneto rituals of courtship and marriage were not easily transposed to Lockleys. For example, a young woman in the Veneto would usually have married a young man from the local area after a priest had vouched for his reputation. In Adelaide, there was no such regulation of marriages.

Within eight years, the four married Veneto men had reunited with their wives and children at Lockleys. Another six men married through different arrangements—some by proxy—while others, like the three Ballestrin men, returned to Italy briefly to find suitable women to marry. At Lockleys, some Veneto men took much longer to attain status as husbands and fathers. One possible explanation for the delay was the small number of women in the Italian community in Adelaide. According to the 1933 census, only one in five South Australians born in Italy was a woman.[63]

---

60 Sala and Baldassar, 'Time to Revisit the Family in Italian-Australian Studies', 2.
61 Stuart Oglethorpe, 'The End of Sharecropping in Central Italy after 1945: The Role of Mechanisation in the Changing Relationship between Peasant Families and Land', *Rural History* 25, no. 2 (2014): 243–60, doi.org/10.1017/S0956793314000089, at 255.
62 Teodor Shanin, 'The Peasantry as a Political Factor', in *Peasants and Peasant Societies: Selected Readings*, ed. Teodor Shanin (Harmondsworth: Penguin Education, 1973), 240–44.
63 O'Connor, *No Need to be Afraid*, 108.

Arrival as a family unit: Francesco and Margherita Marchioro

The exception in the marital arrangements of the Veneto group in the first years was the married couple Margherita and Francesco Marchioro, who landed in Adelaide with their infant daughter, Mary, in February 1926. Margherita's brother, who had arrived in 1922 and developed a terrazzo business in Adelaide, sponsored them and guaranteed work for Francesco. Living as a family unit with an income enabled the couple to put down roots, although they moved between four different boarding houses in search of cheaper rent in the first years after arrival.[64] Within 18 months, a second child, Lina, was born, increasing the incentive for *sistemazione* and permanency. By 1931, after completing the mandatory five years of residency, the Marchioros were the first of the Veneto market-gardener families to become British citizens.

In her interview, Lina thought her parents intended to return to Italy and recalled an incident that, in her mind, related to the option for her parents to re-migrate:

> While they were living in the city in Waymouth Street, my mother told me that she was putting up some curtains and she was having difficulty and then she said: 'Why bother? We're going back in a couple of years.' So, she puts the curtains aside [laughs] … God, she died when she was 97. She was 21 when she came to Australia.[65]

Lina's assumption about her parents' plans to return to Italy contrasts with the lived experience of her mother, who never returned to Italy. After her husband died aged 43 years old in 1945, Margherita developed a profitable market garden and did not remarry.

---

64 Adelina Rismondo nee Marchioro interviewed by Madeleine Regan, Transcript, State Library of South Australia, Adelaide, OH 872/9, 9 June 2020: 16. See also Department of Home Affairs [II] Central Office, A1, Correspondence files, annual single number series [Main correspondence files series of the agency], 01 Jan 1890 – 31 Dec 1969, 1931/6731, NAA.
65 Adelina Rismondo, OH 872/9, 9 June 2010: 16.

Plate 2.9: Margherita and Francesco Marchioro with their first two daughters, Lina and Mary, Adelaide, c. 1927

Source: Photo supplied by Connie Legovich nee Marchioro.

'I BUY THIS PIECE OF GROUND HERE'

Reuniting and creating families in Adelaide

The imperative to reunite and establish families required finance and certainty of accommodation. Four Veneto men who were married when they arrived in 1927—Brunone Rebuli, Domenico Rossetto, Giovanni Santin and Secondo Tonellato—reunited with their wives and children within 10 years. Thirteen children arrived and formed a two-generation community in the *paese* at Lockleys. The children completed compulsory years of education before undertaking full-time work in the market gardens with their parents.

Plate 2.10: Giovanni Santin pours drinks for his own and others' children who had recently arrived from Italy, at Lockleys, December 1935
Note: The other children are from the Panazzolo, Santin and Tonellato families.
Source: Photo supplied by Assunta Giovannini nee Tonellato.

Returning to Italy to marry

Some Italian men returned to Italy to find wives even in the period between the wars. In the decade 1920–30, the average time between the arrival of southern European men and their marriage, either by proxy or during a brief return visit to Italy, was just over eight years.⁶⁶ After seven years in Australia, Antonio and Isidoro Ballestrin and their cousin Giuseppe Ballestrin returned to Vallà for eight months to find wives in the *paese* where they were brought up. The three marriages were conducted within 10 days of each other and, shortly after, the newly married couples left Italy to begin their lives together north of Adelaide.

The marriage of Giuseppe Ballestrin and Cesira Tieppo

Norma Camozzato nee Ballestrin, the daughter of one of these couples, was 75 years old when she discussed the way her parents, Giuseppe Ballestrin and Cesira Tieppo, married in 1934. Norma described her father's return to Italy as 'hunting for a wife', highlighting the generational differences in understanding the roles of women and men in the process of choosing a marriage partner.⁶⁷ Norma reflected on the risk her mother took at 20 years of age: marrying an unknown man, relinquishing physical ties to her family in Italy and migrating to a distant country.

Norma compared the experience of her daughter, Joanne, who moved from Adelaide to Canberra for employment as a young single woman in the 1980s. Referring to her own mother, Cesira, Norma revealed the differing generational values about the role and parenting of daughters and the experience of marriage:

> [W]hen Joanne left home, my daughter left home, she went for a job, she went to Canberra. And my mother turned around to me, she said: 'How could you possibly let your daughter move away from home to go to Canberra?' And I said to her: 'But Mum,' I said, 'You came over to Australia, you left your parents, your family. You came over to Australia with a strange man', because basically she'd only met him and married him. And she said: 'He wasn't a strange man,' she said: 'He was your father.' Okay [laughter].⁶⁸

---

66   Price, *Southern Europeans in Australia*, 137–38.
67   Norma Camozzato nee Ballestrin interviewed by Madeleine Regan, Transcript, J.D. Somerville Oral History Collection, State Library of South Australia, Adelaide, OH 872/37, 21 September 2016: 4.
68   ibid., 5.

Plate 2.11: The Ballestrin family: Cesira and Giuseppe, with children Norma and Lino, Adelaide, c. 1943–44

Note: A third child, Louis, was born in 1950.

Source: Photo supplied by Norma Camozzato nee Ballestrin.

When Norma said 'Joanne left home' and amplified 'my daughter left home', she confirmed the reality of the separation. This contrasts with the expectation for adult children, especially daughters, to stay close to their parents. Norma's elderly mother pointed out that the man she married after a short time was not just any man, 'he was your father', and illustrated the respect held for the role of parents—especially fathers—within the *contadino* family. Norma communicated the incongruity of the circumstances of her mother's path to marriage in contrast with her own experience when, at the age of 25, she married a postwar Veneto migrant in Adelaide. She also revealed the story of her daughter's initiative to move away from home and gain independence to pursue professional opportunities.

Two brothers marry after more than 20 years in Adelaide

Veneto *contadino* customs regarded unmarried adult men as lesser members of the community.[69] Although Alberto and Pietro Berno remained single men in the *paese* at Lockleys for more than 20 years, they acquired the status of leaders because of their hard work, prosperity, knowledge and financial experience. The brothers worked in partnership on a substantial landholding and owned the largest number of glasshouses of all the Veneto market gardeners, ensuring steady, substantial income and identities as successful businessmen.

After the interruption to overseas travel during the war years, the brothers visited Italy separately and became acquainted with women known to the Berno family in Riese Pio X and took the steps to marry them. Remo, son of Pietro and Antonietta Pastro, provided the perspective:

> First my father, and then my Uncle, married but first they worked and they passed 20 odd years of having lived in Australia. So, they were able to stay here in Italy, you know, a year or seven, eight months to find a girl, to get engaged and get married. Dad was looking for a young woman that was able to have a family and who would accept migrating to Australia.[70]

---

69   Robert H. Evans, *Life and Politics in a Venetian Community* (Notre Dame: University of Notre Dame Press, 1976), 118.
70   Remo Berno interviewed by Madeleine Regan, Transcript, J.D. Somerville Oral History Collection, State Library of South Australia, Adelaide, OH 872/46, 27 June 2017: 5.

The brothers married in 1948 and 1951, respectively, and returned to Lockleys with their wives. The two couples lived and raised their families together in a large colonial house in Lockleys in circumstances that resembled the extended *contadino* households in their village of origin. While the brothers managed the market gardens, their wives rotated the weekly domestic roles and care of children with work on the land—an efficient way to organise the household and business, which, at times, was supplemented by employing other workers, including young Veneto migrants after the war.

Marriage by proxy

For some single Veneto men, proxy marriage resolved the problem of selecting a prospective wife from the small number of available Italian women in the Adelaide community in the 1930s and 1940s.[71] Of the three men who married by proxy, two had known their wives before they migrated in 1927. In the formality of proxy marriage, the bride was partnered by a male relative, who stood in for her fiancé during a church ceremony.[72] In the case of Gelindo Rossetto and Adele (Lina) Bordin, who married in 1930, Gelindo's father represented the groom in the wedding ceremony in Bigolino. Lina recalled this arrangement in her memoir:

> It was with a despondent enthusiasm that I prepared for my strange wedding with no husband. I was to marry my husband by proxy, by taking the hand of my father-in-law! The world can only imagine the trembling feelings of doubt and fear experienced by a young girl entering such a union. Village morality frowned on travel for unmarried girls so I had to submit to this loveless ritual in order to eventually be with Gelindo in Australia.[73]

---

71 See Susanna Iuliano, 'Donne Buoi dai Paesi Tuoi [Choose Women and Oxen from Your Home Village]: Italian Proxy Marriages in Post-War Australia', *Australian Journal of Social Issues* 34, no. 4 (1999): 319–35, doi.org/10.1002/j.1839-4655.1999.tb01083.x; Susi Bella Wardrop, *By Proxy: A Study of Italian Proxy Brides in Australia* (Melbourne: Italian Historical Society, CO.AS.IT, 1996).
72 The legal aspects of the proxy marriage were organised by parish priests in Italy and Australia. The groom signed papers that were sent to Italy before the marriage.
73 Rossetto, *Rain in These Shoes*, 65–66.

Plate 2.12: The formal photo of Lina Bordin's proxy marriage, Bigolino, Italy, 1930
Note: Lina (with fur collar) sits between her parents-in-law, fourth from left in the front, as her father-in-law points to her.
Source: Photo supplied by Maria Rosa Tormena.

A second couple in the Veneto market-garden community, Angelo Piovesan and Rosalia Zanatta, had also known each other before their proxy marriage in 1934. If the woman and man were not known to each other, the man asked relatives in Italy to recommend a suitable spouse. A family member who knew the reputation of the prospective bride could make a recommendation—a process that reflected transnational patriarchal control.[74] Unlike those who returned to Italy to find a suitable spouse, a man who married by proxy reduced his costs by paying only a single fare for his wife.

Proxy marriage of Vittorio and Angelina Marchioro

The third example of a proxy marriage is a story of family origin recorded by members of two generations who provide accounts of the 1937 marriage of Vittorio Marchioro and Angelina Marchioro.[75] Interviewed in 1984,

---

74 Susanna Iuliano, 'Choose Women and Oxen from Your Home Village', 324.
75 Although their family names are the same, they were not related.

Vittorio and Angelina reflected on aspects of their proxy marriage. More than two decades later, their sons considered it an antiquated practice in contemporary Australia.

After remaining single for 11 years, Vittorio wrote to his sister in Malo in the province of Vicenza, asking her to recommend a young woman to be his wife. His sister endorsed Angelina, with whom she worked in a silk factory. Through letters, the couple communicated their interest; Angelina was 23 when she agreed to marry Vittorio. At 70 years of age, Angelina recalled contrasting emotions about her decision:

> I worked with the sister, and talking, talking and getting sick of working in the factory and asked if you like to go to Australia. I said just for fun, I said: 'Going to Australia'.[76]

However, Angelina's buoyancy contrasted with the realisation when she began the voyage by ship that she was permanently leaving her family: 'This made me a little bit afraid … a long way to go. Can't come back.'[77] Angelina recalled her arrival at the Port of Adelaide, where 40 Italians welcomed her. She spoke about living in a shed, starting work in the market gardens and beginning married life without knowing another person in Australia. When Vittorio was asked about marrying Angelina, he began by saying: 'This is a story.' It was as though Vittorio acknowledged the proxy marriage as drama and chance. Both Angelina and Vittorio laughed as they recounted their story—memories of their younger selves pledging to a future together and their long partnership in the market gardens.

When Angelina and Vittorio's two sons discussed their parents' marriage in their interviews, they posed questions about starting married life unknown to each other and the significance of this heritage. For example, Romano spoke about his mother's decision to enter the marriage: 'She got married in Italy and my father got married here … [I]t was like thousands of miles apart when they got married separately, virtually.'[78]

---

76 Angelina Marchioro, OH 12, 13 March 1984: 8.
77 ibid., 10.
78 Romano Marchioro interviewed by Madeleine Regan, Transcript, J.D. Somerville Oral History Collection, State Library of South Australia, Adelaide, OH 872/20, 11 June 2021: 3.

Plate 2.13: Angelina and Vittorio Marchioro's official wedding photo, Adelaide, 1938
Source: Photo supplied by Johnny Marchioro.

More than 20 years after his parents' interviews, the couple's older son, Johnny, aged 68, also reflected on the family story:

> So, until 1937, Dad wanted to get married and probably letters were only written once a year, [laughs] and he wrote to Italy, to his sister in Italy and said that he wanted to get married ... Then my mother—or-to-be-my-mother—came to Australia ... She got married before, by proxy, but without seeing my father, and they lived together [laughs] for the next 60 years.[79]

In the interview, Johnny was joined by his wife, Eleonora, and both expressed admiration for Angelina and Vittorio although they implied that the risk was greater for Angelina. Johnny acknowledged the ambiguity of proxy marriage in the phrase 'my mother—or-to-be-my-mother' and expressed pride in his parents' long relationship. Johnny's laughter combined curiosity, self-consciousness and incredulity. He also conveyed the difference in traditions and marriage customs between his parents' time and the 1960s, when he and Eleonora married. Like his parents, Johnny married, and then he and Eleonora lived and worked together as market gardeners until retirement. In contrast to Angelina and Vittorio's story of limited opportunities shaped by migration, the younger couple's experience of meeting and marriage was characterised by independence and choice.

Marriages outside the community

In the early 1930s in Adelaide, two young Veneto men took the radical step to marry outside the Italian community and, in one case, there is evidence that it was condemned by some Anglo-Australians. On the other hand, the Veneto market gardeners seemed to accept the marriages even though they could have been considered a threat to the fledgling community at Lockleys. As Baldassar states: 'Endogamy is important to the maintenance of community ... "Mixed" marriages were perceived as threatening group solidarity.'[80]

---

79 Johnny Marchioro interviewed by Madeleine Regan, Transcript, J.D. Somerville Oral History Collection, State Library of South Australia, Adelaide, OH 872/1, 21 July 2008: 3.
80 Baldassar, *Visits Home*, 254.

Silvano Zampin and Amelia Shaw

Plate 2.14: Amelia Zampin nee Shaw and Silvano Zampin, Adelaide, mid-1930s
Source: Photo supplied by the family.

Silvano Zampin was 21 years old in 1931 when he married 20-year-old Amelia Shaw, the daughter of Irish-Australian parents. Silvano had arrived three years before, sponsored by his older brother, Pietro, who had been in Australia for six years. The marriage took place a year after Pietro's accidental death. Silvano's need to put down roots in Australia was realised in a marriage that set the couple apart from other *veneti* in Adelaide. The marriage also placed Amelia in a challenging position because of the racism towards Italians in Australia at the time; her own family shunned her, reflecting the prevailing racist attitudes towards Italians. In their first years of marriage, Silvano and Amelia lived in boarding houses in the City of Adelaide. Children were born and Silvano worked for several gardeners, including a Chinese man, before they moved to Lockleys and leased land for their own market garden.

Six daughters of Silvano and Amelia who recorded oral history interviews reflected on what they understood about the challenges of marriage between an 'Australian' and an Italian in the 1930s and 1940s. The daughters remembered examples of racist attitudes that their parents endured because of their unconventional marriage, which had even more significance during the war years. The sisters recalled offensive and disrespectful terms used to describe Italians, who were identified as 'aliens'. The young Irish-

Australian woman and her Italian husband experienced generalised racism in the context of their marriage and the formation of their family in Anglo-Australian Adelaide.

On the other hand, without exception, the daughters remembered the high regard in which their mother was held by the Veneto community and recalled the close friendships made and regular social occasions attended by their parents. The acceptance of the marriage of Amelia to Silvano indicates that the Veneto market gardeners could accommodate an outsider and include her and the family in the community. One daughter affirmed the inclusivity of the Veneto market gardeners: 'The Italians accepted her better than the Australians.'[81] This acceptance could indicate the Veneto market gardeners' transcultural response to new circumstances and adaptation to a sense of the future of the community in Australia, marked by an attitude of inclusivity towards the exogenous marriage rather than exclusion or rejection of Amelia and Silvano.[82]

Gino Berno and Jean Dyson

Another Veneto man, Gino Berno, married outside the community in 1933. His wife, Jean Dyson, was the daughter of an Anglo-Australian market-gardener family who lived in the Lockleys area. Jean was 19 and Gino was 24 when they married. The couple and their two children shared a large house with Gino's cousins, who were market gardeners for several years.

Marrying a relative of a first-generation Veneto market gardener

There was significance in a migrant's choice of marriage partner and value in marrying a woman 'known' in the community. Even better was a wife whose family was from the same *paese*—a continuity of the Veneto tradition of choosing marriage partners within the local area. Sixteen years after arrival, Eugenio Zalunardo married Luigia Ballestrin, sister of the two Ballestrin brothers who had arrived in 1927. At the time of their marriage in 1943, Eugenio was 38 and Luigia was 27; she had migrated with her mother in 1938.

---

81 Roma Bordignon nee Zampin interviewed by Madeleine Regan, Transcript, J.D. Somerville Oral History Collection, State Library of South Australia, Adelaide, OH 872/41, 3 February 2017: 20.
82 Riccati, *Italians in Australia*, 8–11.

2. BEGINNINGS IN ADELAIDE

Plate 2.15: The marriage of Eugenio Zalunardo and Luigia Ballestrin, Adelaide, 1943
Note: The group poses for a photo in formal attire, conveying the sense of occasion even though it was the middle of the war.
Source: Photo supplied by Norma Camozzato nee Ballestrin.

Adjustments to life at Lockleys

The Veneto migrants who arrived between 1926 and 1928 negotiated several major adjustments after leaving their family households in the Veneto region. First, they made the transition from their *contadini* origins to life as migrants. Second, they managed the uncertainties of beginning life in Australia as dire economic conditions impacted the population in every part of the nation and discrimination against Italians was widespread. Third, the men were compelled to become itinerant labourers—an unfamiliar experience even for people accustomed to seasonal employment. Fourth, the *veneti* made the transition from immersion in family in their childhood households to being alone and learning to survive on the margins of an intolerant society. The next most significant transformation was seizing the opportunity to lease land at Lockleys and establish market gardens. Finally, reunification or formation of families marked evolution to a new form of *paese* comprising nuclear family households. The first generation of *veneti* created working lives and homes on the market gardens with limited connections to Anglo-Australia. However, they used strategies that demonstrated agency and

65

initiative in seeing the potential in becoming business owners and leasing land to develop market gardens as a livelihood. The early market gardeners displayed 'transcultural identities' in establishing themselves on the land.[83]

The first generation adjusted core elements of Veneto life and *contadino* structures, creatively adapting Veneto culture in their new *paese* even when Anglo-Australian hostility towards Italians challenged their belief in a safe settlement. The opportunities at Lockleys to recast their affinity with the land, become market gardeners and build a cohesive social network as a *paese* are fixed threads in the history of the Veneto market-gardener community in the interwar years.

---

83   ibid., 10.

3
Attachment to land

> The whole area was all market garden, you know. Well, I suppose they had to get a living somewhere … When they come here they couldn't understand much, speak much English, didn't know what to do, so they had to start off something because over there [in Italy], they only had little gardens too, and where we come from [in the Veneto] they used to plant once a year because you'd get the snow that high, every year, I still remember the snow there.
>
> —Lino Tonellato, 2010[1]

As Lino Tonellato reflected on his father's early days as a market gardener at Lockleys, he easily reconstructed the landscape where the first generation of *veneti* had lived as *contadini* with their families in the Veneto region. Lino, who was 84 years old when interviewed, remembered the land in the province of Treviso, and his focus on climate reflected a cultivator's awareness of seasons. He connected ideas about land use and agricultural practices in the Veneto with the experience of the first generation and their efforts to gain a livelihood in family run market gardens at Lockleys. He noted that the climate and geography in the subalpine area of the Veneto were different from the western district of Adelaide. Lino captured the narrative of the Veneto market gardeners, the initiative to preserve their *contadino* heritage of working the land and the adaptations required to establish

---

1 Lino Tonellato, OH 872/10, 16 July 2010: 14.

commercial market gardens in Australia. He provided a gendered view of work, focusing on the male perspective and, as one of the 1.5 generation, conveyed familiarity with the Veneto region.

The path to settlement and ownership for the first generation of the Veneto market gardeners was not simple or quick. Yet, the group successfully negotiated the means to access and work the land and reached their goal of becoming self-employed market gardeners during the 1930s, and landowners by the mid-1950s. This chapter addresses the adaptation of Veneto values and practices through transcultural strategies and the formation of group identity through attachment to land.

Plate 3.1: Lino Tonellato, Adelaide, 2014
Source: Michael Campbell.

The convergence of the *veneti* on fertile land at Lockleys that they developed as market gardens is explained by four factors. First, their origins as peasant farmers in the Veneto provided the motivation and knowledge to live and work on their own land. Second, the group recognised that it was possible to occupy and secure land through the South Australian land tenure system. The third factor is the role of the family as a labour unit, including husband, wife and children—a feature of many early rural settlements of Italian groups in Australia.[2] Fourth, the *contadino* tradition of living in a proximate community explains the formation of an enduring, close settlement of families who shared the same occupation in a *paese* or small village-like cluster within 3 kilometres of one another at Lockleys. While the proximity of the families supported the adjustment of the first generation, the density of the Veneto market-gardener settlement was considered a problem by the Anglo-Australian community, who saw the group as distinctly separate and undesirable.[3]

The destiny of the *contadino*

In Italy the relationship to land defined everyday life, the past and the future for the *contadino*. Families had worked the land for generations in the Veneto region. In the early twentieth century, some families owned land, although inheritance was a challenge because it was impossible to expand landholdings to accommodate increasing numbers of the new generations. When land was carved up to support independent subfamily groups, opportunities to increase the livelihood from harvests were insufficient for large households.[4]

---

2 Pascoe, 'Place and Community', 92–93; Jenkins, *Power of the Land*, 21–23.
3 See Lancaster Jones, 'Ethnic Concentration and Assimilation'.
4 Huber, *From Pasta to Pavlova*, 19–21.

'I BUY THIS PIECE OF GROUND HERE'

Plate 3.2: Angelina and Secondo Tonellato outside the house where the Tonellato family grew up, in Caselle di Altivole, Italy, 1962
Source: Photo supplied by Assunta Giovannini nee Tonellato.

The example of the large Ballestrin family illustrates the extent of poverty in the Veneto between the wars that prompted the migration of extended families. Although it was not the experience of other Veneto market gardeners, the two Ballestrin families in the first-generation group gradually sponsored other members and built a large extended family of three generations in Adelaide before World War II.[5] Four members of one family arrived within three years, 1937 to 1939, including the widowed mother of two men who had migrated in 1927. Egidio (Jimmy) Ballestrin explained that his father was 'called' to Adelaide by his two brothers because the intergenerational household at Vallà was unable to provide adequate food, work and space for all the family:

> They were a very large family, and also a very large extended family living with them, and they had some land but couldn't make ends meet because of the fact that there were just too many. There was all his brothers and sisters … nine of them in all, and also the older children started reproducing and having the children or the grandchildren, if you like, live there with them, and there just wasn't enough to go around … Two of his older brothers, which was Antonio and Isidoro, came to Australia in 1927, and in doing so, then also asked … his other brothers to come out and he came out in the early '30s.[6]

Within the Lockleys market-gardener community, the reunion of the extended Ballestrin family re-created the traditional intergenerational arrangements and was the closest example at Lockleys to the family model of chain migration followed by most other Italian migrants in Australia.

The imperative to work the land was shared by the Veneto market gardeners. In his interview, Aldo Rossetto confirmed that on the passenger list on the ship on which his father and uncles arrived in 1927, the most common occupation described people who worked the land:

---

5   One other family, the Santins, formed a three-generation arrangement on Frogmore Road. Three brothers and their wives worked together on the market garden. Two couples and their families shared a large house with the elderly Santin parents.
6   Egidio Ballestrin interviewed by Madeleine Regan, Transcript, J.D. Somerville Oral History Collection, State Library of South Australia, Adelaide, OH 872/15, 6 June 2011: 1–2.

> I noticed on the *Carignano* list of passengers, it had all 'gardeners,' 'gardeners,' 'gardeners;' along every name they were all market gardeners. They cultivated land as peasants in Italy, lived off the land, and obviously that was the way to go.[7]

Aldo indicated the inevitability of the Veneto cohort applying their knowledge and skills as cultivators of land in Australia. The Great Depression had delayed the process of the first generation of *veneti* putting down permanent roots. However, the group progressively took up leases in the Lockleys area through the 1930s. There the market gardeners differed from other Veneto groups who had settled in Australia between the 1920s and 1970s, who moved through four stages of development in achieving *sistemazione*: temporary work in mining, then agriculture, movement from rural to urban life and employment, to the final stage of self-employment.[8] At Lockleys, the first generation moved to the second and ultimate stage of their working lives as market gardeners, and most remained in that occupation well into the 1970s.

Land at Lockleys

The *veneti* settled on leased properties of between 1.2 and 8 hectares on the northern side of the River Torrens between the City of Adelaide and the St Vincent Gulf. The floodplain and alluvial soil had provided a rich abundance of food for the Indigenous peoples of the area, who had for thousands of years used the river as a source of water and food and its surrounds for cultural practices such as burial sites.[9] The river had been a natural corridor between the hills above the plain and the sea in the west. After colonial settlement in the second half of the 1830s, English settlers developed broadacre farms near the River Torrens in the Lockleys area and records of land titles indicate that subdivision of the large farms had begun by at least the 1890s, when a landholding of 60 hectares was divided into smaller parcels.[10]

---

7   Aldo Rossetto interviewed by Madeleine Regan, Transcript, J.D. Somerville Oral History Collection, State Library of South Australia, Adelaide, OH 872/16, 4 July 2011: 9.
8   Baldassar and Pesman, *From Paesani to Global Italians*, 62.
9   Sharyn Beth Clarke, 'The Creation of the Torrens: A History of Adelaide's River to 1881' (MA thesis, University of Adelaide, 2005).
10 South Australian Certificate of Title, Vol. 585, Folio 2, 1894, Property Title Registry, Land Services SA, Adelaide.

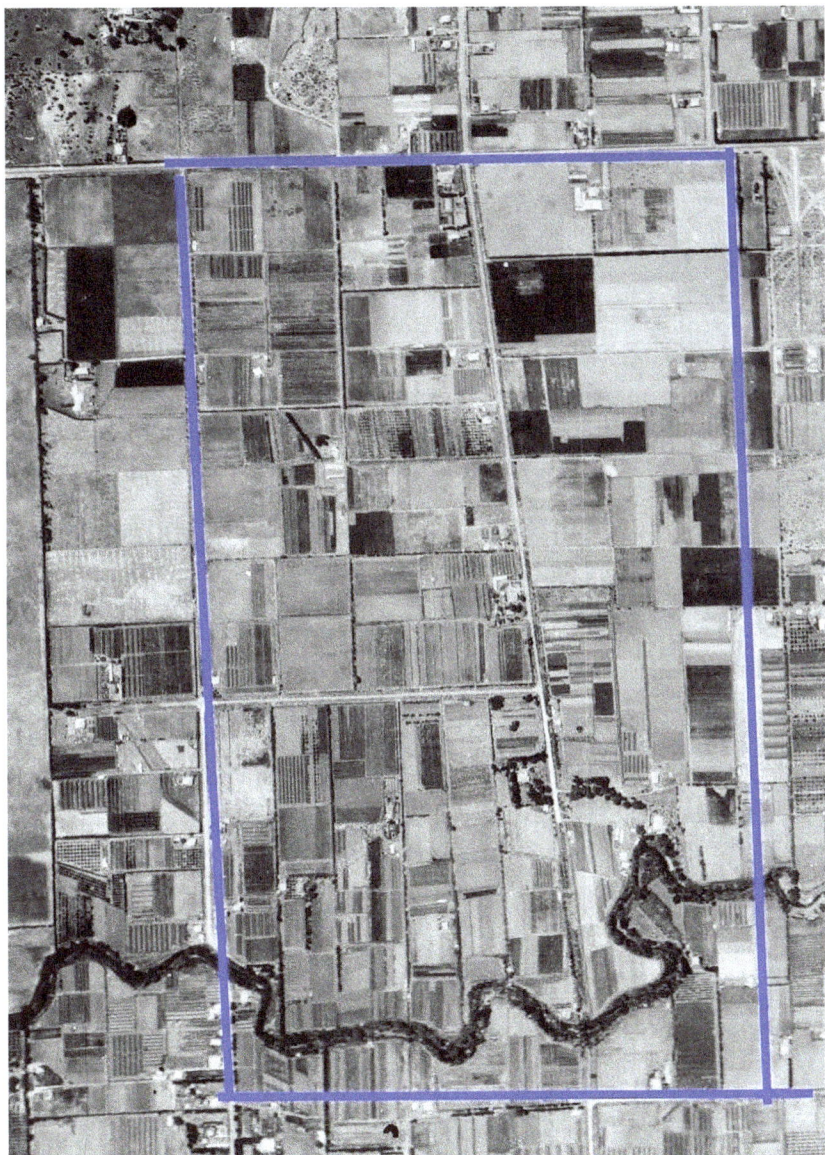

Plate 3.3: Aerial photo showing the approximate location of the Veneto market gardens, 1935
Source: City of Charles Sturt, reproduced with permission.

By the 1930s when the *veneti* took up leases, the area was a mix of large landholdings under crops such as lucerne, dairy farms, small intensive vegetable farms and orchards. Tomatoes were grown in glasshouses in the

Lockleys–Fulham area—a method pioneered by an Englishman, Thomas Skuse, who had arrived in the colony of South Australia in 1865.[11] At that time, apart from the colonial families, small plots of land were leased to Chinese men who grew vegetables for sale at the market from at least the late nineteenth century. After World War I, some returned soldiers were allocated land and Italians from regions including Campania and Calabria worked market gardens in the same area.

The location of the leaseholds secured by the Veneto group close to the River Torrens and about 8 kilometres from the wholesale vegetable market promised optimum conditions for the *contadini* to work land for themselves and establish commercial market gardens. While the river provided water, the earliest years were marked by extensive flooding, which ruined crops, until the government modified the course of the river in the late 1930s. In an article about the experiences of the Tonellato family, the author referred to the River Torrens as 'unpredictable which in dry times, was like a creek painted on canvas, played up when it freely flooded the land destroying the harvest of the farms there'.[12] The desire for land presented risks and uncertainty that were ameliorated by the security of the community.

The *veneti*, land and market gardens

The compact area in which the Veneto market gardeners lived and worked provided physical and social security and a sense of separation from the Anglo-Australian world. The gardens were divided by thick hedges of boxthorn, pine trees or bamboo along tracks that extended away from made roads. Accommodation on the landholdings varied from an early tent dwelling, a former cowshed and iron and wooden shacks that could be dismantled and moved easily, to a large colonial villa acquired by Gino Berno, one of the Veneto market gardeners, during the war. One first-generation woman, Adele (Lina) Bordin, arrived in 1930 to join her husband, Gelindo Rossetto, and found her accommodation was a tent: '[A] hovel—bare and empty—with no gas, no firewood, no electricity and no floor.'[13]

---

11   *Advertiser*, [Adelaide], 5 April 1918: 9. In his obituary, Thomas Skuse was reported to have begun the practice and eventually had 'acres of tomatoes under glass'. Tomatoes became one of the most prevalent crops in market gardens by the time of his death at 70 years of age.
12   Anon., 'C'era una volta una famiglia che viveva in un vagone … = Once upon a Time There Was a Family Who Lived in a Railway Carriage …', *Il Messaggero*, [Rome], June 1986: 17 (translated by Graziella Ledda).
13   Rossetto, *Rain in These Shoes*, 68.

Plate 3.4: Gelindo, Lina and Romeo Rossetto, Lockleys, c. 1932
Source: Photo supplied by the Rossetto family.

Secondo Tonellato solved the problem of housing his wife and five children when they arrived in 1935 by purchasing a disused railway carriage from the South Australian Railways and transporting it to his land at Lockleys. The carriage, or *vagòn*, was a significant landmark in the Veneto community and all narrators recalled its presence near Frogmore Road. The story told most often about its origins was that it was built as the royal train for the tour in 1927 of the Duke and Duchess of York (who later became King George VI and Queen Elizabeth). One of Secondo Tonellato's granddaughters, Sandra Conci nee Santin, remembered what her mother, Rosina, had told her about coming to live in Adelaide in 1935 as a child:

> I know that … she was 12 when she came out. Nonno came out about, I reckon he came out seven or eight years before she did and then she came here and that's when they moved into that carriage because that was the house, he brought out all his family then in 1935.[14]

---

14 Sandra Conci nee Santin interviewed by Madeleine Regan, Transcript, J.D. Somerville Oral History Collection, State Library of South Australia, Adelaide, OH 872/47, 25 August 2018: 4.

Plate 3.5: The Tonellato *vagòn*, Lockleys, 1935
Note: The photo was taken when Elisabetta joined her husband with their five children in June of that year.
Source: Photo supplied by Assunta Giovannini nee Tonellato.

Close occupationally based communities separated from the Anglo-Australian population were evident in other Italian migrant group settlements between the wars. For example, a small group of Sicilian migrants leased market gardens near Geelong in Victoria between 1929 and 1949 although there were just six families who had come from the same village.[15] Settlements of *veneti* existed on farms in the Griffith area in the Riverina of New South Wales and in the Gippsland region of Victoria, where they were more scattered and included the self-employed and wage-earners.[16] The Molfettese fishers in the regional South Australian city of Port Pirie developed a strong community and occupational identity from the late nineteenth century.[17] At Lockleys, the network developed by the market gardeners was a more opportunistic endeavour than the communities formed through chain migration because the Veneto group established themselves without relying on existing social structures.

---

15 Maria Mantello, *Now and Then: The Sicilian Farming Community at Werribee Park, 1929–1949* (Melbourne: Globe Press, 1986).
16 Huber, *From Pasta to Pavlova*; Davine, *Vegnimo da Conco Ma Simo Veneti*.
17 Bromley, 'The Italians of Port Pirie'; Corrieri, *Italians of Port Pirie*.

3. ATTACHMENT TO LAND

A group of market gardeners from north-eastern Bulgaria who had arrived in Adelaide in 1928 began leasing land in the early 1930s at Fulham Gardens, about 2 kilometres west of Lockleys.[18] Like the *veneti*, the men who had been agricultural workers in Bulgaria created a close community and worked hard to establish their gardens before they brought their wives and families to join them, or they married once in Adelaide. In contrast to the Veneto market gardeners, who created their *paese* at Lockleys without a physical hub, the Bulgarian group at Fulham Gardens built a centre and a church for the wider Bulgarian community in the late 1940s.[19]

Although there were other market gardeners in the locality, the Veneto families formed a physically and socially separate *paese* at Lockleys. The Anglo-Australian market gardens were mostly on the periphery of the Veneto settlement and one Anglo-Australian narrator, Rae Ballantyne, recalled that his family had no significant interactions with the Italians. He described the area: 'There was isolated houses here and there … so there was no social life, I suppose, nothing at all.'[20] In contrast, the sons and daughters of the first generation of Veneto market gardeners remember the composition of the area differently and identify families in their own community. For example, Romano Marchioro, a second-generation son born in 1942, distinguished other Veneto families, adding details about their kinship and emphasising that the Anglo-Australians were the exception in the area: 'Well, there was the Tonellatos, there was the Piovesans and the Ballestrins and Zalunardo; he was my godfather. They were all in that area … all Italians. There weren't too many Australians around there.'[21]

The 1.5- and second-generation narrators spoke about the significance of land for their parents. From a distance of 70 years, they provided precise details about the family market gardens, recalling locations, physical features such as the River Torrens, bridges, positions of roads and tracks, ownership of land, boundaries of boxthorn and bamboo, varieties of crops, numbers of glasshouses and the few houses in comparison with open and farmed land. In an aerial photo from the late 1950s, the narrators identified at least

---

18 Kristen Wilkins, *Bulgarian Migration and Market Gardens in the Western Suburbs*, Report submitted to the City of Charles Sturt and the Faculty of Humanities and Social Sciences (Adelaide: University of Adelaide, 2012), 14.
19 The Bulgarians' Educational and Friendly Society, *50th Jubilee Book* (Adelaide: The Bulgarians' Educational and Friendly Society Incorporated, 2000).
20 Rae Ballantyne interviewed by Madeleine Regan, Transcript, J.D. Somerville Oral History Collection, State Library of South Australia, Adelaide, OH 872/21, 25 August 2012: 15.
21 Romano Marchioro, OH 872/20, 11 June 2012: 4.

'I BUY THIS PIECE OF GROUND HERE'

40 individual family farms, including those owned by Anglo-Australians, Chinese, Veneto and other Italians. The nucleus of Veneto families was always their starting point when viewing photos and maps of the area.

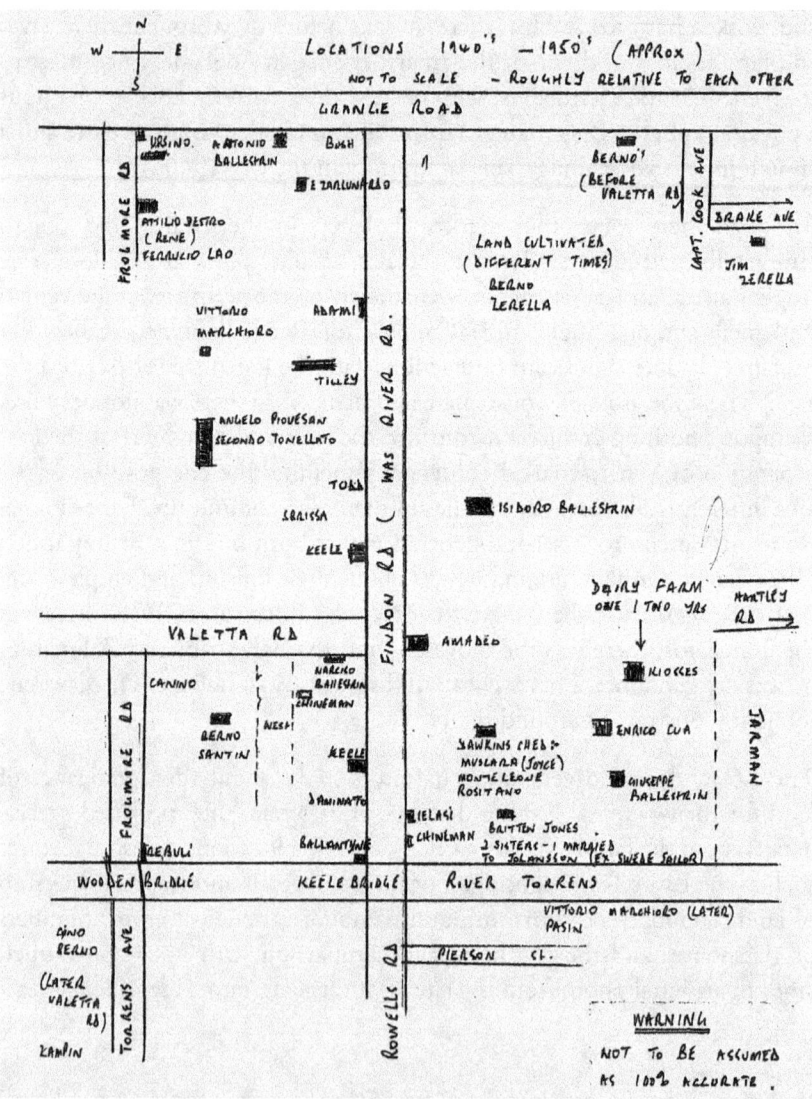

Map 3.1: Map drawn by Lino Ballestrin showing Veneto and other market gardeners in the Lockleys area, 1940s–50s

Note: Some families are not identified west of Frogmore Road between Grange Road and Valetta Road.

Source: Map drawn and supplied by Lino Ballestrin.

3. ATTACHMENT TO LAND

Occupying land as market gardeners

Before World War II, most Veneto market gardeners had engaged with the land tenure system in South Australia as lessees. The first generation demonstrated agency and competency as they engaged with the administrative structures in Australia as migrants who had experienced mobility and insecurity in their first years after arrival.[22] The case of the first Veneto man to own land for a market garden illustrates the challenge of achieving ownership in the 1940s for someone born in Italy. It also demonstrates the advantage of naturalisation in facilitating access to Australian law and acting on behalf of kin to purchase land during the war years. However, the advantage abated when the government restricted the rights of Italians after Italy entered the war with Germany.

An old colonial family, the Butterfields, had owned large landholdings in what was known as the Lockleys and Fulham localities along the River Torrens. In 1942, a Butterfield son sold 6.5 hectares at St James Park (also known as Lockleys) to Gino Berno, who was naturalised in 1938. Gino's cousins Alberto and Pietro Berno had worked as farm labourers on the Butterfield property since about 1930 but were prevented from buying land because they were not naturalised at the time the property was offered for sale. The brothers had first applied to be naturalised in September 1939 and were notified 13 months later that their applications were unsuccessful. When they reapplied in 1944, their applications were rejected on the grounds that the war prohibited the naturalisation of enemy aliens.[23] It is not clear why the brothers did not take the step to become naturalised before 1939 or how the decision was made to sell the property to Gino.

Gino Berno's purchase of land was an extraordinary step for a *contadino* whose family experience of land occupation in Italy had been constrained by the *mezzadria* system, which did not permit landownership. It was also remarkable because the purchase was an example of the resourcefulness

---

22 The example of the initiative to lease land reflects what Ricatti describes as 'the intensity of migrants' lives', demonstrated by the complexity of social and cultural dealings: the experience of nostalgia for what they had known mixed with the challenges of settlement and prospects for the future. Ricatti, *Italians in Australia*, 3, 10.
23 Department of Immigration Central Office, A435, Class 4 correspondence files relating to naturalisation, 01 Jan 1944 – 31 Dec 1950, 1946/4/510, Berno Vittorio Pietro born 18 July 1909—Italian, 1939–1946; Department of Immigration Central Office, A435, Class 4 correspondence files relating to naturalisation, 01 Jan 1944 – 31 Dec 1950, 1946/4/527, Berno Alberto—born 16 February 1905—Italian 1939–1946, NAA.

of the Berno brothers, Alberto and Pietro, who had become involved in negotiations that tested the rigorous wartime regulations. The land transaction became the subject of an extensive investigation by the Attorney-General's Department because of a potential breach of the National Security (Land Transfer) Regulations of 1940, which severely restricted the right of 'enemy aliens' and even naturalised people of enemy origin to acquire land during the war. The Berno brothers were suspected of providing the funds for the sale and Gino was accused of 'dummying' for his cousins. Dummying was an offence under the regulations, which were enacted during the war to preclude enemy aliens from entering into land transactions.

The Commonwealth Investigation Branch questioned the exchange of the large sum of £2,100—the price of the land finalised in May 1942. The government investigator was especially suspicious of the 'mortgage' of £1,600 that had been handed over in banknotes in a lawyer's office. In the Anglo-Australian world, large amounts of cash would generally have been handled by banks whereas the *veneti* were not used to possessing money or entrusting the management of their finances to an institution like a bank. In discussion with members of the 1.5 generation, I learned that even in the 1960s some first-generation *veneti* in Adelaide negotiated loans within families or within the Veneto community because they trusted *paesani* more than banks.[24] The investigators examined Gino Berno's financial history to establish the improbability of his capacity to possess such a large sum of money. While Gino signed the contract in April 1942, the government investigation continued until October 1943, even as crops were planted and harvested on the land.[25]

Antipathy towards Italians in the wider community influenced the results of the investigation. The negativity was particularly evident in an area like Lockleys where the concentration of Italian market gardeners, including the *veneti*, had increased during the 1930s. Across Australia, the clustering of small-scale migrant farmers in some suburban areas made them conspicuous in the 1940s.[26] By July 1942, public opinion had been inflamed and the Commonwealth attorney-general invited citizens to report unlawful land transfer arrangements by enemy aliens or naturalised persons of enemy

---

24   Maria Rosa Tormena, Personal communication, 11 February 2021.
25   Investigation Branch, Central Office, Melbourne and Canberra, A12217, Alien Land Transfer files, single number with L [Land] prefix, 01 Jan 1940 – 31 Dec 1946, L5555, Gino Felice Berno—purchase of property in Lockleys, SA, 1942–1943, NAA.
26   Price, *Southern Europeans in Australia*, 157–58.

origin.²⁷ The public invitation prompted an Anglo-Australian resident of Lockleys to write a detailed letter outlining a case against Italians taking over the area. The resident had previously worked land that Gino Berno purchased and had been required to relinquish the dwelling in which he had lived because of the transaction.

The complainant set out his objections, accusing the 'unnaturalised enemy aliens'—the Berno brothers—of having illegally acquired the land and a large house on the property and describing what he saw as 'this Italian menace, they are allowed to build wood & iron shacks and live in filthy conditions'. The letter alleged that the Italians were not paying taxes and called for action on behalf of 'our Australian boys away fighting for their country', whom he believed should have had preference in matters of land purchases.²⁸ The lengthy investigation of Gino Berno and his cousins extended to other members of the Veneto community who were questioned about their relationships and knowledge of the financial position of the extended Berno family. However, the testimonies of three Veneto witnesses in the community were dismissed as worthless. Ultimately, the Attorney-General's Department found that it could not prove a breach of regulations and the case against Gino Berno and his cousins was not upheld.²⁹ Nonetheless, the allegation of dummying remained an obstacle when the brothers endeavoured to apply for naturalisation in later years.

Disputes about ownership of property also impacted another family in the Veneto group who had applied to lease part of the same property acquired by Gino Berno. Giovanni Santin, a member of the first generation, had moved to Adelaide from country South Australia with his wife and four children in 1941 and leased land across the River Torrens from the Veneto market gardeners for two years. When Giovanni was naturalised in December 1939, his wife, Costantina, and their children were also deemed British subjects. In May 1943, Giovanni applied to lease a section of land from Gino Berno on Valetta Road. However, the application was the subject of another investigation into a possible breach of the National Security (Land Transfer) Regulations because Gino Berno did not have the authority to allow a person to sublet land without permission from the attorney-general. Giovanni's ambition to lease land close to other *veneti* demonstrated his belief that he might later be able to purchase a property large enough to work with his three sons.

---

27 A12217, L5555, 'Gino Felice Berno', NAA; *Advertiser*, [Adelaide], 1 August 1942.
28 A12217, L5555, 'Gino Felice Berno', NAA, 33–34.
29 ibid., 13–14.

The extensive investigation into the circumstances of the subletting of land involved interrogation of Giovanni Santin and his three sons, who had been observed working the 1.4 hectares they had applied to lease. The absence of a formal contract between Gino Berno and Giovanni Santin was regarded as a problem. The authorities would not have been satisfied with verbal agreements about leases and land ownership because the Torrens title system had been adopted in South Australia to identify ownership and transfers of ownership on a certificate of title, avoid disputes over proprietorship and ensure equitable taxation arrangements. The Berno–Santin agreement would have been based on understandings common in the Veneto region. Verbal agreements were considered binding and sound and there was no belief in formal legal contracts.

During the investigation, one of the Santin sons claimed his right to lease and work the land as a 'British subject' because he had been called up and released by the army to cultivate vegetables during the war.[30] The investigation officers highlighted the 'duplicity' and 'unreliability' of the Veneto market gardeners involved in the case; however, after a considerable period, the lease was finally approved. The six members of the Santin family and Gino Berno and his wife and their two sons jointly occupied the large house on the property on Valetta Road. In 1950 the Santin family bought their own, larger property on Frogmore Road within 2 kilometres of the Berno land.

Denial of an application to own land

In a different case, the attorney-general refused an application to purchase land made by a Veneto market gardener who had been naturalised in 1939. After leasing 1.8 hectares in the Lockleys area for several years, Gelindo Rossetto and his wife, Lina, aspired to own their own land for market gardens. In 1942, Gelindo applied to purchase 3.6 hectares on Frogmore Road, near other *veneti*. Gelindo was able to cover the asking price of £2,600 with a 10 per cent deposit and stated that he could make a cash payment of £1,600, which included a loan of £220 from his brother-in-law. The report that informed Gelindo of the rejection of his application implied criticism

---

30 Investigation Branch, Central Office, Melbourne and Canberra, A12217, Alien Land Transfer files, single number with L [Land] prefix, 01 Jan 1940 – 31 Dec 1946, L7183, Giovanni Santin—purchase of property Lockleys, SA, 1943–1944, NAA.

of the verbal agreement.³¹ Gelindo's income from both his mica mine and his market garden was robust and would have satisfied the requirements of repaying the bank loan.

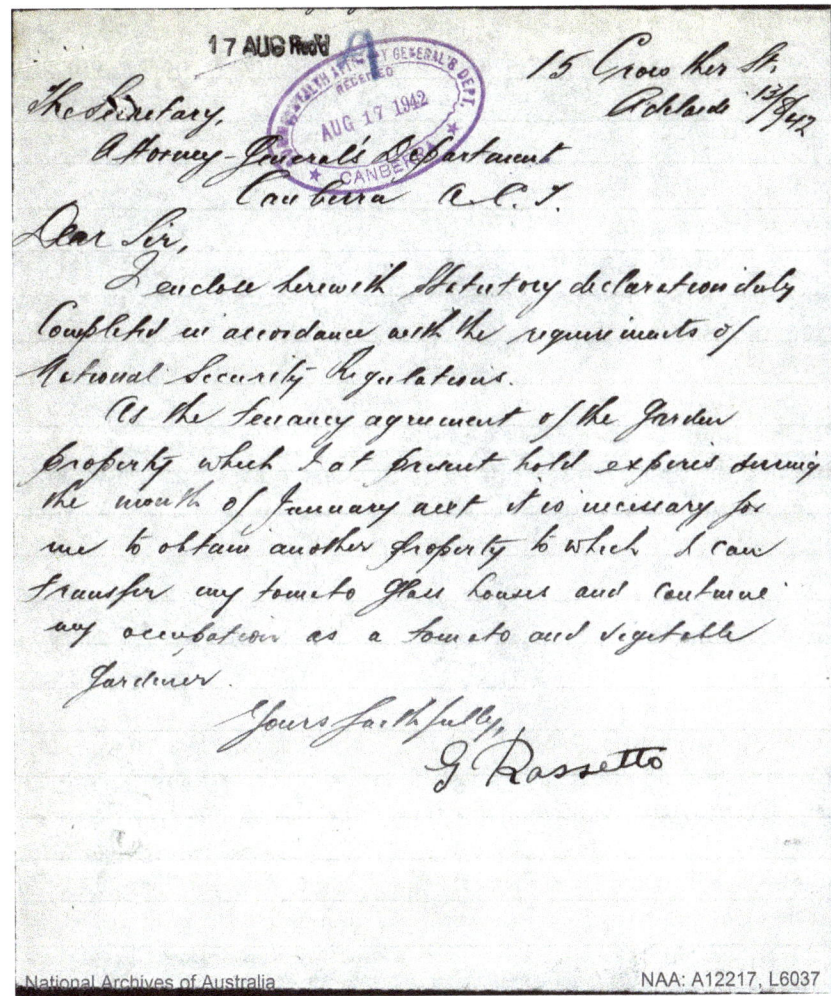

Plate 3.6: Gelindo Rossetto's letter to the attorney-general requesting early consideration of his application to buy land for his market garden, 13 August 1942
Source: Investigation Branch, Central Office, Melbourne and Canberra, A12217, Alien Land Transfer files, single number with L [Land] prefix, 01 Jan 1940–31 Dec 1946, L6307, Gelindo Rossetto—purchase of property Findon, SA, 1942–1942, NAA, 23.

---

31 Investigation Branch, Central Office, Melbourne and Canberra, A12217, Alien Land Transfer files, single number with L [Land] prefix, 01 Jan 1940 – 31 Dec 1946, L6307, Gelindo Rossetto—purchase of property Findon, SA, 1942–1942, NAA, 10–11.

Gelindo's experience as part-owner of a mica mine gave him the confidence to request a speedy response to his application to purchase the land at Lockleys. His determination is evident in two letters he wrote to the Commonwealth attorney-general. Gelindo requested that the application be approved quickly because the lease on the property he was working was due to expire and he needed to relocate his glasshouses to the new property in time for the tomato-growing season.[32] In the letter dated the same day as his application, Gelindo explained the imperative to move his glasshouses.

Gelindo's plan to set up his new market garden included employing his youngest brother and another Italian man to work the land while he worked in the Northern Territory at his mica mine—a labour model that echoed customary structures of co-working land in the Veneto region. His absence from the market gardens suggests a parallel to the role of the *padrone*, who owned land and contracted *contadini* to work for him in return for half the produce under the *mezzadria* system. Although he received considerable income from the mica mine, Gelindo wanted to keep his connection to working the land by purchasing and cultivating a market garden when he returned to Adelaide for seasonal tasks such as planting and harvesting. In addition to imitating the role of a *padrone*, Gelindo was also reshaping the Veneto's traditional seasonal employment model.

In November 1942, after an inquiry by the Investigation Branch in Adelaide, the Attorney-General's Department notified Gelindo Rossetto that the contract of sale had been refused under the National Security (Land Transfer) Regulations.[33] While the Investigation Branch conceded that there was no evidence to suggest that Gelindo was disloyal or of poor character, the decision rested on three facts that adversely affected his ambitions. First, in 1942, the war was a factor because the Australian Army was engaged in combat with the Japanese Army in New Guinea and fear in the community had increased since the bombing of Darwin earlier that year. Second, the land Gelindo aspired to purchase on Frogmore Road, close to a bridge, was classified as being in a strategic frontline military location should an invasion occur, and the report acknowledged that plans had been formed to remove the Italian families in such circumstances. Finally, four Anglo-Australian market gardeners in the area who belonged to the local Lockleys sub-branch of the Returned Soldiers League and were soldier-

---

32   ibid., 24–25.
33   ibid., 3.

settlers campaigned against the right of Italians to purchase land and wrote testimonies outlining strong concerns about the enemy aliens. Two statements also referred to the Bulgarian market gardeners in the district, implying that Bulgarians were also a threat to Anglo-Australian property owners.[34]

The campaign against enemy aliens mirrored the hostile views of World War I veterans in other parts of Australia where southern European communities had established market gardens or farms close to soldier settlers and/or had bought the land that soldier settlers abandoned as unviable.[35] The four local soldier-settler market gardeners condemned the large number of Italians, whose 'behaviour at all times was most offensive' and who could potentially sabotage local bridges and munitions factories in the event of an invasion. The returned soldiers portrayed the area as an 'Italian colony' where previously there had been only British residents.

The statements of the soldier settlers echoed contemporary public opinion built on racism, wartime insecurity, fear and nostalgia for an Anglo-Australia already changed by the presence of southern European migrants. The inspector in the Adelaide office of the attorney-general pointed out errors in the statements, such as the gross overestimation of the number of Italians in the area, and confirmed that Italians had applied for land transfer in many locations across the state. Yet, the report also contained opinions that mirrored prevailing anti-Italian sentiments. It included details about the lives of the Veneto market gardeners, such as their perceived low living standards.[36] It also censured their long working hours—practices that were seen to threaten Anglo-Australian employees. The fears of the petitioners proved sufficient for the Australian Government to deny the application and Gelindo and Lina continued to lease the small landholding for their market garden. Gelindo maintained his involvement in the mica mine in the Northern Territory—another version of asset ownership in Australia.

---

34 ibid., 10–15.
35 Maria Mantello, 'Their Words … My Words … Our Words: A Reflection on Oral History with Reference to Italian Immigrant Identity in the Werribee Community during World War 2' (BA Hons thesis, University of Melbourne, 1981), 34–36; Price, *Southern Europeans in Australia*, 214–15.
36 This judgement had been promulgated since at least the 1920s when public servant Lyng described Italians as 'Mediterranean types' who 'are backward and the living standard of the people low.' Lyng cited in Catherine Dewhirst, 'The "Southern Question" in Australia: The 1925 Royal Commission's Racialisation of Southern Italians', *Queensland History Journal* 22, no. 4 (2014): 316–32, at 326.

'I BUY THIS PIECE OF GROUND HERE'

Land and minerals in the Northern Territory

The Veneto tradition of seasonal and 'out' work provided the model for two Veneto men to regularly leave their market gardens in the care of their wives, other kin and neighbours while they worked on mica mines in the Northern Territory. Although they did not have mining experience, the desire for land, security of employment and income motivated many Veneto men to mine for mica in the remote desert.[37] The mines were about 1,700 kilometres north of Adelaide and 200 kilometres north-east of Alice Springs. Numbers of *veneti* in the wider community in Adelaide worked in the mica mines, including several married couples who lived and raised children there. Although Gelindo Rossetto and Angelo Piovesan came from different villages in the Veneto, they had become close friends through the market-gardener group at Lockleys and their bonds were strengthened when Angelo became godparent to one of Gelindo's sons.

In the mid- to late-1930s, after leasing land for market gardens and settling their wives and small children on their properties in Lockleys, the two men saw a financial opportunity to own shares in a mica mine. Dino Piovesan explained his father's reason for working in the mine:

> Dad went up to the mica mines for a short time, to get some money, to earn a little bit better living because the market garden was only just set up and wasn't producing much income.[38]

The financial return from mining was particularly lucrative during the war because mica was used in electronic equipment, thermal insulation and airplane instruments. It had been mined in small-scale operations from the late nineteenth century in the Harts Range and Italian miners, many from the north of Italy, were a large presence on the mica fields, particularly in the 1930s and 1940s.[39] The extended Veneto market-gardener community was involved in the mica treatment chain, from its extraction, hand-cutting and transportation to Adelaide, where it was processed in a factory owned by a Veneto man who employed many young Veneto women in the 1940s and 1950s.

---

37 See Baldassar and Pesman, *From Paesani to Global Italians*, 64–65; O'Connor, *No Need to be Afraid*, 125–27; Hugo, 'Mica Mining at Harts Range', 156–229.
38 Dino Piovesan, OH 872/17, 23 September 2011: 7.
39 Hugo, 'Mica Mining at Harts Range', 92–102.

3. ATTACHMENT TO LAND

Plate 3.7: Gelindo Rossetto at the Spotted Tiger mica mine, Northern Territory, 1930s
Source: Photo supplied by the Rossetto family.

The prospects for attaining *sistemazione* were more likely for market gardeners than for miners because the cultivation of vegetables continued to meet demand and was undertaken within a stable community environment, whereas mica mining was dependent on specialised demand and involved working in a remote location with the emotional cost of separation from family.[40] Gelindo and Angelo accepted the isolation and demanding work in the mines and managed cycles of planting and harvesting in their market gardens with visits and assistance from family members, *paesani* and paid workers.

The impact of distance and separation was a challenge for miners when a family experienced difficult circumstances in Adelaide, as reported by Gelindo's daughter Lena, who recalled a crisis:

> Then my Dad went up to the Harts Ranges, he was away for a few years, but he used to come home now and then, but the aeroplane used to take about 12 hours from Alice Springs to Adelaide … As a matter of fact, when my eldest brother died on the 1st of November [1938], my Dad was still in Harts Ranges, and it was hard to get messages to him. Somehow or other, somebody from Alice Springs had to go to the mine and tell Dad that my brother was dying. He tried to get back to Adelaide before he died, and the doctors in the Children's Hospital kept him on oxygen to keep him alive until my Dad arrived back.[41]

Gelindo Rossetto and Angelo Piovesan were naturalised in the late 1930s and, although they had mined at Harts Range before the war, they were initially prohibited from holding a miner's right because of the National Security (Land Transfer) Regulations, which also applied to naturalised enemy aliens. In 1941, permission was granted to Italians and other enemy aliens to take up mining rights, probably to meet the increased demand for mica during the war. In that year, Gelindo and Angelo reapplied for mining approval with two other Italians and an Anglo-Australian man; the application was approved by the Investigation Branch in Canberra. Gelindo's application to purchase land for a market garden was refused in 1943 when he used the

---

40   Two women interviewed for the project spoke about their experience of living at the mines with their families. See Armida Mattiazzo nee Biasetto interviewed by Madeleine Regan, Transcript, J.D. Somerville Oral History Collection, State Library of South Australia, Adelaide, OH 872/12; and Bruna Rossetto nee Battaglia interviewed by Madeleine Regan, Transcript, J.D. Somerville Oral History Collection, State Library of South Australia, Adelaide, OH 872/33.
41   Lena Moscheni nee Rossetto interviewed by Madeleine Regan, Transcript, J.D. Somerville Oral History Collection, State Library of South Australia, Adelaide, OH 872/32, 28 August 2014: 18.

same administrative processes associated with the National Security (Land Transfer) Regulations. The difference in the two applications related to the use of land: the mine was producing mica that was an essential commodity required for the war effort. The cultivation of fresh vegetables, particularly during the war years, was also essential; however, the enemy alien threat to homogeneity was viewed as a greater risk in the urban area of a state capital and partially explains the government's drive to regulate land transfers to Italian migrants. While Gelindo did not return to full-time work in the garden, Angelo returned and worked the market garden at Lockleys with his wife and sons until his sudden death in 1949.

From leaseholds to ownership

From the 1930s, the *veneti* leased plots of land mostly under annual agreements. Some narrators recalled a regular childhood task of taking the rent money to a landowner at Lockleys on behalf of their parents. The image of the child delivering rent to landowners echoes the *padrone–contadino* relationship within the *mezzadria* system in the Veneto. It was never possible for a *contadino* family in the *mezzadria* structure to earn an income from the tenancy arrangements since it was a life of subsistence. However, as tenants in Adelaide, they could earn an income from the land they leased and were able to improve and increase production and accumulate funds to eventually purchase their properties.

Ownership of land for the Veneto market gardeners was a definite step towards stability, permanency and the formation of identity in Australia.[42] The turning point for the Veneto market gardeners at Lockleys occurred after the war when the regulations restricting enemy aliens from purchasing land were reversed and families moved from being tenants to owners.[43] Acquiring a certificate of title demonstrated ownership of freehold land in perpetuity—a significant goal for the migrant families. In his interview, Bruno Piovesan used the example of his family to interpret the process of determining ownership of property. He traced transactions from leaseholds

---

42   Baldassar and Pesman, *From Paesani to Global Italians*, 65; Davine, *Vegnimo da Conco Ma Simo Veneti*, 49.
43   The first two families, the Rebulis and the Marchioros, were able to purchase land before 1950. See South Australian Certificate of Title, Vol. 1095, Folio 118, 27 February 1947; South Australian Certificate of Title, Volume 1986, Folio 84, 2 July 1948, Property Title Registry, Land Services SA, Adelaide.

in the 1930s to the time when the first-generation, and some of the 1.5-generation, families bought their land, to the 1960s, when landowners began to subdivide their land:

> In those years the occupiers of the land had first option to purchase. Of course, we had five acres [2 hectares] and that was it; other people had twelve acres [5 hectares]. But when they come to survey it with proper means, with *better* means than they had in those years [when land was subdivided for leaseholds], people finished up with thirteen, fourteen acres [5.2–5.7 hectares] for their ten acres [4 hectares]. We finished up with about six acres for five acres [2.5 for 2 hectares] … But [it] didn't make any difference anyway, in those years, you occupied that area and that's what you kept.[44]

Adapting *contadino* traditions of landownership

In the 1950s the Veneto families bought land using contractual partnership arrangements that differed markedly from the patriarchal structures of the *contadino* working households. In the Veneto region, the male head was dominant in all aspects of the household, in the fields, in financial matters and in decisions about labour and crops. Adult men were under the authority of their fathers in roles of 'superordination–subordination' and if a family lived on and worked the land, sons were unable to 'own' it until the death of their father.[45] In the Tonellato family, Secondo and his four sons had worked together on leased land at Lockleys for several years until the older ones married and established their own market gardens. As married men, they acquired land separately, which they worked with their wives. Albert explained the circumstances that enabled him and his wife, Mary, to purchase land:

> They [the two younger brothers] started to work with Dad. Still, me and my older brother went out; not too far out … And then [in] 1952 or '51 we bought land on Findon Road. With no money, never had any money. Those years, friends were friends. You asked them, can they lend you a bit of money, if they had them, they'll give it to you. And they did.[46]

---

44   Bruno Piovesan interviewed by Madeleine Regan, Transcript, J.D. Somerville Oral History Collection, State Library of South Australia, Adelaide, OH 872/5, 3 December 2008: 8 [emphasis in original].
45   Huber, *From Pasta to Pavlova*, 20, 25, 29.
46   Albert Tonellato, OH 872/4, 3 October 2008: 6.

3. ATTACHMENT TO LAND

Albert illustrated the familial and *paesani* bonds and trust shared in the market-gardener community that made it possible to borrow money and become a landowner. Albert used 'we' to refer to himself and Mary, who worked with him on their market garden, although he was identified as the proprietor of the 2 hectares they purchased in 1950.[47]

By the early 1950s, Secondo's two youngest sons, Lino and Nano, joined him in a partnership formally written into the certificate of title as 'tenants in common'. They signed the legal documentation for landownership as equal partners. In a further extension of the benefits of land tenure in Australia, the father and two sons sold their first property to another Italian market gardener and purchased a larger holding.[48] Not only were they landowners, but they also became vendors, creating a structure to develop a partnership between generations in a family and transforming their identity as migrants into that of capable business operators.

Unlike the patriarchal regulation and fragmentation of land among *contadini* in the Veneto, the market-gardener group engaged with land tenure. Some families with adequate landholdings were able to subdivide and gift a parcel to their adult children when they married. Johnny Marchioro observed this practice: 'They took pieces of the land that their fathers were working, they started working it for themselves, so that's how big it was.'[49]

Exceptions to the configuration of landownership demonstrate the adaptations made by the first generation of Veneto migrants as they purchased land after the war. Isidoro Ballestrin bought land in 1953 with his brother and a friend as 'tenants in common'. The case of Vittorio Marchioro and his sister-in-law, Margherita Marchioro, defied the customs of Veneto family relationships and gender hierarchies. They had first formed a partnership to lease and work the land together at Lockleys in the mid-1930s because the ill health of Margherita's husband prevented him from working in glasshouses and he became a wage-earner. Margherita had a strong drive to work the land and, in 1937, when Vittorio married and brought his wife, Angelina, from Italy to the market garden, the arrangements for working the land continued. When Margherita was widowed in 1948, she bought a property with Vittorio as 'tenants in common' with a loan from an Italian man who owned a grocery shop in the city.[50]

---

47 South Australian Certificate of Title, Vol. 2100, Folio 188, 1950.
48 South Australian Certificate of Title, Vol. 1991, Folio 123, 1951.
49 Johnny Marchioro, OH 872/1, 28 July 2008: 25.
50 South Australian Certificate of Title, Vol. 1986, Folio 84.

'I BUY THIS PIECE OF GROUND HERE'

A woman signing a contract with her brother-in-law challenged the strict gendered relationships of a Veneto *contadino* household and transgressed the patriarchal structures of landownership that prohibited women in the Veneto region from being involved in property or financial matters. Although similar conventions about male ownership of property applied to women in the Anglo-Australian culture at the time, the incidence within the Veneto tradition of a sister-in-law and brother-in-law establishing a partnership would have been unimaginable. The partnership of the Marchioro in-laws was yet another adaptation of the Veneto model of landownership: two women and one man owned land and worked together on the same market garden.

The partnership between the in-laws allowed Margherita to achieve her ambition to live and work as a market gardener in Adelaide. Her ability to earn an income as a widow and support her three daughters placed her in a comfortable economic position and enabled her to build what her daughter Connie called 'her dream home'.[51] The market gardens provided opportunities to modify the traditional roles of women and men. The Veneto group gained benefits from the migration experience, including freedom from some gendered and paternalistic constraints on family relationships as well as the opportunity to exploit the possibilities of owning land in Australia through legal contracts. The examples of the new contractual arrangements within families and extended families for buying (and selling) land provide evidence of the agency of the Veneto market gardeners to further their aspirations to achieve *sistemazione*. The first and 1.5 generations demonstrated their capacity to use legal and administrative structures as a 'transcultural strategy for orientation and emplacement' in Australia.[52]

The turn from patriarchal control to new parallel arrangements within the family is illustrated in a further example of transforming gender relations in land ownership. In 1953, cousins Giuseppe and Ermenegildo Ballestrin bought 8 hectares of land on the River Torrens at Flinders Park. They had leased the property from the early 1940s and chose to purchase it as 'tenants in common'. In 1954, Ermenegildo returned to Italy to marry and brought his wife, Norina, to Adelaide. At that time, Giuseppe had been married for 20 years to Cesira and they had three children. Both women worked with their husbands on the market gardens cultivating large crops of celery and glasshouse tomatoes. In 1955, the two men applied to change the land title

---

51   Connie Legovich nee Marchioro interviewed by Madeleine Regan, Transcript, J.D. Somerville Oral History Collection, State Library of South Australia, Adelaide, OH 872/11, 10 January 2011: 4.
52   Ricatti, *Italians in Australia*, 132.

certificate to include the names of their wives on the documentation. They were the only couples among the Veneto market gardeners who included their wives' names as joint legal owners of the property. While the reason for adding the women's names is not known, it is evidence of Veneto men readjusting the priorities of male inheritance and control of land from the Veneto region to their new circumstances at Lockleys.

The desire to achieve *sistemazione* was a feature of the lives of Veneto families. It was a material aspiration that the market-gardener husbands and wives worked hard to attain through owning the land they worked at Lockleys. The goal of ownership was likely motivated by their *contadino* heritage and their strong attachment to the land.[53] Through ownership of property including a house, they achieved the material and symbolic aspects of *sistemazione*. It was a pursuit that also involved the participation of children in first-generation families.

Plate 3.8: The Ballestrin families preparing celery for sale at market, Flinders Park, late 1950s
Note: From left to right: Celso Tieppo, Cesira, Giuseppe and Lino Ballestrin, Primo Berti and Ermenegildo Ballestrin.
Source: Photo supplied by Ric and Angelo Ballestrin.

---

53   See Mariastella Pulvirenti, 'The Morality of Immigrant Home Ownership: Gender, Work and Italian Australian *Sistemazione*', *Australian Geographer* 31, no. 2 (2000): 237–49, doi.org/10.1080/713612245, at 238. Pulvirenti analyses *sistemazione* in the context of postwar migrants and home ownership.

'I BUY THIS PIECE OF GROUND HERE'

Children's contributions to purchasing land

Those families whose children had arrived with their mothers in the 1930s were advantaged in the pursuit of land ownership because they contributed to the labour unit in the early years of establishing the market gardens. Some in the 1.5 generation worked with their parents, which created a pathway for the children to progress to become owners of their own market gardens. Men in the first generation who married after arrival in Australia had to wait until their children were old enough to add them to the family workforce. Sons recalled that they were not paid for their labour and contrasted their experience with their peers in the broader Italian community who worked for wages and had more independence from their family. The two Anglo-Australian men interviewed for the project spoke of similar circumstances: the dependence on the family work unit and its impact on young people, who were expected to give their labour to the market garden. In some Veneto households at Lockleys, the imperative to own land required children to labour in the market gardens and some daughters were required to become wage-earners to contribute to the family project.

The Zampin family

The last Veneto couple to purchase land in the 1950s was Silvano and Amelia Zampin, who had nine children. Although they had been unable to buy the property they had leased since the 1930s, the Zampins bought 1 hectare close to the Lockleys area in 1954 when their youngest, the only son, was a baby. Silvano was naturalised in 1937 and the imperative to support his large family had taken precedence over the purchase of property. In contrast to other families in the Veneto community who spoke dialect in the home, the language in the Zampin household was English.

In interviews, six Zampin daughters presented memories of their father's role in their family life and culture, which limited their secondary education to the compulsory years. The focus for many years was ownership of land. The daughters stated that their wages contributed to the family's endeavour to purchase land. The eldest daughter, Milva, did not complete primary school and her labour was divided between assisting her mother with the care of the younger children and working with her father in the garden. When old enough to legally enter the workforce through employment, in the Brazzale mica factory in Adelaide, Milva contributed her wages to the family fund. She recalled her parents' achievement when they finally purchased their land and home, reporting 'they were in heaven'. However, Milva's priorities were different, and she looked back at the imperative to contribute to the family goal, which was attained after she had married: 'We more or less put our money in the bank every week or Dad put our money in the bank to buy that land and I didn't reap the benefit of it.'[54]

Milva's sisters left school at 14, the legal age at which compulsory education ended, and handed their wages to their father. He put aside a proportion to pay for their weddings. The fourth daughter, Christine, reflected on the family custom of completing only the compulsory years of schooling:

> Dad said: 'When you're 14, you have to leave school.' So, we just did what Dad said and didn't complain about it because my other sisters had to leave at fourteen, so I just went along with it as well. You had no choice.[55]

Plate 3.9: The Zampin family, Lockleys, c. 1954
Note: Silvano is holding Peter.
Source: Photo supplied by the Zampin family.

---

54   Milva Rebuli nee Zampin interviewed by Madeleine Regan, Transcript, J.D. Somerville Oral History Collection, State Library of South Australia, Adelaide, OH 872/36, 27 March 2016: 19.
55   Christine Zampin interviewed by Madeleine Regan, Transcript, J.D. Somerville Oral History Collection, State Library of South Australia, Adelaide, OH 872/42, 26 February 2017: 8.

It was not unusual for the ambitions of children in migrant families to be subsumed by the material goals of their parents.[56]

The values that Silvano brought with him from the Veneto underlined his expectations for life in Australia: work on, and ownership of, land; independence; family life; stability; and a future for his children. While Silvano married outside the Veneto community, his reliance on patriarchal structures and *contadino* family relationships saw him enlist his children in the plan for land ownership. The Zampins' son, Peter, died in an accident at the age of 18—a sad event that closed the opportunity for continuity of the market garden in the next generation.

The first generation of the *veneti* pursued the *contadino* desire to cultivate land in the *paese* at Lockleys. The early initiative to lease landholdings, develop knowledge of methods of cultivation and crop selection enabled them to enter the market economy, work hard and later achieve prosperity when there was demand for land for housing. The Veneto market gardeners achieved *sistemazione* for their families through acquiring and working land. The sense of security and belonging on the land characterised the *paese* at Lockleys.

---

56   Baldassar and Pesman, *From Paesani to Global Italians*, 159–60.

4
Family life and labour

Giancarlo Marchioro: I remember digging some whole glasshouse with a fork, me and Dad, by hand. Like the fork was the ordinary fork they use in the garden: yes, we had to dig—

Madeleine Regan: How long would that take?

Giancarlo Marchioro: Oh, it'd take you three hours.

Madeleine Regan: Two men?

Giancarlo Marchioro: Yes. Yes, because it was a hundred and twelve-foot [34 metres] long and you had to dig all of it, it was fifteen-foot [4.6 metres] wide and a hundred and twelve foot-long. So, you didn't have time to say, 'Oh, I'm tired' [laughs].

—Johnny Marchioro, 2008[1]

Johnny Marchioro's description of father and son together, digging soil in a glasshouse by hand to prepare for the planting of the tomato crop provides a context for examining family life and labour in the Veneto market-gardener community. In the Veneto region, a larger intergenerational group was involved in working the family land and tomatoes would not have been cultivated because of the cooler climate. The image contains the continuity of the *contadino* tradition and the adoption at Lockleys of cultivation in glasshouses, embodied in the first-generation father and second-generation son.

---

1   Giancarlo Marchioro interviewed by Madeleine Regan, Transcript, J.D. Somerville Oral History Collection, State Library of South Australia, Adelaide, OH 872/1, 21 July 2008: 10–11.

'I BUY THIS PIECE OF GROUND HERE'

Plate 4.1: Giancarlo (Johnny) Marchioro and his father, Vittorio, tending tomatoes in a glasshouse, Bolivar, 1976
Source: Eleonora Marchioro.

Family structures changed in the process of migration and the Veneto market gardeners adapted household roles to assist their *sistemazione* at Lockleys. The family as a labour unit altered traditional gendered roles and impacted the authority of men and women. In addition to their domestic work and the care of children, women gained a new role through working on the market gardens. The involvement of women opens new knowledge about gendered roles in Italian families in the interwar years. Children were incorporated into the family workforce and increased the prospects for additional production of vegetables.

Adapting the *contadino* model

More than 40 per cent of Italians who arrived in South Australia between 1927 and 1940 had worked on the land as labourers or farmers before migration.[2] Like other Italian *contadini*, the Veneto group used age-old intensive farming practices and recast them to suit Australian conditions. The pressures of supply and demand in a commercial market were elements of

---

2 O'Connor, *No Need to be Afraid*, 115.

a new economic context that contrasted with their experience of subsistence farming in the Veneto. The Veneto market gardeners at Lockleys forged new practices and planted crops according to the location of their land, access to water, availability of labour and the demands of the market. Those whose land was near the river cultivated more celery and potatoes while those who relied on groundwater concentrated on glasshouse tomatoes. Most in the group, realising their dependence on a regular supply of safe water, helped one another to sink bores to ensure consistent surface irrigation along the furrows of planted vegetables, including in glasshouses. As Lino Tonellato explained: 'They had put a bore in, they did it themselves, they dug out a hole and put a bore in and they found water … [I]t was only one hundred and eight feet [33 metres] deep, but it was beautiful water.'[3]

Lino's description of the quality of the bore water indicates the significance of the natural resource for the success of crops. Initially, the group grew 'outside' vegetables such as onions, cabbages, cauliflowers, beetroot, tomatoes, trombone (squash), celery and potatoes that did not require the microclimate of a glasshouse. Although not used in the Veneto farming tradition, glasshouses had been important infrastructure for the cultivation of tomatoes in the western peri-agricultural area of Adelaide since at least the first decade of the twentieth century.[4] Acquiring knowledge about the commercial market and with increased revenue, the first generation of Veneto market gardeners diversified their practices and adapted to cultivate tomatoes in glasshouses.

Lino Tonellato recalled that his father did not have glasshouses when Lino arrived in Adelaide as a child with his mother and siblings in 1935. Similarly, Lina Rismondo remembered the absence of glasshouses in the early years and explained: 'Nobody had glasshouses then, [they] couldn't afford to buy them.'[5] With income from the sale of vegetables, and in response to market demand and the suitability of the Lockleys area, the *veneti* purchased second-hand glasshouses from growers who no longer required them. Lino Tonellato recalled: 'We bought them mostly second-hand, people had them, they sold out and the new ones were too dear, they couldn't afford [them]. Every time we shifted [the glasshouses], we used to make an extra one, one or two.'[6]

---

3   Lino Tonellato, OH 872/10, 16 July 2021: 5–6.
4   Barry Philp, 'Glasshouses Tomatoes', in *History of Agriculture in SA* (Adelaide: Department of Primary Industries and Regions, Government of South Australia, March 2012), www.pir.sa.gov.au/aghistory/industries/horticulture/glasshouse_tomatoes2.
5   Lina Rismondo nee Marchioro, OH 872/9, 9 June 2010: 6.
6   Lino Tonellato, OH 872/10, 16 July 2010: 8.

Plate 4.2: Romildo Santin, Valetta Road, early 1940s
Source: Photo supplied by Christine Rebellato nee Mattiazzo.

The purchase of second-hand glasshouses suggests the first-generation group interacted with local Anglo-Australian market gardeners or at least made contact through the market environment. It also suggests the *veneti* (and other Italians) were replacing Anglo-Australian market gardeners, who were leaving the occupation, steadily transforming the profile of growers in the Lockleys area.

Without substantial capital investment, members of the Veneto group were able to establish their market gardens and keep their costs low because family members provided the labour.[7] This approach to establishing market gardens 'with low capital but high labour inputs' was also adopted by Chinese market gardeners in Australia and New Zealand.[8] The work was constant and mostly done by hand, beginning with the preparation of the soil. In the glasshouses, rows of holes were drilled to insert tomato seedlings. The cultivation process included acquiring and sowing seeds, planting seedlings, watering, weeding, picking, sorting and grading, and packing in half-cases. According to Johnny Marchioro, families collected their own tomato seeds:

---

7   O'Connor, *No Need to be Afraid*, 116.
8   Joanna Boileau, *Chinese Market Gardening in Australia and New Zealand: Gardens of Prosperity* (Cham, Switzerland: Palgrave Macmillan, 2017), doi.org/10.1007/978-3-319-51871-8, 150.

> We used to make our own seed at the end of the season squashing our tomatoes … [W]e tried to pick the perfect ones—squash them, and with the rest of the tomato we'd make sauce; and make our seeds and dry it off and ready to plant in January, in February, sow it and start off again.[9]

Market gardeners shifted glasshouses every two years until fumigation was introduced in the 1950s to reduce pests and diseases that could destroy crops.[10] The first-generation men took the vegetables to the East End wholesale produce market in Adelaide usually three days a week. Working days were long and some narrators recalled getting up at 3 am on market days to assist their parents to sell the vegetables. Johnny Marchioro recalled the intensive days when he worked with his parents in the 1950s:

> Busy season, Mum and Dad and myself would have to start at six and finish at six and not much time for stopping or anything like that. But it was long hours—that's without going to market; market days was three o'clock.[11]

Creating the family work unit

In the first years at Lockleys, the lone men established their market gardens with support from other *veneti* with the goal of becoming self-reliant before they brought their wives and children to join them or set themselves up to marry. After families were reunited or marriages had taken place, labour on the market gardens was shared between husbands, wives and children. The cooperative arrangements existed to a greater degree than in the model of the *contadino* family farm in the Veneto region, where gender roles were more strictly defined in terms of domestic routines and work in the fields. In the Veneto, women assisted in the fields only during harvest or when the family labour force was diminished because men were absent for seasonal work in other places.[12] After three or four years of schooling, sons began work on the land while daughters were allocated domestic chores in preparation for their role as wives.

---

9   Giancarlo Marchioro, OH 872/1, 21 July 2008: 8.
10 ibid., 34.
11 ibid., 8.
12 Huber, *From Pasta to Pavlova*, 20–21.

In the emerging Veneto market-gardener community in Australia, new patterns reflected stronger reliance on the nuclear family rather than an intergenerational unit. Women and men worked together to complete the tasks associated with cultivating and harvesting vegetables. Women had responsibility for domestic animals such as cows and poultry; they made cheese and butter and killed chickens. They also tended kitchen gardens and orchards that increased household self-sufficiency and, of course, were responsible for preparing meals, completing household chores and caring for children. Once old enough, children were allocated tasks according to age, gender and skill.

Even when men and women worked side-by-side, much of the work remained gendered. For example, men usually managed the heavy work, which in the early years included digging soil by hand, ploughing with horses and watering, which could involve pumps and accessing bores, wells or the river. Later, families accumulated funds to purchase equipment such as tractors and rotary hoes, which reduced the amount of hand digging before planting. Men usually operated machinery, as observed by Noemi Campagnolo nee Zalunardo: 'I know my Dad bought a lot of machines and things but I don't remember because mostly I was at school … but that was men's stuff … you're not into that.'[13]

Most men acquired a driver's licence although two Ballestrin cousins who were partners in a large market garden did not drive and depended on relatives to transport their produce to the railway yards for sale at the markets in Melbourne. Two women in the Santin families learned to drive, which was unusual in the first-generation Veneto market-gardener community. Anna Santin nee Mattiazzo reflected on the advantages gained, including independence, when she and her sister-in-law Rosina received their driver's licences: 'Lucky I learnt to drive … Rosina and I … we learnt to drive so we could go and do our shopping and that, without the men, dragging them along.'[14]

---

[13] Noemi Campagnolo nee Zalunardo interviewed by Madeleine Regan, Transcript, J.D. Somerville Oral History Collection, State Library of South Australia, Adelaide, OH 872/29, 20 March 2014.
[14] Anna Santin nee Mattiazzo interviewed by Madeleine Regan, Transcript, J.D. Somerville Oral History Collection, State Library of South Australia, Adelaide, OH 872/24, 17 April 2013: 31–32.

That women usually did not obtain a driver's licence points to the conventional gendered roles and expectations at that time that resulted in less freedom of movement for them.

There was a strict gender demarcation for selling vegetables. Men took the produce to market or the railway station for consignment to interstate markets while women and older children graded and packed vegetables like tomatoes. Although children sometimes accompanied their fathers to the market in the early morning, the men engaged with the world of business beyond the boundaries of the market garden. This was a custom observed by both Italian and Anglo-Australian market gardeners. Men sold vegetables at the market, assuming the role of 'trader'—a reflection of societal values about men's work. Socialising with their peers in the market hotel or café after trading was built into the routine of market days. Women carried on with the physical labour in the gardens, maintaining the daily seasonal tasks while the men were at the market up to three mornings a week.

Patriarchal structures and norms were reproduced with the male head of the household mostly responsible for managing family finances—a common practice also in Anglo-Australian families at the time. The Veneto model of the male head of the *contadino* household taking control of the family finances was transplanted to the family market-garden business at Lockleys. However, in at least one context, second-generation children handed their wages over to their mother. Norma Camozzato nee Ballestrin's mother managed the family finances and Norma had to hand over her pay: 'I'd have to ask her for the money. She would give it to me, but she wouldn't let me keep my wages.'[15]

Some narrators reflected on the achievements of their father and assigned him 'pioneer' status in reverential and mythical terms.[16] For example, a 1.5-generation member, Albert Tonellato, referred to the experiences of his father and Angelo Piovesan. The two men had arrived on the same ship in 1927 and it appears that although they had lived in villages about 20 kilometres apart, their families had some connections before emigration.[17]

---

15 Norma Camozzato nee Ballestrin, OH 872/37, 21 September 2016: 22.
16 See Marie-Françoise Chanfrault-Duchet, 'Narrative Structures, Social Models and Symbolic Representation in the Life Story', in *Women's Words: The Feminist Practice of Oral History*, eds Sherna Berger Gluck and Daphne Patai (New York: Routledge, 1991), 81–82.
17 See Angelo Piovesan, 'Links between the Piovesan and Tonellato Families', *Veneti Market Gardeners 1927 Blog*, 29 November 2020, venetimarketgardeners1927.net/links-between-the-piovesan-and-tonellato-families/.

Angelo was single and 22 while Secondo Tonellato was 10 years older and married with five children. At Lockleys, Angelo and Secondo lived on adjacent market gardens and worked together before they were joined by their wives and, in Secondo's case, his five children, in the 1930s.

Albert and his wife, Mary, provided an insight into the legacy of the role of the men in establishing the community at Lockleys:

> Albert: It was bad for them. Dad and Mum, like Dad and Piovesan there, they had nobody. Worse still, they were a lot worse than us.
>
> Mary: Being the first settlers.
>
> Albert: In the first that came out.[18]

Albert and Mary, both aged in their eighties when interviewed, referred to the first generation as pioneers confronting obstacles without the support of extended family in their quest to establish themselves in Australia.[19] The inclination to designate first-generation migrant men as pioneers in 'heroic' roles is a phenomenon also noted in narratives of Italian migrant men in England.[20] The status and meaning ascribed to the masculine role and the lone migrant men—'first settlers' confronting the challenges in a new country—detract from the role of women, who were also first-generation migrants making their way in unfamiliar circumstances. The idealisation of the heroic masculine migrant contrasts with the limited frames of domestic and motherhood roles and reduces the agency of migrant women, who were also significant participants in the processes of settlement.

---

18 Albert Tonellato, OH 872/4, 3 October 2008: 27.

19 The image of the early migrants as 'first settlers' points to the complexity of the history of migration in Australia in the context of Australian settler-colonial history, which renders Indigenous peoples invisible. See Ricatti, *Italians in Australia*, 62–71; Daphne Arapakis, 'Ethnic Compartmentalisation: Greek Australian (Dis)Associations with White Australia and Indigenous Sovereignty', *Journal of Intercultural Studies* 44, no. 6 (2023): 799–817, doi.org/10.1080/07256868.2023.2192468; Ann Curthoys, 'An Uneasy Conversation: Multicultural and Indigenous Discourses', in *The Future of Australian Multiculturalism: Reflections on the Twentieth Anniversary of Jean Martin's The Migrant Presence*, eds Ghassan Hage and Rowanne Couch (Sydney: Research Institute for Humanities and Social Sciences, University of Sydney, 1999), 277–93.

20 See Anne-Marie Fortier, *Migrant Belongings: Memory, Space, Identity* (London: Routledge, 2000), 48–49. See also Raphael Samuel and Paul Thompson, 'Introduction', in *The Myths We Live By*, eds Raphael Samuel and Paul Thompson (London: Routledge, 1990), 17–18.

Women in the market gardens

An analysis of the roles of women in the narratives of the Veneto market-garden community balances the conventional focus on men and male household heads that dominates historical accounts of migration. For this task, it is necessary to go beyond generalisations and identify the different circumstances of Italian women in the experience of migration that transcend images of passivity, submission or invisibility. The focus on individuals is impossible to reconstruct through official documents. For example, married women were viewed as dependants under Australian immigration policies, visible only in relation to their husbands and, at times, were omitted from the details provided on 'incoming passenger card' documentation. They were frequently identified in Australian migration policy and census records within a narrow status of domestic occupation. In passenger statements gathered between 1927 and 1940, the occupations of Italian women in South Australia were almost exclusively classified as 'home duties'.[21] Veneto women on the market gardens contributed as partners rather than as dependants, in addition to their domestic and parenting responsibilities. Their contribution to the market gardens was a vital aspect of the family economy.

Plate 4.3: Luigina Zalunardo nee Ballestrin with Noemi and Maria Gina Ballestrin nee Andreazza with Dolfina, c. 1947, take time off from the market gardens to care for their babies
Source: Photo supplied by Noemi Campagnolo nee Zalunardo.

---

21   O'Connor, *No Need to be Afraid*, 115.

This study builds on the practices of early feminist oral historians who promoted initiatives to record oral histories to ensure that women's experiences were documented, respected and preserved.[22] Through oral histories of individual women's experiences, the diversity of their circumstances, roles and agency is explored and valued. For example, Egidio (Jimmy) Ballestrin, aged 72 when interviewed, reflected on the extent of his mother's role. He recalled daily life in his parents' market garden and the distribution of work, observing the imbalance in his parents' roles: 'My mother and father both worked the glasshouses, probably I'd like to say equal, but maybe not quite equal because my mother would have to then go and cook and do all the household duties.'[23]

Jimmy clearly acknowledged his mother's work in maintaining family life and in cultivating the market gardens. The active participation of women in the family labour unit differs from the experience of the patriarchal structures in the Veneto *contadino* family where 'men laboured as a team under the direction of the head of the household' and women were assigned a subordinate position after marriage under the scrutiny of the eldest woman in her husband's family.[24] At Lockleys, young married women could advance to the role of matriarch and manage domestic duties combined with work in the market gardens without the oversight of a mother-in-law. However, Jimmy also acknowledged the 'double shift' that his mother and other women assumed in the Lockleys households: the domestic and agricultural tasks.

When I asked Lino Ballestrin whether wives worked with their husbands in the market gardens, he replied that 'they were slaves [laughter] to the garden, to be honest.'[25] His laughter suggests a level of discomfort with the extent of his mother's work in the market garden. The son of a Calabrian family who worked as neighbours to Veneto market gardeners at Lockleys used the same term, 'slaves', to describe the work of his mother and siblings. He critiqued husbands who expected their wives 'to work seven days a week for probably on average fourteen hours a day at killing physical toil'.[26]

---

22   Sherna Berger Gluck, 'Has Feminist Oral History Lost Its Radical/Subversive Edge?', *Oral History* 39, no. 2 (2011): 63–72, www.jstor.org/stable/i40061538; Sherna Berger Gluck and Daphne Patai, *Women's Words: The Feminist Practice of Oral History* (New York: Routledge, 1991), 1–3; Abrams, *Oral History Theory*, 71–74.
23   Jimmy Ballestrin interviewed by Madeleine Regan, Transcript, J.D. Somerville Oral History Collection, State Library of South Australia, Adelaide, OH 872/15, 6 June 2011: 3.
24   Huber, *From Pasta to Pavlova*, 20, 23.
25   Lino Ballestrin, OH 872/40, 22 November 2016: 10.
26   Paul Depasquale, *My Path to the Brownlow* (Adelaide: Pioneer Books, 2009), 92–93.

4. FAMILY LIFE AND LABOUR

Plate 4.4: The Ballestrin family: Narcisio, Lina, Maria, Jimmy and, in front, Silvano and Norina, Flinders Park, c. 1959
Source: Photo supplied by Lina Campagnaro nee Ballestrin.

Although the married women in the Veneto market-gardener families were free of the constraints of the hierarchical *contadino* household, the absence of an older generation meant women could not share childcare with grandparents. The one exception was in the extended Santin family, where the grandmother supported her three married sons and their wives who worked together on a large landholding on Frogmore Road, by providing childcare and meals. The three Santin couples cultivated a large range of vegetables on their property. Two of the couples, their children and the first-generation parents shared an intergenerational household comparable with those in the Veneto region.

Women nurturing transnational families

Several narrators reported an additional role undertaken by their mothers: the responsibility to maintain contact with families through writing letters and nurturing the emotional or 'affective' aspects of transnational relationships.[27] Women also took responsibility for providing transnational material assistance to families back in the Veneto region. For example, Dino Piovesan explained that his mother sent material goods to her and her husband's families in Italy when its postwar poverty contrasted with the

---

27   Amanda Wise and Selvaraj Velayutham, 'Transnational Affect and Emotion in Migration Research', *International Journal of Sociology* 47, no. 2 (2017): 116–30, doi.org/10.1080/00207659.2017.1300468.

relative wellbeing of his parents in Adelaide. He indicated the strong sense of connection to relatives separated by migration and communicated the idea of 'home' also being in Italy:

> The parcels that my mother used to make: coffee, old clothes that my father wouldn't wear, she would send them home by surface mail. It took about three months to get there, but they were greatly appreciated when they got there.[28]

The sending of objects suggests that migrant families embodied a practice of home and belonging that can be understood as an example of 'transnational homing processes'.[29] The market gardeners who had achieved a level of comfort at Lockleys were able to send domestic objects that they knew were needed by relatives in their home village in the Veneto region—continuity of the idea of 'home'. Assunta Giovannini nee Tonellato remembered that her family put together parcels to send to relatives in both Italy and Canada after the war. She recalled that packages contained children's clothes, while coffee was included as a prized item for the relatives in Italy. She recalled that she followed her mother's instructions and wrote addresses on the sugar bags or other heavy paper in which the packages were wrapped before they were posted overseas.[30]

In another example of this transnational material culture, Diana Panazzolo nee Santin, a second-generation woman born in 1950, recalled the packages her mother sent to her aunties in Italy. Diana explained that the parcels included clothes she had outgrown, which were packed along with coffee beans, and a cigar was always added for her *nonno*.[31] Sandra Conci nee Santin recalled that her mother continued to send parcels to Italy even after she married in 1967. She remembered that soap was included in the assortment of items that were packed up for her relatives in Caselle di Altivole.[32]

Marrying into a market-gardener family

When a woman outside the community married into a Veneto market-gardener family there was no period of transition or apprenticeship. In 1949, Anna Mattiazzo, a 1.5-generation woman from a family in the wider

---

28 Dino Piovesan, OH 872/17, 23 September 2011: 3.
29 Accarigi, 'Transcultural Objects, Transcultural Homes', 192–93.
30 Assunta Giovannini nee Tonellato, Personal communication, 25 February 2023.
31 Diana Panazzolo nee Santin, Personal communication, 7 September 2023.
32 Sandra Conci nee Santin, OH 872/47, 25 August 2018: 22.

Veneto community, married Vito, the second of the three Santin sons, who owned a large market garden. Anna's family lived in the city, and she had worked in two factories before her marriage at the age of 22. Interviewed at the age of 86, she recalled the quick adaptation to life on the market gardens and the sudden switch from wage-earner as a single woman with time for leisure to wife and market gardener with limited free time. She had met Vito through the wider Veneto network in Adelaide because the Santin family bought their meat from Anna's father, who owned his city butcher shop. Engaged for five years—an unusually long period—Anna recalled that she had enjoyed a varied social life that had included seeing films twice a week.

Anna began her marriage in the regulated routines of a market-gardener family. She moved into the Santin household, which she and Vito shared with her parents-in-law, younger brother-in-law and his wife. The eldest brother lived with his wife and family in an adjacent house. This family set-up replicated the patrilocal-virilocal arrangements of the traditional intergenerational Veneto household where a married woman moved in with her husband's family. When I asked Anna whether she had a honeymoon, she chuckled and said she had to begin work with her husband immediately:

> Got married on the Saturday, on the Monday, I went to cut celery [laughs] … Oh well, you just picked it up. They gave you a knife in your hand and go down with your backside up and cut celery.[33]

In 1950, the Santin families bought 4.5 hectares on Frogmore Road, previously owned by another Italian family, 1 kilometre from the property they had leased from Gino Berno. The intergenerational arrangements continued as children were born to the three couples, with the older generation providing support. Anna explained the arrangements: '[W]e all, the six of us … three brothers and three sisters-in-law, all worked [in the] garden.'[34] Anna's mother-in-law managed some of the domestic arrangements to support the working lives of the families:

> We all … worked. Nothing but work in the garden all day, mother-in-law used to do the cooking, and we used to help her afterwards, wash up and clean the houses … Mother-in-law used to look after the kids. We used to come in and feed them, lunchtime, and she'd look after them.[35]

---

33   Anna Santin nee Mattiazzo, OH 872/24, 3 April 2013: 12, 15.
34   ibid., 15.
35   ibid., 32.

'I BUY THIS PIECE OF GROUND HERE'

Plate 4.5: The marriage of Vito Santin and Anna Mattiazzo, Adelaide, 1949
Source: Photo supplied by Anna Santin nee Mattiazzo.

The glory of a new home

Anna was 45 years old when she moved into a new home and managed a separate household for the first time, in 1972. In response to a question about the difference it made to have her own home, Anna was most animated:

> Oh gee. I think it was everybody's dream those days to buy, build a house that you liked … I remember we never took any of the old furniture from the old house, we bought everything new, so I was in my glory![36]

Her use of 'glory' suggests Anna's triumph, pride and joy; it communicates her achievement of independence and the luxury of a modern, newly furnished residence. While the migrant home is a place of 'comfort and intimacy' and evidence of *sistemazione*, it can also serve as a place for a display of material achievement.[37] Anna claiming her own home suggests a new sense of 'emplacement', which Ricatti explains in the context of migrants' achievement of economic stability. Rather than moving away from Lockleys and undertaking 'a shift from community-oriented to status-oriented emplacement', Anna and her husband (and her two brothers-in-law and sisters-in-law) remained at Lockleys on houseblocks carved from the market gardens after they were sold.[38] The couples enjoyed the financial rewards of their labour over many years and each built a new house that provided comfort, independence, security and opportunities to furnish and enjoy a 'material anchor'.[39]

Anna's experience of moving into a new home is consistent with the findings made by Pascoe, whose study of an Italian migrant family who established a large vegetable-growing business in southern Queensland in the 1930s showed that they prioritised work and economic security. The family lived in basic accommodation and delayed fulfilment of their desire for a grand house.[40] Giovanni Rebuli, whose relatives were market gardeners, reflected

---

[36] ibid.
[37] Daniela Cosmini, Diana Glenn, Maria Palaktsoglou, and Eric Bouvet, 'The Making of Home in a New Land: A Study of the Significance of Personal Objects and Cultural Practices of Aging Italian and Greek Migrants in South Australia within a Transnational Context', *Italian American Review* 8, no. 1 (2018): 1–22, doi.org/10.5406/italamerrevi.8.1.0001, at 6–7.
[38] Ricatti, *Italians in Australia*, 38–39.
[39] Paolo Boccagni, 'What's in a (Migrant) House? Changing Domestic Spaces, the Negotiation of Belonging and Home-Making in Ecuadorian Migration', *Housing Theory and Society* 31, no. 3 (2014): 277–93, doi.org/10.1080/14036096.2013.867280, at 286.
[40] Robert Pascoe, *Open for Business: Immigrant and Aboriginal Entrepreneurs Tell Their Story* (Canberra: Office for Multicultural Affairs, Department of the Prime Minister and Cabinet, 1990), 23.

on the importance of owning a house for Italian migrants: 'In Australia, starting to create an identity … you do start to create a sort of belonging to where you immigrated once you start creating roots there. So, a house is setting roots to a place where you're living.'[41]

Acquiring a (new) home is an example of a 'transcultural strategy for orientation and emplacement' and the processes that migrants take to establish themselves, adapt to new circumstances and achieve permanency with their families. This idea mirrors the Australian dream of homeownership.[42]

A mother challenges the order

When circumstances threatened the future of the family labour unit, some women created solutions and demonstrated their capacity to adjust the practices of Veneto *contadino* households and find new approaches. For example, when women in market-gardener families were unexpectedly widowed with young children, they confronted the challenges of managing parenting, labour, income and security. At Lockleys, three women on market gardens were widowed at a relatively young age in the 1940s. In two families, the sons preserved familial structures and assumed responsibility for the family business. In Margherita Marchioro's case, she was widowed when her husband, who had been chronically ill, died in 1945. She had three daughters, the youngest just seven years old.

At the age of 40, Margherita adapted to her new circumstances with energy and efficiency. She applied the previous experience of working in partnership with her brother-in-law and sister-in-law and enlisted her 18-year-old daughter, Lina, to share the work of cultivating tomatoes in 16 glasshouses. They increased production, which enabled Margherita to accumulate enough capital to build her own house on a block she purchased within walking distance of her market garden. Lina recalled her mother's achievement:

> She built a lovely house and I suppose she had that satisfaction that she'd got what she wanted, a lovely house, furnished it nicely, so … after living all those years in a wooden/iron place, you can imagine. A joy to have it![43]

---

41   Giovanni Rebuli interviewed by Madeleine Regan, Transcript, J.D. Somerville Oral History Collection, State Library of South Australia, Adelaide, OH 872/48, 21 September 2018: 44.
42   Ricatti, *Italians in Australia*, 132; Pulvirenti, 'The Morality of Immigrant Home Ownership', 238.
43   Lina Rismondo nee Marchioro, OH 872/9, 15 November 2010: 50.

Plate 4.6: Mary, Connie and Lina Marchioro, Adelaide, c. 1946
Source: Photo supplied by Connie Legovich nee Marchioro.

Having achieved ownership of her house, Margherita transformed the prospects of two of her daughters. First, she supported Lina to move away from the market gardens and train as a dressmaker because she recognised her creative skills. At the age of 21, Lina became part-owner of a couture business with an Anglo-Australian woman and they deliberately chose to locate their studio in a wealthy suburb where they knew clients would be able to afford their garments. The eldest daughter, who was intellectually disabled, assisted her mother in the market garden and the third daughter, Connie, born in 1938, was also able to take opportunities beyond the market-gardener life:

> When I left school, I started working in a fashion house. I started doing dressmaking. I continued sport, tennis and basketball which I loved. And on Sunday nights I'd go to the Italian Church dance.[44]

Margherita permitted two of her daughters a level of independence not offered in most families in which patriarchal structures constrained opportunities for young women.

---

44 Connie Legovich nee Marchioro, OH 872/11, 10 January 2011: 4.

'I BUY THIS PIECE OF GROUND HERE'

A daughter challenges the order

Plate 4.7: Norma Ballestrin on the family property, Hartley Road, c. 1956
Source: Photo supplied by Norma Camozzato nee Ballestrin.

The traditional role of women in *contadino* families was not always easily followed by the second generation in Australia. Daughters who received more education than their mothers and were exposed to different cultural practices in their schooling in Adelaide observed possibilities other than the direct pathway from the market garden to marriage. In one family, a daughter challenged the model. Norma Ballestrin, an only daughter with an older and younger brother, was required to leave school at 14— the minimum school-leaving age at the time. In contrast, both of Norma's brothers were among the few in the Veneto market-gardener families who completed their secondary education.

Interviewed at the age of 75, Norma recalled the decision she made to disregard her parents' expectations that she stay at home to undertake domestic responsibilities:

> Well, I left school at fourteen and [pause] the noise from home came out that I was going to stay home and work the garden, not work the garden, work the house, do the cooking, the washing and all that. And I thought: 'Like fun!' So, I went up and looked at the paper … I saw it and went and applied for a job.[45]

From her perspective in later life, Norma remembered the expectation that she would be directed into domestic responsibilities as 'noise' rather than familial obligation. In her mother's experience in the Veneto region, choices were limited by family and social standards about the status of daughters, who, at a certain age after living and working within the household, were eligible to become wives. As the only daughter, Norma was expected to assume duties in the house to free her mother to work more hours in the market garden. Norma confirmed after her interview that 'the boys had to be educated, but being a girl, I would stay at home to do housework whilst Mum worked the garden'.[46] However, as an adolescent, Norma defied gender conventions and initiated entry into her own working life outside the family, which she maintained until she was 22 years old. She worked in the office of a financial organisation in the City of Adelaide.

When I asked Norma about her mother's role in the family, her initial response was about work in the garden and she enumerated the number of tasks undertaken by her mother:

> OH: How much work did your mother do in the garden?
>
> NC: Always, she was always in the garden. Always. That was it. That was her life …
>
> OH: And looking after the children?
>
> NC: Well, yes.
>
> OH: And cooking?
>
> NC: And cooking, all that, you know. But that was her life. She went out into the garden and she'd say … when I was around … when I was young enough to understand, she'd say: 'I'm going out to the garden. Do this, do that!' I was trained, I used to look after the house, but I didn't like it [laughter].[47]

---

45 Norma Camozzato nee Ballestrin, OH 872/37, 21 September 2016: 21.
46 Norma Camozzato nee Ballestrin, Additional comments after her interview, ibid., 21.
47 Norma Camozzato nee Ballestrin, OH 872/37, 21 September 2016: 16.

Norma clarified aspects of her mother's role and emphatically declared that it was primarily in the garden. She then turned to her own life and the gendered expectations of daughters in a household like hers. As an adolescent, Norma may not have recognised that she was being 'trained' for marriage, however, with the distance of 50 years, she laughed and acknowledged that her mother was pressing her towards a future as a wife. Norma's laughter was at a view of her younger self. She was aware of the difference between the values of her mother and her own and realised that she could have been constrained to a life of domesticity rather than having independence and a working life outside the family. Her laughter highlighted the point that narrators in oral history interviews can re-evaluate a past event and acknowledge with amusement their behaviour and changes in their identity and roles over time.[48]

Norma recalled that when she married at 25—older than many of her peers—her parents were happy and relieved that her husband, Lino, came from a town close to their *paese* in the Veneto. Lino had arrived in Australia in 1952 and, by the time he married Norma, he had built his own home on the other side of Adelaide, a considerable distance from her family and the community at Lockleys. I asked Norma how important it was for her parents to know her husband's origins:

> [V]ery important because they could talk to him in their own language and he wasn't one of those Australians, the riff raff, you know ... Yes. I think it was pretty important. And they were pleased.[49]

Norma's choice of marriage partner reflected the customary pattern in the Veneto *paese* of choosing a husband from the same locality, which was viewed as a way of maintaining Veneto identity within the family. Her parents also did not have to accommodate a son-in-law from outside the community, let alone an Australian 'riffraff'. Norma's reflections on the impact of gendered roles within the family demonstrate that it was possible for second-generation women to reshape these role definitions in the Veneto community and live more independently than women in her mother's generation.

---

48 Ned R. Norrick, 'Humour in Oral History Interviews', *Oral History* 34, no. 2 (Autumn 2006): 85–94, at 92–93.
49 Norma Camozzato nee Ballestrin, OH 872/37, 21 September 2016: 24.

A single woman in the community

Daughters and sons who did not marry challenged conventions in the Veneto community. In the group of extended families at Lockleys, one sister and brother remained single. Maria Rosa Tormena, a niece of two first-generation market gardeners, arrived in Australia with her parents and brother in 1940, just months before Italy entered the war against the Allies. Before she left school at age 14, she played competitive team sports. As a wage-earner, she pursued her love of sport, changing jobs frequently to allow her to play in state softball championships and travel interstate. Maria Rosa explained that working life was secondary to her participation in sports:

> I used to be very involved in sport then so if that job interfered with the sport, I'd go off doing my sport, you know, interstate. It'd be every year around March and we'd go interstate, a different state each year. And if I couldn't get the time off, I'd say, well, I'd leave and hope for the best. But I never, ever had trouble getting jobs.[50]

Maria Rosa co-founded the Sturt Softball Club in 1963 and it became one of the largest women's softball clubs in Adelaide.[51] She later became a coach and, after active roles, travelled regularly to world series competitions. She explored her passion, resisting conformity to the expectations of marriage and a subordinated position to a husband. Maria Rosa's account of living in the Veneto community in Adelaide contrasts with the experience of other women in the 1.5 generation and even the second generation who, as expected, married and raised children. Her life was very different from her women cousins in Adelaide, who married and raised children with their husbands. However, most second-generation women left school for employment and some continued working after marriage—evidence that the roles of women in the Veneto market-gardener families were expanding.

---

50 Maria Rosa Tormena interviewed by Madeleine Regan, Transcript, J.D. Somerville Oral History Collection, State Library of South Australia, Adelaide, OH 872/19, 15 June 2012: 18.
51 Madeleine Regan, 'The Tormena Family', *Veneto Market Gardeners 1927 Blog*, 15 November 2020, venetimarketgardeners1927.net/?s=Tormena+family.

'I BUY THIS PIECE OF GROUND HERE'

Plate 4.8: An independent young woman with her Zundap scooter: Maria Rosa Tormena, Adelaide, c. 1953

Source: Photo supplied by Maria Rosa Tormena.

Children's roles in the market gardens

As the roles of women evolved, the status of children in the Veneto market-gardener families also changed. The *contadino* custom was to put children to work for the family as soon as possible and, consequently, the first generation of *veneti* had received very little schooling, usually no more than four years. At Lockleys, the first-generation parents complied with legislation that required children to attend school until age 14 at that time. However, children in this cohort contributed to the market gardens in combination with their schooling. The financial success of the family enterprise depended on the contribution of every member, including children of primary school age. Francesco (Frankie) Ballestrin recalls assisting his parents to shift glasshouses:

> My cousin and myself, [our] homework … was to drill holes and put up a row of posts each night we come home from school. Our parents would prepare the rails on the ground and that was the start of setting up your glasshouse. And we put the rail in, then they'd have the rail on top of it and then we'd come home and nail the rafters in. You know, they'd show us what to do, sort of thing. And then carry on from there. And then slide the glass and all the rest. It wasn't easy.[52]

While narrators described the challenges of the physical tasks and the time required to participate in the cultivation processes, they qualified their memories. They confirmed that hard work was the convention for most children in market-gardener families, including in other Italian families and Anglo-Australian households. In another of the Ballestrin families, son Jimmy asserted that the incidence of children working with their parents was not excessive:

> We were taught that we had to help, from a young age, and thinking back on it, we worked very hard as kids but thought nothing of it because all my friends did exactly the same and I didn't hear any of them complain. We didn't seem to think it was a chore at all, it was just something that was done.[53]

---

52   Francesco Ballestrin, OH 872/7, 12 December 2008: 8.
53   Egidio Ballestrin, OH 872/15, 16 June 2011: 3.

On the other hand, some felt the burden of working in the market gardens as children. For example, Dino Piovesan recalled the difficulties of shifting the glasshouses and his desire to be at the beach rather than having to take apart and rebuild the glasshouses in summer:

> So, they would just be shifted post, pane of glass by pane of glass, and it had to be done in the hottest months of the year, after the last crops were out, in January and February. Again, I can remember as kids we dearly would have loved to go to the beach, but sometimes there just had to be glasshouses that had to be shifted. The glasses were that hot, you'd pick up two or three glasses at a time and you would almost drop them because they would be sitting in the sun, and really so hot that they were hard to handle.[54]

At the end of her interview, Bruna Semola nee Zampin evaluated the demands of working in the family market gardens as she was growing up: 'I wouldn't like to go through it again [laughs]. I've had enough of that … I know it was hard for us, I know it was hard for Mum and Dad. I know I wouldn't like to do it again.'[55]

Bruna referred to the challenges of the hard physical work and the time involved in maintaining the family market-garden business, and expressed empathy for her parents. At the same time, she acknowledged the ordeal of the constant work required in the garden. It is likely the views of narrators at the time of interview were influenced by contemporary thinking about women's right to education and employment and, for both men and women, the range of career paths they might have taken. While they recalled their obligations and the arduous work that reduced their leisure or homework time, the narrators also acknowledged that it was common for parents in market-gardener households, including the Anglo-Australian families, to require the concerted effort of all members.

There were some gendered divisions in children's work, particularly after school. Sons, especially in the 1.5 generation, undertook increased responsibilities in the market gardens in preparation for their future role and the likelihood that they would inherit the family business. In the second generation, the expectations were not as absolute; however, some children were required to assume adult responsibilities in situations where their parents could not complete business transactions because of their language

---

54 Dino Piovesan, OH 872/17, 23 September 2011: 35.
55 Bruna Semola nee Zampin, OH 872/39, 8 November 2016: 33.

and literacy levels. In one family, because his parents could not read or write, a son, when he was eight or nine years old, wrote cheques, accompanied his father to the bank, paid accounts and acquired early knowledge of the business administration of the market gardens.[56]

Generally, daughters in the second generation were not expected to work in the market garden after they left school. Daughters were not likely to have a future on the land unless they married into a market-gardener family. Their experience differed from their mother's because they had received more education, even if only to compulsory age, and they were permitted to work outside the home.

Delineation between work on the market gardens and schooling

The first-generation *veneti* assumed that the land and market-garden livelihood would be passed onto their sons in the tradition of the Italian *contadino* family. In this model, education beyond compulsion was not important. A similar approach seemed to exist in the Anglo-Australian families, which suggests that education was not a priority for a young man who was groomed to inherit a market garden.[57] The apprenticeship in the market garden was more prized than completing secondary education.

Many narrators provided evidence that the complexity of tasks in the market garden increased with children's age. Noemi Campagnolo nee Zalunardo recalled learning how to pack tomatoes: 'I think it was 12, 13 and then you'd graduate, and you learn other things. But that was my job when I was that age.'[58]

Noemi's cousin Lina looked back on her role in the glasshouses as a schoolchild:

> I always remember helping Dad tying up strings for the tomatoes in the glasshouses, I think there were about five rows … I had the job of the low rows so it was my job and I always remember doing French knots of those tomato plants … That was one of the jobs and that was done after school or in the holidays or weekends.[59]

---

56   Melbourne Recchi interviewed by Madeleine Regan, Transcript, J.D. Somerville Oral History Collection, State Library of South Australia, Adelaide, OH 872/31, 18 June 2014: 7.
57   See Rae Ballantyne, OH 872/21, 25 August 2012: 22.
58   Noemi Campagnolo nee Zalunardo, OH 872/29, 20 March 2014: 8.
59   Lina Campagnaro nee Ballestrin, OH 872/28, 13 March 2014: 9.

Bruno Piovesan, interviewed at age 71, recalled the division between school life and working in the gardens:

> I remember coming home from school, didn't even know what homework was because we had our chores to do: take the leaves out of the glasshouse when they were pruning tomatoes; hoe around the side of the glasshouse so insects wouldn't get inside of the glasshouse. Always something to do [pauses and laughs]. We were kept busy all the time. There wasn't a question of having nothing to do, that's for sure.[60]

Bruno communicated his amusement while remembering that his labour was more valuable to the family than completing homework. However, like most second-generation sons in the community, Bruno was enrolled at a Catholic school and his parents paid school fees, which suggests families respected the moral education of young people provided by religious orders. Yet, work in the market garden took priority outside school hours. Bruno and his two brothers became even more involved in working in the garden as young adolescents when their father died. In many families, regard for education had to wait for the next generation.

Daughters, education and the market gardens

Although the Veneto families complied with the legislation in South Australia and children attended school for the compulsory years, there was an exception. In the Zampin family, Sandra refused to enrol in secondary school because she did not like being a student and had been bullied because of a 'turned eye' that affected her appearance. Although corrective surgery had made some difference, Sandra explained in her interview that she had been self-conscious and had endured bullying in primary school.[61] In 1959, when Sandra left school aged 12, her parents were required to obtain permission from the state Department of Education and guarantee her employment, which, of course, was in the family market garden.

---

60   Bruno Piovesan, OH 872/5, 4 October 2008: 3.
61   Sandra Semola nee Zampin interviewed by Madeleine Regan, Transcript, J.D. Somerville Oral History Collection, State Library of South Australia, Adelaide, OH 872/44, 27 April 2017: 4, 15, 17, 26.

About two years later, her parents visited Italy and were away for seven months. They trusted their daughter to manage a tomato crop in the glasshouses.[62] Sandra explained that her father had planted tomatoes before he left:

> They were about six inches [high] and while he was away, I had to string them and I knew how to prune and tie so there was nine glasshouses [laughs] and while he was away, I did all that.[63]

Some in the community were surprised Sandra was given the responsibility at just 14 years of age, although her father had asked his *paesani* to look in on her occasionally. She recalled with pride and amusement an incident that occurred when she was managing the glasshouses in her parents' absence:

> Dad was in Italy … I was in the glasshouse doing something, and I could hear these voices and I thought: 'What's going on?' So, I went outside: 'Hello Sandra. We've come to help you.' And I said: 'To do what?' And they said: 'To prune the tomatoes.' And I said: 'Okay.' [Laughs.] And they looked in and their hats come off. And they says: 'We'd better go home and do our own. She's finished.' [Laughs.] I'll never forget that day. They just [pauses] couldn't believe that I had just finished doing these nine glasshouses and they were going to come and help me so that I wouldn't get behind. [Pauses.] And they said: 'When did you start?' I said: 'Last week. I'm finished.' And they're standing there, scratching their head [laughs].[64]

Sandra reconstructed the encounter with the older market gardeners and proudly recalled her effort in pruning the tomato plants. She enjoyed retelling the story of the incident and the shock when the men saw her achievement. She summed up this experience by adding: 'So, Dad had money in the bank when he come home.'[65] While she was paid for her work, Sandra reported that her father took half her 'wages' for board and a proportion was paid into a bank account for her future wedding costs.[66]

---

62 There were approximately 700 tomato plants in a standard glasshouse. Johnny Marchioro, Personal communication, 22 February 2023.
63 Sandra Semola nee Zampin, OH 872/44, 27 April 2017: 17.
64 ibid., 17–18.
65 ibid.
66 ibid., 23.

'I BUY THIS PIECE OF GROUND HERE'

Plate 4.9: The marriage of Arturo Semola and Sandra Zampin, Lockleys, 1966
Source: Photo supplied by Sandra Semola nee Zampin.

Noemi Campagnolo nee Zalunardo completed the compulsory years of secondary school while working with her father on the market garden. She referred to the necessity of observing the weather in relation to the glasshouses:

> No homework. No homework. And did what had to be done at home, grading tomatoes, putting papers in half-boxes … Well, depends what the weather was like. If it was nice weather, you leave them [glasshouses] open. If it was cold, you used to shut the doors, you went around the whole 25 of them and closed all the doors.[67]

Noemi also helped to care for her chronically ill mother until she died when Noemi was 18 years old. In both cases, Sandra and Noemi took on roles as co-workers with their fathers and reduced the need to employ people from outside the family.

---

67   Noemi Campagnolo nee Zalunardo, OH 872/29, 20 March 2014: 12.

Family business arrangements

Veneto families developed their own business arrangements to manage external commercial transactions and comply with taxation reporting requirements. The need for accountability to the state contrasted with subsistence life in Italy where the purpose of labour on the land was to feed the household without gaining income. In traditional peasant societies, opportunities to improve financial status or acquire wealth were unattainable. In Australia, the market gardeners worked to support their families, but it was possible to also make a profit and become prosperous.

At Lockleys, recordkeeping was usually managed within families and several narrators reported assisting their parents with documentation. Notebooks were often used to list expenses, sales and income. When some owners had difficulties meeting the bookkeeping requirements for taxation purposes, they employed accountants to address compliance with government regulations. Some larger families formed partnerships and spread their business responsibilities. In the case of two Ballestrin cousins and their wives who co-owned an 8-hectare property, the financial arrangements were casual and involved an older family member, Isidoro, who had his own market garden but assisted his brother and cousin and their wives with financial matters. The processes are described by one of the sons, Lino:

> That was a fifty:fifty arrangement. One didn't have excess over the other one … They didn't do any books. There was no such thing as books … [T]hey had a strange arrangement where often a lot of paperwork and bills were paid by Isidoro Ballestrin. And what they'd do once a year, [is] get under the shed with all their notes and bits of paper and say: 'Oh, you owe me $20 for that' and 'I owe you $50.' And it sort of, settled out things like that but there was no bookkeeping as such.[68]

During the initial years when production was modest, it was viable to rely on family members for all labour on the market gardens. Over time, some families employed casual labourers including relatives or other Italians who lived locally to assist with harvesting. In an exceptional case, which illustrates a transformation of the family labour unit, the Berno brothers employed an Anglo-Australian man, as Remo recalled: 'And then we had people, one of the … labourers that used to work with us lived there for a long time. His name was Albert Wyatt and he was almost part of the family.'[69]

---

68 Lino Ballestrin, OH 872/40, 22 November 2016: 20.
69 Remo Berno, OH 872/46, 18 June 2014: 7.

Plate 4.10: A group of young Veneto men in front of the Santin house, 1962
Source: Oscar Mattiazzo.

This arrangement represents a departure from the *contadino* model of subsistence and reliance on family and indicates a new kind of authority in employment relationships, which suggests the confidence of the Berno brothers to manage a small commercial business in Australia.

After the war, some of the young Italian migrants who were sponsored by the first generation worked for families either as paid labour or as *paesani* who were paid in-kind with vegetables. Some young men who were employed in factories near Lockleys fitted their work in the market gardens around their shifts when it was time for picking. As Diana Panazzolo nee Santin explained, the Santin families asked young men who were *paesani* from the Veneto for assistance in the 1950s and 1960s:

A lot of the men that used to work at Holdens [*sic*] that used to come on a Tuesday night, weekends, they used to come and help and then they'd bring produce home ... Sort of something for them. I know every year Dad used to buy them a bottle, they used to buy them a bottle of whisky or something, at Christmas time, to say thank you. But I don't think there was money exchanged.[70]

Identity at Lockleys

The identity of the Veneto group as market gardeners evolved from the mid-1930s when they began taking up leaseholds and it remained intact and bounded until the 1960s when subdivision brought changes. The first generation of Veneto men shifted from the marginal position they held in the early years after arrival in Australia and grasped economic and commercial opportunities that they could never have realised in Italy. Husbands, wives, sons and daughters participated in the family economic unit in unexpected ways and new partnerships were forged with extended family members. While they looked back to Italy for rules about familial loyalty and the heritage of cultivating the land, the imperative to develop and acquire commercial market gardens enabled the first generation of Veneto migrants to modify and reshape practices. Through their market gardens, families developed a new identity in Australia within the community and created physical and social stability for the second generation.

---

70 Diana Panazzolo nee Santin interviewed by Madeleine Regan, Transcript, J.D. Somerville Oral History Collection, State Library of South Australia, Adelaide, OH 872/27, 13 September 2014: 9.

5
Life within the community

Madeleine Regan: We're coming to the end of the interview, Assunta. But what would you like people to know about, today, about this particular area?

Assunta Giovannini: Well, in this particular area like that you said, Madeleine, in those days there were just these migrants that arrived, tried to make a living, tried to make something for themselves, they worked hard and they all kept in touch with one another and everyone seemed to have got on with everyone else. There was no arguments, there were no quarrels it was just that all the families helped one another and you were all classed as friends, you know, if something happened to someone the other one would know and it all seems to be in that square, there. And they all kept close contact, and it's good to remember that these people, they all looked out for one another.

—Assunta Giovannini nee Tonellato, 2014[1]

Assunta Giovannini nee Tonellato's memories of the early days of the community of market gardeners at Lockleys reconstruct her experience of the *paese* in the interwar years. Responding to a question about the area, Assunta immediately directed her focus to the history of the community. Like other narrators, she remembered growing up within family structures, work and a social network in the market-gardener community. Assunta communicated the shared experience of living among families whose members enjoyed trust, solidarity and security in everyday life and support in times of need.

---

1   Assunta Giovannini nee Tonellato interviewed by Madeleine Regan, Transcript, J.D. Somerville Oral History Collection, State Library of South Australia, Adelaide, OH 872/6, 9 October 2014: 37.

Plate 5.1: Assunta Tonellato and her uncle Secondo Tonellato, Frogmore Road, c. 1952

Source: Photo supplied by Assunta Giovannini nee Tonellato.

A second-generation woman interviewed at age 77, Assunta remembered an idealised community and communicated nostalgia for a past that differed from her present life. She visualised the comfort and safety of the community created by the first generation in her formative years.[2] Assunta also conveyed the loss of that first generation, her connections to the community and hinted that her own experience and identity could be lost. Assunta had previously referred to the intimacy of relationships within the *paese*: '[In] the early years all the old people kept close together.' Her reference to the 'old people' reflected her respect and affection for the first generation of women and men who established the community at Lockleys.

The first generation of market gardeners developed their work and family lives and created a regional identity as *veneti* rather than as a group from the same village or family line. The market gardens at Lockleys became sites of independence and financial success for individual families who maintained some traditional structures and rituals of the Veneto region, which provided a sense of the transnational connection to place. This chapter examines the social arrangements that provided the foundations for the *paese* that supported families and the community from the 1930s to the 1970s.

Community and assimilation

The examination of the Veneto community of market gardeners is set against the assimilationist policies and public opinion in the interwar years in Australia. Writing about the settlement of Sicilians in Australia and their origins, social scientist Constance Cronin argues that the Australian Government did not have strategies to manage the presence of southern European migrants. Without official structures, migrants established themselves in their own ethnic communities.[3] Rather than being pushed into a location, the Veneto market gardeners were drawn to the availability of land at Lockleys and the opportunity to earn a livelihood, transforming their experience as *contadini*. The possibility of cultivating land to earn a livelihood was an enticement and the aggregation of the Veneto group at Lockleys enabled the formation of the *paese*.

---

2   Assunta was raised by her Tonellato uncle and aunt when her mother died soon after her birth. Assunta later chose to be adopted by them.
3   Constance E. Cronin, *The Sting of Change: Sicilians in Australia* (Chicago: University of Chicago Press, 1970), 131–32.

At Lockleys, interactions that brought meaning to their everyday lives included sharing a language, relationships with kin and proxy family members, social activities and cultural customs and practices that were means of 'increasing internal solidarity'.[4] The first-generation Veneto market gardeners also brought with them images of their origin villages to counter the discomfort of being 'the other' in a climate of open hostility during the 1930s and 1940s as they established themselves at Lockleys. In contrast, the young Italian immigrants who experienced the postwar devastation and poverty in Italy generally were less bound by their 'imagined, romanticised construction of the Veneto village'.[5]

The social lives of first-generation men and women in the market-gardener families were contained within the *paese* and wider Veneto network in Adelaide and they did not seek opportunities to move beyond this. Leon Bernardi, a relative of a market-gardener family, observed the limited interactions of the first generation of Italians with non-Italians in Adelaide when he arrived as a young man in the late 1950s: '[T]he Italian community was quite close and even though they respected the Australian community ... mixing was rare, particularly the oldies. And the kids were brought up at school ... [T]he parents were more cliquey with the Italian community.'[6]

The interactions of the first generation with the public domain were limited to two main areas of external communication: the twice or thrice weekly wholesale fruit and vegetable market and attendance at the Catholic Church. Unlike their experience in the Veneto, presence at weekly mass was more a voluntary act than a necessity to profess their faith under the authority of the priest. In the village, the priest had been 'the most powerful man in the commune, and determined the amount of the annual crop to donate to the parish and advised about voting and selection of marriage partners'.[7] The *veneti* at Lockleys did not have to answer to a local priest because the structures of the Catholic Church were different in Australia and they were not under the same scrutiny as *contadini* experienced in the villages in the Veneto. Some Veneto families attended Sunday mass while

---

4   Simone Marino, 'Beyond Authenticity: An Ethnographic Reflection on Italians in Australia and Italians in Italy', *Journal of Sociology* 58, no. 4 (2022): 588–604, doi.org/10.1177/14407833211016090, at 593. Marino makes the point in relation to Calabrian migrants in Adelaide that the first generation maintains practices and values or a sense of the village that they embodied when they first arrived.
5   ibid., 599.
6   Leon Bernardi interviewed by Madeleine Regan, Transcript, J.D. Somerville Oral History Collection, State Library of South Australia, Adelaide, OH 872/65, 16 June 2022: 32.
7   Huber, *From Pasta to Pavlova*, 26.

in others only the women and children fulfilled the obligation.⁸ However, the full community attended religious rites of passage such as baptisms, first holy communions, confirmations and weddings, and enjoyed the celebratory occasions held in packing sheds on market gardens.

The Veneto market gardeners turned to the *paese* at Lockleys as they developed their livelihoods, settled their families, created a community and achieved *sistemazione*. Beyond the *paese*, the Australian Government's White Australia policy emphasised difference and public opinion denounced Italians and other non-British migrants on ethnic grounds. In the period between the wars, Italian immigration was viewed as 'a problem'.⁹ British migrants were publicly acknowledged and welcomed as more desirable citizens than 'white aliens' like Italians. In the years after the report of the 1925 Ferry Royal Commission on Increase of Aliens in Queensland, concern about settlements like the Veneto market gardeners at Lockleys had circulated in the wider Australian community. Commissioner Ferry advised Commonwealth and state governments against 'the formation of alien groups [that were] all anti-British in sympathy and outlook'.¹⁰ As Dewhirst argues, the Ferry report embodied the xenophobic beliefs that were prevalent in the 1920s and promoted further regulation of non-British immigration, particularly of southern Italians.¹¹ While the report exposed the prevalent public views, it went further, as it 'epitomised overt racism within the political and social fabric of the state and Commonwealth'.¹²

In the absence of assistance from governments and other institutions, individual Veneto families, like many other southern European migrant groups at the time, found support within their community. Consequently, the incentive to assimilate was limited at least until the Australia-born children went to school. While they may have withdrawn from the inducement of assimilation, the Veneto market gardeners became naturalised and had a vision of settling permanently in Australia and providing a future for their children. Eight of the first generation were naturalised within 11 years of arrival. The war interrupted the processing of Italian applications for naturalisation. By 1947, all the first-generation market gardeners in Australia were

---

8   Mass was celebrated in Italian every Sunday at the Catholic parish at Flinders Park for several years during the 1950s.
9   N.O.P. Pyke, 'Some Reflections on Italian Immigration into Australia', *The Australian Quarterly* 18, no. 4 (1946): 35–44, doi.org/10.2307/20631402, at 35–36, 44.
10 Thomas Arthur Ferry, *Report of the Royal Commission Appointed to Inquire into and Report on the Social and Economic Effect of Increase in Number of Aliens in North Queensland* (Brisbane, 1925), 25.
11 Dewhirst, 'The "Southern Question" in Australia'.
12 ibid., 328.

naturalised. Although the Veneto group was self-contained in their *paese* at Lockleys, they did not create formal structures such as a commercial centre or a cultural organisation like the Bulgarian community 2 kilometres away. This was, perhaps, an outcome of the relatively small population between the wars and the size of the group settlement of Veneto market gardeners. The *veneti* engaged with commercial and market activities and health services outside the Lockleys area. On trips to the market in Adelaide, the first generation patronised the grocery and butcher shops owned by Veneto families who had arrived in the 1920s as participants in an 'economically interconnected ethnic community'.[13] It was many years before the Veneto market gardeners joined cultural organisations outside their *paese*.

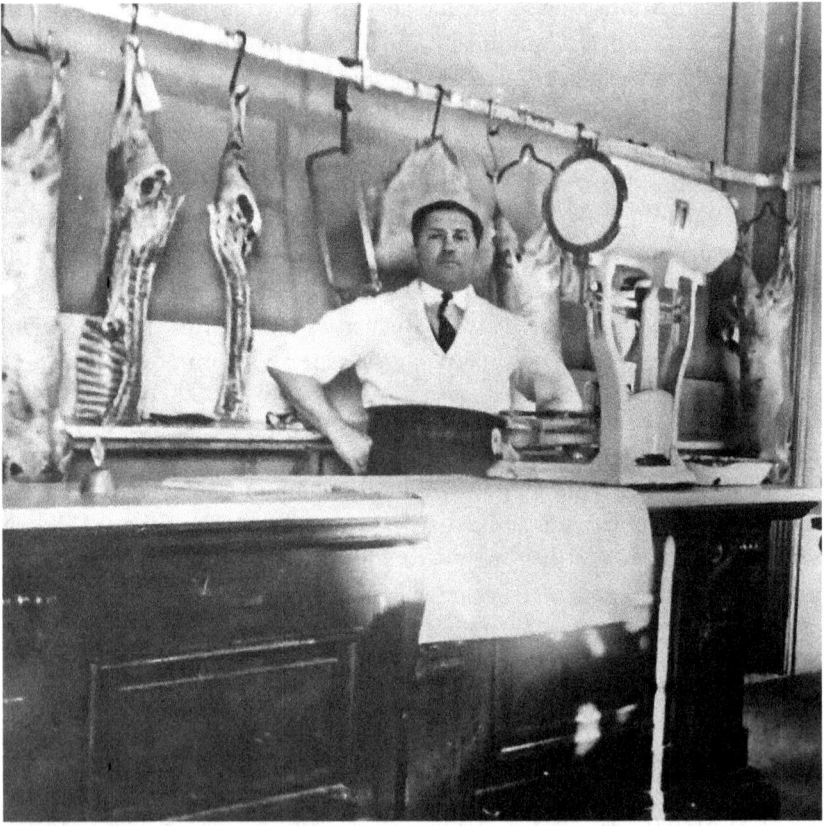

Plate 5.2: Emilio Mattiazzo in his butcher's shop, City of Adelaide, 1940s
Source: Photo supplied by the Santin family.

---

13   Micaela di Leonardo, *The Varieties of Ethnic Experience: Kinship, Class, and Gender among California Italian-Americans* (Ithaca: Cornell University Press, 1984), doi.org/10.7591/9781501721250, 154–56.

The close community

As in any community, the Veneto market gardeners experienced the positive aspects of their close relationships and proximity, but these undoubtedly brought limitations and uneven experiences for some. Most narrators were members of the second generation and were not focused on sharing the subjective meaning of how their parents experienced life in a small community with other *paesani*. There were suggestions that some tensions existed and these included difficult behaviours, disputes about ways of operating businesses and moral opinions about the conduct of the second generation and the suitability of some marriages. Arrangements in some households and the use of space created intrafamily discord. For example, some families continually received relatives who migrated after the war and, for some, this resulted in discomfort and lack of privacy. Women had extensive responsibilities within families and did not enjoy the same opportunities as men to spend time away from the family.

The lives of children were dominated by the family business and some in the second generation were unable to achieve their hopes of a future away from the market gardens. The generational conflict was also evident in some families as the second generation became less attached to home. Another point of difference was articulated in respect to the more comfortable socioeconomic position experienced by the 'new Australian' postwar migrants compared with those who arrived between the wars. However, it does appear that, overall, for the first generation, the benefits outweighed the challenges of living in the *paese*. It seems that they valued the close network within the boundaries set at Lockleys as they adapted to life in Australia and endured challenges that existed outside the *paese*. The narrators were not drawn to providing negative views of their families.

In their reflections, second-generation narrators offered an interpretation of the community as they recalled it or had heard about it from their parents. They were comfortable speaking about life in their families and their identity as market gardeners and were loyal to their relatives. There was distance from difficult incidents for which there were no records or formal allegations and from personalities in the first generation who may have been controversial.[14]

---

14   Thompson and Bornat identify influences on the oral history interview and the transmission of memory, which is an individual experience but also influenced by the collective identity. The influences on the interview relate to both the interviewer and the narrators. Narrators may not have felt comfortable articulating memories of negative aspects of family or community in the context of a project that was transmitted publicly. Thompson and Bornat, *The Voice of the Past*, 207–13.

With the birth of children, new opportunities to form more formal relationships in the *paese* opened. The role of godparents was the most significant of the internal formal bonds that *paesani* developed within the early community. In the Catholic tradition, parents select significant adults and ask them to become godparents at baptism and confirmation to provide a loving presence and possible role as guardians in their godchild's life. In the Veneto culture, a female godparent was known as a *santola* (plural, *santole*) and a man as a *santolo* (plural, *santoli*). A study of the godparent relationship in Calabrian families in Adelaide, known as *comparatico*, identifies a similar 'family-type relationship based not on blood or marriage', but on '"spiritual kinship" that connects the family of the child with the family of the godparent'.[15] Godparents reinforced the close and enduring connections of care among the first generation of market-gardener families and created intergenerational bonds that were important for the Veneto families who did not have other relatives in Australia. In the absence of extended family, godparents became aunts and uncles.

Plate 5.3: The baptism of Louis Ballestrin, Hartley Road, c. 1951
Notes: Louis is held by Norina Ballestrin, with his godfather, Gino Berno, at left, and his father, Giuseppe. Note the half-cases stacked behind the group.
Source: Photo supplied by Norma Camozzato nee Ballestrin.

---

15   Marino and Chiro, 'Family Alliances and "Comparatico"', 111.

Plate 5.4: A group of Veneto women with Irene Destro, Frogmore Road, c. 1946
Note: Irene Destro is fourth from left in striped top.
Source: Lina Marchioro.

Vittorio and Angelina Marchioro took the unusual step of choosing an Anglo-Australian woman, Irene Destro, as godmother for their first-born son, Johnny. Irene's husband, Attilio, had emigrated from the same village as Vittorio and married Irene soon after his arrival in 1927. Although not market gardeners, the Destro family lived on the neighbouring property and, as Johnny Marchioro indicated, it was considered an honour to be invited to be a godparent: 'When I was baptised, she [Irene] held me for the christening.'[16] The image of the child being 'held' suggests trust, intimacy and exclusivity in a role chosen by the parents. The Marchioro family demonstrated openness in giving the respected status of *santola* to an Anglo-Australian woman who became a *paesana* (villager) through that role.

Irene (Rene) Destro was remembered by some narrators as the person who introduced the Anglo-Australian practice of baking cakes for children's birthdays. Romano Marchioro recalled that his family was transformed by Irene's custom of celebrating birthdays: 'We were lucky we were one of the first people that used to have birthday cakes because of our Australian

---

16 Johnny Marchioro, OH 872/1, 21 July 2008: 28.

influence.'[17] Irene had a wider impact on the Veneto community through her role assisting women by interpreting at doctors' appointments and because she and her husband allowed the *veneti* to use their telephone, which, for some time, was the only one in the community. Assunta Giovannini nee Tonellato explained:

> Rene Destro. She married an Italian, Destro … [S]he was the only one in that area to have a phone. Now, if anyone had to make a phone call, they all had to go to her and she … seemed to be an interpreter for everybody.[18]

Johnny Marchioro's godfather or *santolo* was Pietro Berno, who, at the time of Johnny's birth in 1940, was a single man. In a congruence characterising the intimacy of *paesani* relationships, Johnny's parents were asked to be *santoli* when Pietro and Antonietta Berno's second son, Remo, was born in 1953. Johnny maintained contact with his *santolo* even after the Berno family returned to Italy to live in 1969 and he visited Pietro when he and his family went to Italy for the first time in 1975.

The birth of children and selection of their godparents reinforced ties within the community that were often maintained beyond childhood and transnationally. For example, Diana Panazzolo nee Santin, born in 1951, continued to communicate with her godmother from the time she returned to live in Italy in 1969 until her death in 2013.[19] When a child was confirmed at about 11 years of age, a sponsor was chosen and this role also assumed status within a family. In the following excerpt, Dino Piovesan conveys the significance of both roles. He used the general Italian masculine and feminine terms *compare* and *comare* for confirmation sponsors and the Veneto word *santolo* to describe the godfather relationship:

> As far as the Italian community is concerned, that is a very important relationship, because if you ask someone to be *compare* for you, a sponsor for your child, that person, that family has a special significance after that, and they remain friends forever, shall we say. There was not so much a bond but a special relationship between those who were *compare* and *comare* … Gino Berno … was my *santolo*, the word *santolo* meant more than the name itself. He was the person to be respected, the *santolo*.[20]

---

17 Romano Marchioro, OH 872/20, 11 June 2012: 4.
18 Assunta Giovannini nee Tonellato interviewed by Madeleine Regan, Transcript, J.D. Somerville Oral History Collection, State Library of South Australia, Adelaide, OH 872/6, 15 July 2010: 9.
19 Diana Panazzolo nee Santin, OH 872/27, 18 October 2013: 22.
20 Dino Piovesan, OH 872/17, 23 September 2011: 11.

Plate 5.5: Baptism of Peter Zampin, Adelaide, c. 1953
Notes: From left: Gino and Irma Berno, Silvano Zampin (holding Peter), Elisabetta and Secondo Tonellato. Front: Christine and Virginia Zampin.
Source: Photo supplied by the Zampin family.

Although it was part of the religious framework, the godparent relationship was treasured within the network of relationships that supported the Veneto market-gardener families.

Bonds within the community

The bonds within the community were continuously strengthened through a range of daily and seasonal interactions. For the Lockleys Veneto group, the most important bonds were the relationships, customs and conduct that stemmed from their collective history, shared language, culture, religious background, co-location and common occupation—elements that created a homogeneity also noted by Bromley in his study of the Molfettese fisher community in Port Pirie.[21]

---

21   Bromley, 'The Italians of Port Pirie', 207.

Shared language

Although the Veneto group shared a dialect, there were variations related to the eight different places of origin in the first generation. Because most had received minimal education, their command of standard Italian was limited and they communicated by adapting different Veneto dialects. In the first generation, the need to learn to speak English was largely dispensable, particularly for women, who were less likely than men to participate in the commercial world outside Lockleys. Dino Piovesan recalled his mother's view of English: 'Mum always used to say jokingly, "You don't need to speak English to spend money. All you need is money."'[22]

Even if the market gardeners had been motivated to learn English in the first years after their arrival, there was no opportunity because the Australian Government did not provide official language programs for adult migrants until 1947, in a policy response to the mass migration of Europeans after World War II.[23] Because their parents did not speak fluent English, children in many migrant families used transcultural skills to act as translators and interpreters. Individuals in the 1.5 generation of the Veneto market-gardener community often undertook this role for relatives in the first generation and those who arrived after the war. One woman who had been educated to the third year of secondary school in Adelaide was known to assist Veneto women at medical appointments, often in gynaecological consultations.

A 1.5-generation man who had attended the compulsory years of schooling helped newly arrived Veneto migrants with transactions such as purchasing a car. He was also asked by postwar *veneti* to be power of attorney and executor of wills. Another man, who had arrived at the age of 11 and received three years of secondary schooling, became a business owner and qualified as a justice of the peace. He was called on by Italians who preferred to speak about legal and administrative matters with a native Italian-speaker. In this way, the 1.5 generation demonstrated the application of transcultural strategies and processes and used their agency to engage with the social, economic and cultural aspects of daily life in Australia by assisting people who were less proficient English speakers.[24]

---

22 Dino Piovesan, OH 872/17, 23 September 2011: 12.
23 Jean I. Martin, *The Migrant Presence: Australian Responses, 1947–1977* (Sydney: George Allen & Unwin, 1978), 83–84.
24 Ricatti, *Italians in Australia*, 132.

In the context of the generational gap in language proficiency, some second-generation narrators recalled assuming the role of interpreter for first-generation relatives in formal transactions that required complex discourse such as in hospitals, government, financial or legal institutions. For example, when Lina Rismondo nee Marchioro was a primary school student, she translated for her uncle in a meeting with a taxation officer. Lina was asked to vouch for the honesty of her uncle, Vittorio Marchioro, although she was uncertain about the financial details relating to his income, when she interpreted for him:

> at the Taxation Office when he had to do his income tax, and I didn't know what he was talking about [laughs]. I remember once the tax, the one that was talking to us asked me: 'You're not telling lies, are you?' I said: 'No.' I don't think they believed me when I said, 'Uncle wasn't making much money.' And I had to tell them there wasn't much money. And: 'You're not telling me lies, are you?' I said: 'No' [laughs].[25]

Lina was compelled to defend her uncle although, as a young girl, she was unsure about the context—a cause for her laughter as an 83-year-old in the interview. The situation had a deeper meaning for both Lina and her uncle because within the patriarchal structures of a Veneto family, a male adult relative would normally never have yielded power to a young girl in any circumstances.

Adapting relationships

Relationships were adapted in response to new circumstances in the *paese*. When three first-generation men died at a relatively young age in the 1940s, members of the community supported their families in their loss. Without assistance from the *paesani*, the economic status of the three families would have been severely compromised. The extent of support and practical assistance provided to the families illustrates the maturity and cohesion of the community. In the event of the death of the leading man in a Veneto village, close relatives would have enveloped the bereaved family and given additional support. At Lockleys, the web of connectivity strengthened within the *paese* because of the commitment to provide care and support

---

25 Lina Rismondo nee Marchioro, OH 872/9, 9 June 2010: 13.

as proxy family members. For example, Guido Rebuli recalled that Pietro Berno, a Veneto neighbour, was attentive to the needs of his mother after his father's death in 1947 when Guido was nine years old:

> Peter Berno, Piero Berno. He was the person in those years ... if somebody needed help ... He wasn't a guardian over the rest of them, but he was very good with people to help them when they needed help. And of course, by that time, Dad had gone so he knew, and he used to pop through there [and ask my mum]: 'Nana, is everything alright?'[26]

A new kind of leadership

Pietro Berno and his brother Alberto became informal leaders within the emerging community despite both remaining single for more than 20 years. Although their bachelor status was contrary to the *contadino* culture because of the positive regard afforded to the status of husband and father, the brothers were respected for their hard work and prosperity and were invited to become *santoli*. The community, which had already incorporated two Anglo-Australian wives since the 1930s, also accepted the single status of the Berno brothers in a further adaptation of the *contadino* model of kin and family. Although narrators did not identify class divisions in the Veneto market-gardener group, it appears that the Berno brothers achieved prominence because of their business success and role in providing advice to *paesani* at Lockleys. Similarly, in a study of a Veneto community in Victoria's Gippsland between the wars, those men who had achieved prosperity gained respect and authority. Although real class divisions were not identified there, men who had attained substantial financial status and gave advice and support to their peers formed a proxy class hierarchy through their leadership roles.[27]

From a poor *contadino* family, the Berno brothers had worked hard to prosper in Australia and acquired a form of patriarchal authority. Veneto man Angelo Innocente, who arrived in 1951, referred to the Berno brothers as 'the bank for the Italians' because they lent money to the newly arrived and assisted them with finding employment: '[T]hey opened more doors

---

26 Guido Rebuli interviewed by Madeleine Regan, Transcript, J.D. Somerville Oral History Collection, State Library of South Australia, Adelaide, OH 872/25, 24 April 2013: 13.
27 Davine, *Vegnimo da Conco Ma Simo Veneti*, 52–53.

for us to work.'[28] In 1963, the role of the Berno brothers in the wider Italian community in Adelaide was noted in an article in a section featuring 'Men of the Community' in the Australian Italian newspaper *La Fiamma* ('The Flame').[29] A special supplement of the paper was dedicated to Italians in South Australia, a history of migration and the successful settlement of various individuals and groups. The Berno brothers were selected with five other Italians to represent Italian market gardeners in the state. In their reflections in the article, the brothers attributed their success to luck, hard work and mutual agreement in their partnership.

Although the brothers' reputation was comparable with the kind of influence and authority a leader such as a mayor or a priest might have exercised in a Veneto village, they were also appreciated for their generosity and, later with their wives, for hosting social occasions in their large packing shed.

Plate 5.6: Pietro and Alberto Berno, Valetta Road, early 1960s
Source: Photo supplied by the Berno family.

---

28 Angelo Innocente interviewed by Madeleine Regan, Transcript, J.D. Somerville Oral History Collection, State Library of South Australia, Adelaide, OH 872/8, 5 January 2009: 21.
29 'La comunità Italiana di Adelaide', *La Fiamma*, [Supplement], October 1963: 23.

While the Veneto community recognised the Berno brothers as leaders, the judgement of the Australian Government was less favourable. In 1944, they were seen as being not 'fit subjects for Naturalization'.[30] Although they were also regarded as a security threat, two main arguments were used against them. The first related to a 'suspected offence against the Land Transfer Regulations'—a reference to the purchase of land by their cousin in 1942. The second was a report made by the Department of Taxation because the brothers had not submitted legitimate tax returns for the years 1937–42. Alberto and Pietro paid the overdue sum with a penalty and were able to avoid legal proceedings, but their naturalisation was denied and they waited another two years before new applications were approved.[31]

Customs and conduct

The Veneto group balanced the preservation of customs with new opportunities away from work that were available in Lockleys because there was time for leisure. The close living arrangements facilitated a community social life and activities ranged from events for families and men's recreation to women's home gatherings and children's play.

Recreation in the *paese*

Some social activities that were customary in the Veneto region were adapted and valued by the community at Lockleys. In the Veneto, the main family social activity outside the household was the outing to attend Sunday mass or religious festivals. Other leisure pursuits were few although men visited the local *osteria* (tavern or inn), where they played cards. Men also played games of *bocce*, the Italian form of lawn bowls. At Lockleys, families participated in community social occasions. In addition to cards and bocce, market gardeners visited other *veneti* who lived in Adelaide on the way back from selling vegetables at the market. Women's social life outside the household was limited and, apart from community social events, confined mainly to the domestic sphere through receiving or visiting relatives.

---

30   Department of Immigration, Central Office, A435, Class 4 correspondence files relating to naturalisation, 01 Jan 1944 – 31 Dec 1950, 1946/4/4527, Berno Alberto—born 16 February 1905—Italian, 1939–1946, NAA. The same documentation was produced for Pietro Berno (435, 1946/4/510, NAA).
31   'Pietro Berno', 435, 1946/4/4527, NAA.

5. LIFE WITHIN THE COMMUNITY

Some narrators recalled visiting families in the wider Veneto community in the city or suburbs at weekends. While some religious rites of passage such as baptisms, first holy communions and confirmations were largely intimate occasions attended by family, weddings drew the wider Adelaide Veneto community together. In the following excerpt, Maria Rosa Tormena, a member of the 1.5 generation, responds to a question about attending weddings in the Veneto community:

> They used to end up, I think, [with] a hundred and fifty to two hundred people at their weddings … Certainly all of Lockleys, the Italians of Lockleys plus the ones that they got to know … Once they had to take their tomatoes to the market, the East End market, and we lived in town, they used to call around and maybe they'd have a glass of wine or a coffee so you got to know them that way, you know. You visited one friend and they took you to the other one. Which doesn't happen now, does it?[32]

Recalling the socialising between members of the first generation of the *veneti*, Maria Rosa reflected on the ease of making connections within the wider Veneto community in Adelaide in the 1950s. Some *veneti* in Adelaide, like Maria Rosa's family, were relatives of market gardeners or *paesani* from the same villages. Families adapted the custom of visiting and socialising, or *fiò* (in the Veneto dialect), as a way of maintaining intergenerational relationships in the community. *Fiò* was a custom brought from the Veneto, where extended families would gather at night in the warmth of the stable, which was under the main roof of the intergenerational household.

Fiò took on new significance at Lockleys as it was easy to visit other families who lived within walking distance and it was possible to do so at the end of the working day after dinner. As Silvano Ballestrin explained, the whole family would be involved:

> We would often go to *fiò* and visit all of our relatives and friends and they would visit us as well. Once or twice a week, usually after dinner, we would hear our parents talking to each other, saying something like: '*Andemmo a fiò?* [Shall we go visiting?]' '*Va ben, andove demo?* [All right. Where shall we go?]' '*A ben, andemmo da Yiyo Toneato* [Oh well, let's go to Luigi Tonellato]' … [T]he family would walk from our Valetta Road home to friends' and relatives' places after dinner during the evening *fiò*. For example, from Valetta Road, our

---

32 Maria Rosa Tormena, OH 872/19, 25 May 2012: 13.

family would walk two and a half kilometres to the Marchioros at the end of White Avenue, stay for two to three hours and then walk back later that night. A five-kilometre all round walk.[33]

The market-gardener families enjoyed group outings including picnics in the Adelaide Hills and an annual activity that developed after the war when they were more prosperous and had bought trucks. Each New Year's Day, families organised a trip to St Kilda Beach, 30 kilometres north of Lockleys, an outing that included people from the wider Veneto community. Families shared a day of socialising, crabbing, eating and playing games. Many narrators recalled the pleasure of being together as a group, which was memorable because families took time off from the market gardens. Noemi Campagnolo nee Zalunardo, a member of the second generation, recalled her parents taking her to the event and her delight at the annual occasion:

> I remember them going to St Kilda. Oh, it was fun. It was fun. It was really good ... With a truck with everybody at the back of the truck, not now, you have to have seatbelts. Yea, the back of the truck singing ... Oh gosh, there was a lot of them that used to go, we used to have a truck full, follow the leader, it was good, it was nice.[34]

Plate 5.7: Group of Veneto families, St Kilda, early 1950s
Source: Photo supplied by Noemi Campagnolo nee Zalunardo.

---

33 Silvano Ballestrin, 'Narciso Ballestrin and Maria Dotto Family', *Veneto Market Gardeners 1927 Blog*, 12 July 2020, venetimarketgardeners1927.net/narciso-ballestrin-and-maria-dotto-family/.
34 Noemi Campagnolo nee Zalunardo, OH 872/29, 20 March 2014: 10.

Packing sheds as halls

Some market gardeners transformed their packing sheds from sites of labour into venues for community events. Some large sheds were substitutes for or the equivalent of the *piazza* or central square, the main meeting place in an Italian village. Maria Mazzarolo nee Compostella used the term 'halls' when she explained how packing sheds were transformed into venues for large social occasions.[35] Maria made a distinction between the halls that were hired for wedding receptions and the packing sheds that accommodated gatherings of the community, where the celebrations could continue into the night without restrictions on the finishing time:

> They used to have weddings, you used to go to the halls and the next day, you gathered around … [S]o you used to go to Bernos' or Santins' sheds and they used to congregate there and of course, there was no time limit there.[36]

Plate 5.8: Confirmation party for Robert Berno and John Torresan, Berno packing shed, Lockleys, 1959
Source: Photo supplied by the Berno family.

---

35 Maria Mazzarolo nee Compostella interviewed by Madeleine Regan, Transcript, J.D. Somerville Oral History Collection, State Library of South Australia, Adelaide, OH 872/30, 23 April 2014: 6.
36 ibid., 7, 8.

In interviews, various Veneto families were named as providing their sheds for community celebrations and social occasions—for example, the Berno brothers and their wives. Remo Berno remembered that when his sister Diana was confirmed, six other children including relatives and his parents' godchildren were guests of honour in a shared celebration in the family packing shed.[37] Adrian Tonellato, from the second generation, described the community as 'like the family' and contrasted individual endeavours on the market gardens with the participation of the group in celebrations: 'Everybody [was] on their own, but when we had a party, everyone used to come there in the shed.'[38]

Gendered social activities

Before World War II, when the families were establishing their gardens, the social activities were limited to *fiò*, Sunday-afternoon *bocce* hosted by a Veneto man who lived several kilometres from Lockleys and, for some, attendance at mass. After the war when freedom of movement resumed for Italians and the market gardeners were more financially secure, social activities increased, particularly for men. Men congregated at Isidoro Ballestrin's packing shed on Sunday afternoons to spend time together, and sons were often present before they embarked on their own social lives. Adrian Tonellato recalled the gatherings when he was a boy:

> [Isidoro] had the shed and he used to buy the beer and they used to sit in the shed and talk about old times, about Italy … Every Sunday. They used to go there, what? About 11 in the morning … and come home about 6 or 7 at night … [I]n those days, they didn't own cars, or they had bikes or they walked.[39]

Adrian's 92-year-old mother, Italia, was present during his interview and confirmed that women stayed home on Sunday afternoons. Both mother and son laughed about the differences between social activities for women and men, implying that the role of women then was definitely in the domestic world, apart from the times when couples visited one another with their children. The separation of women and men in social life was particularly evident in post-wedding events when guests finished off kegs of beer and leftover food. This was the case the day after the marriage of Anna Mattiazzo and Vito Santin in 1949.

---

37   Remo Berno, OH 872/46, 27 June 2017: 28–29.
38   Adrian Tonellato, OH 872/35, 19 November 2015: 23.
39   ibid., 15.

5. LIFE WITHIN THE COMMUNITY

Plate 5.9: Veneto group the day after Anna Mattiazzo and Vito Santin's wedding, Lockleys, 1949
Source: Photo supplied by the Santin family.

After the arrival of the postwar migrants, most of whom were young men, the range of social activities expanded. The Sbrissa family from the Veneto—although not members of the first-generation group—created a *bocce* court on their market garden and established a formal public competition, the results of which were published in the Italian page of the Catholic weekly newspaper.[40]

Children and recreation

Under the rigid working days and patriarchal structures of the traditional Veneto household children were not afforded planned leisure time. However, first-generation parents at Lockleys created occasions for their sons and daughters to enjoy activities away from the market gardens. Although assigned jobs, narrators spoke of opportunities to go for bike rides, play informal games of tennis or cricket or go into Adelaide with

---

40 'Grande Gara Bocciofila a Lockleys il 20 giugno, 1954 [Great Bowls Competition at Lockleys on 20th June 1954]', [*L'Angelo degli Italiani* (No. 889)], *Southern Cross*, 11 June 1954: 10.

their mothers and walk along the river or visit the zoo. Veneto market-gardener families took advantage of Adelaide's climate and proximity to the beach and organised outings for the children. Several narrators, such as Francesco Ballestrin, remembered trips to the beach on hot summer days during school holidays:

> [I]n the summer, Dad used to grow tomatoes, and around Christmas time when it was too hot and we were on school holidays we used to [go] down the beach all the time, every day, under the jetty there. And all the group round here [Lockleys,] cousins, aunties and uncles and friends, the whole mob of us used to go down the beach and pass the day away that way because it was very hot in those years and no air-conditioning and all in tin shacks. I mean there was no insulation, no nothing, and [it was] like an oven.[41]

Plate 5.10: Maria Berno and daughter Lucy with cousins Diana and Marisa Berno, Glenelg Beach, Adelaide, c. 1962
Source: Photo supplied by the Berno family.

---

41   Francesco Ballestrin, OH 872/7, 14 January 2009: 33.

Assunta Giovannini nee Tonellato recalled joining children from neighbouring families for play and leisure using the area around the houses and market gardens, including her house, which was the railway carriage on Frogmore Road:

> We used to go around our place, we used to make it like a dirt track and we would ride our bikes and that was our entertainment, riding our bikes around the house [laughs], and nearly knocking the old ladies over and playing cricket there on the courtyard in the front, or tennis or whatever we were doing.[42]

Guido Rebuli, whose father died when he was nine years old, showed talent in sports when he was at school and represented South Australia in interstate football and cricket championships. The opportunity to compete in elite sports at a young age was unusual in the Veneto group. Although some other young men played in league football teams, Guido participated in national schoolboys' championships. Guido recalled his family's support for his sporting trips:

> I got picked in the State Schoolboys—Under 14, but you know, most of us were only 12 or so … Well, the football carnival was in Hobart. Went for cricket, went to Sydney with the State, this is State schoolboys … [W]e went with the school, teachers and all and the teachers come around home and said, this is where we're going to go and my brothers were there, being the fathers for me. And she [Mum] was quite happy.[43]

Guido's story emphasises the freedom he was given to develop his sporting life and he ascribes the paternal role to his older brothers, who assented to the interstate travel. While some children—foremost boys—were permitted to participate in the Anglo-Australian competitive sports environment, their parents organised family social life within the Veneto community. Two other sons of Veneto market-gardener families, Johnny Marchioro and Aldo Rossetto, played league football for Adelaide teams.

---

42 Assunta Giovannini nee Tonellato, OH 872/6, 15 July 2010: 33.
43 Guido Rebuli, OH 872/25, 24 April 2013: 15.

Preserving customs

At Lockleys, families preserved food customs from the Veneto region, which formed both a material continuity with their origins and a symbolic and emotional link that carried a sense of Veneto identity between the two locations of the transnational migrant families.[44] The customs of making particular food dishes were sometimes shared with other market-gardener families and strengthened Veneto identity and bonds within the *paese*. The first-generation Veneto families were almost self-sufficient, growing much of the food consumed at their own table and making their own wine. In the early years, women used produce from their market gardens and domestic vegetable plots and orchards, milked cows to make cheese and butter and raised chickens. Later, other customs were introduced that signified increased prosperity and access to resources. Some families arranged with other households for more expensive annual activities such as killing a pig to make salami or buying (and sometimes picking) grapes in bulk to make and bottle wine.[45]

Johnny Marchioro remembered his parents' energy for the seasonal tasks that enabled them to preserve traditions from Italy:

> I think they used to go to Reynella and get their grapes for the wine. He [Dad] made a cement tank and when the wine season was—back in would have been April, May … we used to squash it, jump in the barrel and squash it by foot, and they'd make our own wine. Yes, that was like a seasonal thing. Like you'd make your own tomato sauce and the wine time came you'd make your wine, and wintertime you'd make your own salami, too, for the family.[46]

---

44   See Wise and Velayutham, 'Transnational Affect and Emotion in Migration Research'.
45   See Madeleine Regan, 'Autumn and Wine-Making', *Veneto Market Gardeners 1927 Blog*, 21 March 2021, venetimarketgardeners1927.net/autumn-and-wine-making/. See also Aida Innocente, Gino Innocente, and Mary Innocente, 'Making Salamis—Part 1', *Veneto Market Gardeners 1927 Blog*, 2 May 2021, venetimarketgardeners1927.net/making-salamis-part-1/, and 'Making Salamis—Part 2', 16 May 2021, venetimarketgardeners1927.net/making-salamis-part-2/.
46   Johnny Marchioro, OH 872/1, 21 August 2008: 24.

5. LIFE WITHIN THE COMMUNITY

Plate 5.11: Ermenegildo Ballestrin unloading grapes for making wine, Flinders Park, late 1950s

Source: Photo supplied by Ric and Angelo Ballestrin.

Egidio Ballestrin reflected on his parents' food and wine customs:

> In those days especially, they all liked to have their glass of wine, and wine wasn't that easy to come by here in Adelaide, the type of wine they were used to drinking, and also the type of foods that they were used to eating … weren't readily available. I think it was very important because … you know, there's always something of home … [T]hey liked to keep … their Italian lifestyle, and might I say, perhaps improved on the Italian lifestyle that they had because of the poverty over there.[47]

Egidio registered the difference between the first generation's initial efforts to preserve customs from 'home' and their adaptation once families attained a more robust economic position in Australia. His view was repeated by other narrators who acknowledged that the annual ritual of killing a pig to make salami became viable after the first generation gained financial stability.

The preservation of dialect has been important in some families whose older members sometimes prefer speaking it to English. The dialect is particularly noticeable in the context of food customs. Many second-generation and, in some cases, third-generation *veneti* have retained Veneto and/or Italian words and phrases to describe traditional foods and dishes. For example, narrators spoke of *polenta e baccalà* (polenta and stockfish), *risi e bisi* (rice and peas), *carciofi* (artichokes) and *crostoli* (a sweet, deep-fried pastry dusted with icing sugar). Families who continue annual customs such as making tomato sauce and cooking traditional dishes at Easter and Christmas acknowledge that these rituals connect them to their parents and the traditions of their ancestors. Christine Rebellato nee Mattiazzo explained in a blog on the Veneto market gardeners' website the significance of Easter customs for her family:

> Over the years Easter time has been a time for our family to be together to enjoy each other's company, a time to keep our traditions, a time to enjoy food with a focus on keeping our loved ones alive.[48]

The food traditions are an example of the second and third generations maintaining a material connection to their ancestors in the Veneto region.

---

47   Egidio Ballestrin, OH 872/15, 6 June 2011: 5.
48   Christine Rebellato nee Mattiazzo, 'Polenta e Baccalà: More Than a Meal', *Veneto Market Gardeners 1927 Blog*, 5 April 2020, venetimarketgardeners1927.net/polenta-e-baccala-more-than-a-meal/.

Plate 5.12: Peter Rebellato and his father-in-law, Oscar Mattiazzo, deboning stockfish for *baccalà*, West Lakes, Adelaide, 2009

Source: Christine Rebellato nee Mattiazzo.

Transnational connections

The market gardeners maintained transnational connections with their families and villages in the Veneto through material objects, communication, return visits and, more recently for the second and later generations, through technology. Some in the first generation maintained a form of transnational connection through the material objects they brought with them from Italy. Some narrators described a few examples in their interviews. It is not surprising that material objects were not available to the second generation since the men who came on their own experienced a high level of mobility and did not move into their own accommodation on the market gardens for several years after arriving in Adelaide.

Three examples of material objects brought from Italy demonstrate the transnational links created by the first generation of Veneto market gardeners. When Costantina Santin nee Visentin joined her husband, Giovanni, in 1935, she was accompanied by her four children. Among the possessions she brought with her was a large, black-framed picture of Saint Anthony of Padova under glass. Saint Anthony is beloved by Italian people and known as the patron saint of the poor and the sick. The picture of Saint Anthony was always placed above Costantina's bed.[49] The family donated it to a Catholic parish church in Adelaide after her death because it was too large to display in their modern homes and their attachment to the saint differed from that of Costantina.[50]

Oscar Mattiazzo, who arrived as an 11-year-old with his mother in 1934, spoke about prized family objects his mother brought from Italy. Oscar's father had been in South Australia for seven years trying to find work before he arranged for the migration of his wife and son. In a sign of the permanency of the migration, Oscar's mother, Virginia, brought with her a liqueur set, a carafe and six small etched glasses. At the time of the interview, just one glass remained; it was decorated with a gondola, which would have been a reference to Venice. Oscar explained that his parents would never have used the liqueur set even though his mother 'treasured' it. He reflected on his parents and acknowledged that his mother had an appreciation of beautiful things because her father was a merchant while Oscar's father

---

49   For discussion of religion and migration and the significance of religious objects and rituals for sustaining transnational devotional practices and observance of faith, see Cosmini et al., 'The Making of Home in a New Land', 8–12.
50   Diana Panazzolo nee Santin, Personal communication, 7 September 2023.

5. LIFE WITHIN THE COMMUNITY

was from a *contadino* family. Oscar added: 'Of course, we never had the opportunity or the money to buy anything that was good. These things here must have been given to my mother and my father.'[51]

Oscar's daughter, Christine, was present at the interview and suggested that the liqueur set had probably been a wedding gift—a treasured object unfamiliar in the everyday life of the Mattiazzo family.

A collection of linen is a third example of material objects carried from Italy to Australia between the wars. Lena Moscheni nee Rossetto remembered that her mother, Lina, brought a chest that contained clothes, embroidered sheets and towels—items that embodied the desire for permanent settlement, domesticity and *sistemazione*. After Lina was married by proxy in 1930, she arrived in Australia to find that her accommodation was a tent and it was a few years before she enjoyed moving into a home in Adelaide. The linen, which Lina had embroidered, remained in the family and some was passed onto Lena and a daughter-in-law. Lena explained the origin of the embroidery:

> [My mother] would have done some, and other people, like her relatives, maybe, her sisters … They'd sit around at night and sew. She brought a lot of stuff … not crockery or things like that, just linen stuff, towels.[52]

The linen represented the dowry custom in which young women engaged in making household linen items as training for marriage and domestic life.[53]

A final example of material objects raises questions that the first generation may have asked about the official procedures for naturalisation. When members of the first generation of Veneto market gardeners applied for naturalisation, they were required to relinquish their Italian passports.[54] The loss of the passports communicated inhospitality and disregard for the migrants' nationality, which, of course, was the basis of the White Australia policy. The *contadini* who had separated from their family in the Veneto must have valued their passports as a material and symbolic link to Italy.

---

51 Oscar Mattiazzo, OH 872/13, 13 April 2011: 155.
52 Lena Moscheni nee Rossetto, OH 872/32, 28 August 2014: 6–7.
53 See Cosmini et al., 'The Making of Home in a New Land', 12–14.
54 I was surprised to handle the passports at the National Archives of Australia in Canberra that had been held by the first generation who had arrived in the 1920s. I thought about the emotional cost of being separated from their identity document.

Surrendering their passport and renouncing their Italian nationality to become British subjects must have caused some ambivalence as they swore allegiance to King George VI.

Transnational communication and visits

The first generation corresponded with their families in Italy by mail, which took weeks, and some narrators remembered adding messages to their grandparents when their parents wrote letters. One of the first-generation men received photos of his three children sent by his wife in the six-year period between his migration and their arrival in Adelaide.[55]

Some in the first generation made return visits to Italy in the 1960s, by which time they had made an income that could fund extended trips, which were usually by ship. Early visits sometimes provided opportunities for children to develop relationships with grandparents, aunts, uncles and cousins whom they met for the first time. However, not all those in the first generation made the return journey to Veneto. Of the 19 who arrived between 1926 and 1928, six did not go back and three men had died at an early age. According to their children, three others were not interested in returning to their birthplace because their memories of poverty and hardship were troubling. For example, Francesco Ballestrin recalled his father's attitude and his commitment to remaining in Australia, not needing to see remaining family or his place of origin: 'Dad never, ever wanted to go back to Italy and he never did, because of probably the starvation they had there.'[56]

Several second-generation narrators stressed that their parents identified Adelaide as 'home' rather than their birthplace in the Veneto. After they made return visits to see their families, they were happy to resume their stable and comfortable domestic work and life at Lockleys.

---

55   Elena Rebuli has photos of her grandmother, father, uncle and aunt taken in Bigolino, Italy, and sent to her grandfather. She also has a postcard sent to her grandfather at an address on Kangaroo Island in South Australia between 1927 and 1931 when he was working to accumulate funds to pay for the migration of her grandmother and their three children.
56   Francesco Ballestrin, OH 872/7, 5 January 2009: 41.

Plate 5.13: Maria and Narciso Ballestrin and their daughter Norina are farewelled on their first return visit to Italy by friends and family among the crowds at Outer Harbour, Adelaide, 1965

Source: Photo supplied and annotated by Silvano Ballestrin.

Romano Marchioro, the son of first-generation market gardeners, spoke fondly of his parents' relatives in Italy with whom he maintained connections after some of them visited Adelaide:

> I think if I went back to Italy, I'd always be welcome to where they come from even though they're all thinning out. I'm losing a lot of cousins, we've only got one aunt left. She must be getting close to a hundred, I'd say. Umberto's grandmother—she come here [pause] three times, I think, she came. She come with my Mum's sister together one year.[57]

Romano's statement 'back to Italy' expresses a familiarity and affinity with his parents' birthplace although he was born in Australia. He uses the first person, initially in singular, 'I', and then moves to specify 'we' as he reflects on the loss of his ageing relatives in the Veneto. He conveys his sense of identity and belonging to an extended family separated by migration although reconnected by visits. Romano also spoke of his two aunts who made visits to Adelaide when it was possible to make a quicker journey

---

57 Romano Marchioro, OH 872/20, 11 June 2012: 19.

by plane. Romano clearly illustrated the existence of transnational links within families that were parted in the 1920s. Visits by Italian relatives were celebrated in the market-gardener community and reflected the strength of the ties between the two *paesi*: in the Veneto and transplanted at Lockleys.

Interactions beyond the community

While it was possible to contain many aspects of Veneto traditions within the *paese* at Lockleys, families also interacted with institutions outside the community to access services and other needs. Economic life, education and religion were three areas of external contact identified in a study of the Italian community in the Ovens Valley in Victoria that were regarded as 'necessary' on the continuum of increasing interactions with the Anglo-Australian world.[58] Apart from the market, the Veneto community had contact with the education system and the Catholic Church. These transactions were challenging for the *veneti* because in both institutions there was an emphasis on assimilation and communication in English, and the first generation generally did not have extensive opportunities to learn English.

Education of children

Children in the 1.5 and second generations attended school from the mid-1930s to the 1970s when education was a means of assimilation and reflected Australia's monocultural policies and values. Generally, the 1.5-generation narrators did not provide many details of their Australian schooling although several alluded to the challenges of enrolling in classes below their age level because they could not speak English when they arrived. Even in the 1950s when Australia increased its non-English-speaking population with mass migration initiatives, schools did not provide dedicated programs to assist children who spoke only their first language. The government's goal was to guide non-British migrants to conform with the existing Anglo culture and schools served an 'assimilationist function'.[59]

---

58   Daphne Eunice Phillips, 'Italians and Australians in the Ovens Valley Area: A Sociological Study of Interaction between Migrants and the Host Population in a Rural Area of Victoria' (PhD diss., The Australian National University, Canberra, 1970), 384.
59   Martin, *The Migrant Presence*, 90.

In Italy, while the Catholic Church permeated civil life, a Catholic school system did not exist. In contrast, in Australia, the church viewed Catholic schools as an essential platform for the formation of faith for children and young people in Catholic families. Lacking familiarity with the Australian Catholic Church, the first-generation market gardeners mostly sent their children to the local government school. Yet, some parents were persuaded by priests to remove their children and enrol them in the local Catholic schools.

In the 1930s after the Tonellato children had arrived, they were enrolled in the government school within walking distance of their home. Lino Tonellato recalled that the parish priest asked his father to transfer his children to the Catholic school. When Mr Tonellato said he could not afford it, the priest paid for the cost of tram fares and thereafter the children attended the Catholic school.[60] Lino Ballestrin gained good results and, through the advocacy of an Italian priest, received a scholarship based on his performance in his fourth year of secondary school in the city.[61] He reported on his parents' detachment from decisions about his education and the context of his future working life:

> They just left it up to me … [T]hey were too concerned with the garden … [A]t home, my parents gave me no indication, guidance of what I should be doing. So, another friend of mine and myself, together, we went around to the Public Service office in King William Street to talk about getting a job in the Public Service. That's how it happened.[62]

The intervention of the priest enabled Lino to complete his secondary schooling and pursue a career in the Commonwealth Public Service— an exceptional example of occupational mobility in the second generation of the Veneto community at Lockleys.

---

60   Lino Tonellato, OH 872/10, 16 July 2010: 5.
61   In 1952 Lino was awarded one of six inaugural *borse di studio* (scholarships) based on his results in Year 11. 'L'Angolo degli Italiani (No. 7)', *Southern Cross*, 11 July 1952: 3.
62   Lino Ballestrin interviewed by Madeleine Regan, Transcript, J.D. Somerville Oral History Collection, State Library of South Australia, Adelaide, OH 872/40, 22 November 2016: 14, 15.

The role of the Catholic Church

Respect for the authority of the clergy was a fundamental element of the religious, social and cultural frameworks in Italian villages.[63] Angelina Marchioro, who left Italy in 1937, remembered the influence of the local priest in Monte di Malo: 'Everybody go[es] to church … [T]he priest knew all the families in the little town … [T]hey were very strict in the town, the priests.'[64] Interactions with the Catholic priests in Australia were different. In the interwar years, Italians in Australia had to overcome obstacles like language and other cultural differences in the Catholic Church. Irish clergy had dominated Australian parishes and the training of priests since the nineteenth century. In the archdiocese of Adelaide in 1939, where parishes covered extensive suburban areas, two-thirds of the 65 diocesan priests were Irish.[65]

Although the population of Catholics born in Italy increased in the interwar years, the Catholic Church did not provide for the differences in their observance of faith. From the late 1920s, the church in Adelaide organised occasional visits from Italian priests who travelled from Victoria for short periods to minister to the needs of the Italian community. In 1927, Father Vincenzo De Francesco visited Adelaide and reported to his superior in Naples his concern for the many Italians who did not participate in religious life in Australia.[66] Most Italian migrants at the time did not have permanent work or stable accommodation and did not embrace any institutions that were not related to their material existence. Consequently, it was not surprising that the participation of Italians in Catholic parishes was low because at this time they were not welcomed into the Irish-Catholic culture and they could not see 'their *Italianità* mirrored' in the church.[67]

Italians were not fully accepted as a cultural group in the Catholic Church in Adelaide until after World War II.[68] In 1946, Archbishop of Adelaide Matthew Beovich, whose father was European, began to address the needs of Italians and appointed an Italian priest to minister to the Italian community in South Australia. Between 1946 and 1949, Father Paul Zolin brought the

---

63   Huber, *From Pasta to Pavlova*, 26–27.
64   Angelina Marchioro, OH 12/1, 13 March 1984: 5, 7.
65   Josephine Laffin, *Matthew Beovich: A Biography* (Adelaide: Wakefield Press, 2008), 105.
66   Vincenzo De Francesco SJ, *Letters to Naples: A Neapolitan Writes Home about His Work in Melbourne, 1919–1928*, ed. and trans. Aniello Iannuzzi (Ballan: Connor Court, 2010).
67   O'Connor, *No Need to be Afraid*, 131–32.
68   ibid., 131.

Catholic Church to the Italian community, made pastoral visits and offered translation and interpretation services.[69] Father Zolin provided pastoral care to Italians in the City of Adelaide, in suburbs including 'Lockleys' and in regional areas including Port Pirie.[70] After the war, with the increased numbers of Italians, the archdiocese arranged for a weekly Italian mass conducted by Italian priests in the Flinders Park church—the parish closest to Lockleys. In 1949, another Italian priest was instrumental in founding the Catholic Italian Welfare Association to provide social and material support to Italian migrants in South Australia. The association organised weekly dances for young, single Italian men in city halls that belonged to the Catholic Church.[71]

Although many of the families attended church, the Veneto market gardeners did not develop networks there because it did not offer an inclusive community experience, nor did they participate in the various service associations or social groups. However, in 1952, some of the Veneto men organised a distinctive quasi-religious celebration, *la cuccagna*, in the church grounds at Flinders Park, with the approval of the parish priest. Historically, the priest in the Irish-Catholic tradition organised religious events or occasions that were held on parish property.[72] Generally, religious celebrations in church grounds were limited to rites such as a first holy communion party for the class of students. Expressions of faith in the Irish model were more private and individual, confined to the church buildings, schools and family homes. However, *la cuccagna* broke with the conventional practices of the Catholic parish with a public expression of community enjoyment loosely related to a religious context.

The event at the Flinders Park parish provides an example of an unusual collaboration with the Anglo-Celtic parish priest, who supported the event. The families adapted a Veneto tradition and organised a lively procession of horse-drawn carts decorated with flowers, streamers and balloons, which moved from the market gardeners' houses to the church grounds accompanied by a boy playing his piano accordion. At the church grounds,

---

69   See Monica Tolcvay, 'Community and Church: Italians in South Australia in the Early Post-War Years', *Italian Historical Society Journal* 7, no. 2 (1999): 4–8.
70   Daniela Cosmini and Diana Glenn, *La Seconda Casa: The Second Home—A History of the South Australian Italian Association* (Adelaide: South Australian Italian Association, 2021), 36.
71   ibid., 36–37, 42.
72   See Stefano Girola, 'Saints in the Suitcase: Italian Popular Catholicism in Australia', *The Australasian Catholic Record* 80, no. 2 (2003): 164–74, at 170–71; Tony Paganoni, 'The Italian Community in Australia: Historical Notes on Pastoral Care, its Development to Date and Future Options', *The Australasian Catholic Record* 84, no. 2 (2007): 185–203, at 195.

teams of men climbed a greasy pole competing for a trophy. Veneto men from an eastern Adelaide suburb also competed and were accompanied by their Italian parish priest. After the greasy pole competition, the families socialised and shared a picnic. It created a spectacle and social occasion for the local Veneto families and single men who had recently arrived from Italy.[73]

Lina Campagnaro nee Ballestrin recalled *la cuccagna* and the excitement it provided as entertainment permitted by the parish priest:

> My Dad was involved with the church—I remember he was part of a *carnevale*—we dressed up a cart, decked it all up with flowers and things and they drove it from, or they took it from our house to the church and they all climbed on, all these young guys climbed on it. And then they had these greasy pole competitions. So, you know. It was excellent. It was a form of entertainment.[74]

The local Anglo-Australian community, which was not used to public demonstrations of faith, would have seen the pageantry of the procession and the public display of religious tradition as a striking performative act. The group at Lockleys took the initiative to craft what Lina Campagnaro nee Ballestrin identified as a *carnevale*—an enjoyable form of entertainment rather than a more restrained Anglo-Celtic expression of faith.

According to Paganoni, although it took decades after the large wave of postwar Italian migration to occur, the Catholic Church's move away from the security of the Irish model was in part because of the contribution of Italians and other migrants who brought religious-cultural practices from their countries of origin.[75] The participation of Italian migrants in the life of the Catholic Church in the 20 years after the war assisted with the processes of 'forging a new mentality'.[76]

In 1950, the Catholic Church reflected the Australian Government's assimilationist policies with the publication of a bishops' Joint Pastoral Letter that encouraged Catholics to facilitate 'the assimilation of our new

---

73 See Silvano Ballestrin, 'Parties and Festivals', *Veneto Market Gardeners 1927 Blog*, 12 July 2020, venetimarketgardeners1927.net/?s=Parties+and+Festivals.
74 Lina Campagnaro nee Ballestrin, OH 872/28, 13 March 2014: 7.
75 Paganoni, 'The Italian Community in Australia', 193–203.
76 ibid., 198.

settlers into a way of life that is Catholic and Australian'.[77] Some second-generation narrators recalled that their families were generally welcome at the local Catholic primary school although there was a distinction with those whose parents had more experience of interaction with Anglo-Australia. Some of the 1.5-generation parents who had some schooling in Australia were fluent English speakers and were more accustomed to relating to Anglo-Australian culture and became involved in the school. Sandra Conci nee Santin's recollection of sports-day stalls provides a picture of the advantage of inviting market-gardener families to contribute their vegetables to fundraising initiatives:

> [B]ecause they were market gardeners … [my parents were involved in] every sports day, they used to take fruit and veg—more vegetables than anything—and used to sell them, just to raise money. And they used to make the coffee with cake and biscuits, so my aunties were all involved with that.[78]

However, Teresa Mazzarolo nee Zampin, whose parents migrated after the war and spoke little English, remembered the exclusivity of the mothers' club in the 1950s: '[I]t was the Australian ladies.'[79]

Some second-generation narrators remembered that in the late 1950s when the Italian population was larger, the same parish in which the annual *cuccagna* was held offered opportunities for young women and men from Italian families to participate in social programs and competitive sports. Lina Campagnaro nee Ballestrin, who was born in Adelaide, recalled attending dances organised by a group in the local church, and young Italian men who had arrived from Italy in the 1950s were included in the events. Lina said that in the context of providing for the needs of young people, 'the Church was important'.[80] In 1961, the first priests in the Scalabrinian religious congregation from Italy were installed in a new parish within walking distance of the market-gardener families at Lockleys. Their presence reflected the commitment of the archdiocese to supporting the pastoral care

---

77 Joint Pastoral Letter of the Australian Catholic Bishops 1950, cited in Frank W. Lewins, 'The Catholic Church in Australia: An Agent of Assimilation', *Clearing House on Migration Issues* no. 391 (1980): 1–6.
78 Sandra Conci nee Santin, OH 872/47, 25 August 2018: 10.
79 Teresa Mazzarolo nee Zampin interviewed by Madeleine Regan, Transcript, J.D. Somerville Oral History Collection, State Library of South Australia, Adelaide, OH 82/64, 17 December 2021: 30.
80 Lina Campagnaro nee Ballestrin, OH 872/28, 13 March 2014: 7.

of the Italian Catholic community in the western suburbs of Adelaide.[81] The proximity of the church to the market gardens revived memories of the location of the church in the heart of villages in the Veneto region.

The authority of the Catholic Church over families

The influence of Catholic priests extended beyond the education of children to the morality of family life. Leon Bernardi, who arrived in Australia as a young man after the war, summed up the tradition of the expansive, unquestioned authority of the priest in an Italian village:

> There was also a lot of respect for the Church, because if you had a problem with the law, you'd go to the priest. And he would solve it for you because there was no money for lawyers, [we] didn't know what lawyers were, didn't know what dentists were. But there was a lot of respect for, and the priest had to solve a lot of marriage problems, a lot of legal problems of damage.[82]

Three examples illustrate the control priests exerted over the lives of market-gardener families and their kin in the 1940s and 1950s. The first shows the role of the Catholic Church in endorsing the virtue of marriage and the nuclear family. In the second example, a young girl tests her agency in the context of the Catholic sacrament of confession. The third case provides an insight into the relationship of young Italian women to the church.

Guido Battaglia migrated to Adelaide from Caselle di Altivole in 1927—the same year that two other market gardeners from the same village arrived. The two market gardeners had reunited with their wives and families within eight years, however, the Battaglia family was still separated after 12 years and Guido had never seen his youngest daughter, who was not born when he left. The parish priest in the village advocated on behalf of Maria Battaglia and her three daughters using the transnational network of the Catholic Church to communicate with the parish in the City of

---

81 The Capuchin religious congregation of friars from Italy had been at Newton, in the eastern suburbs of Adelaide, where there was a large community of Italians, from 1949. At that time, the archbishop of Adelaide asked the Capuchin order to assist with the pastoral care of Italians in the area.
82 Leon Bernardi, OH 872/65, 16 June 2022: 14.

Adelaide with instructions for Guido to reunite with his wife and children. In 1939, Maria arrived in Adelaide and joined her husband, accompanied by her three daughters.

In the second example of the authority of the church, Bruna Rossetto nee Battaglia experienced the intervention of a priest in intimate family matters in 1942. When Bruna fell in love with Giuseppe Rossetto, whose brother was a market gardener, she was 16 and Giuseppe was 30 years old. After Bruna's father forbade the marriage, a young Irish-Australian priest counselled him to agree to the couple marrying in the church. Although Bruna's father consented to the marriage, he did not attend the ceremony and prevented his wife and other children from attending the church or the small party afterwards. Interviewed when she was 89, Bruna communicated her negative feelings towards her father and relief at the mediation of the priest even though he was obviously aware of her youth and the age difference with her husband. The priest assumed the authority expected of the village pastor in Italy, but in this case, he supported an atypical marriage and advocated on behalf of the couple in opposition to the bride's father.[83]

In the third example, the role of the church provides a context for examining the ambiguity between religious observance and the emerging adult identity of a young woman, Lina Rismondo nee Marchioro, who remembered her experience of a weekly ritual. Lina and her friend, Teresa, a neighbour from a conservative southern Italian market-gardener family, travelled by tram to a parish church every Saturday night to recount their 'sins' and receive the sacrament of confession. The experience of making their confession was their weekly outing—a date:

> [H]er father was so strict but he'd let her go to confession so [laughs] we'd go to confession every Saturday night … and halfway there, there were these boxthorn bushes, and we'd get behind the bushes and put lipstick on, and then [laughs] go to confession [laughs]. And all we'd tell the priest was that we used to put lipstick on, and look, and we were 18 and 19 years of age … and we thought we were wicked. That's dreadful. Talk about naïve [laughs], and the priest, I can just imagine now when I look back, he must have thought it was so funny, the same girls every Saturday night going to confession.[84]

---

83 Bruna Rossetto nee Battaglia, OH 872/33, 18 December 2014: 11–14.
84 Lina Rismondo nee Marchioro, OH 872/9, 5 May 2011: 75–76.

'I BUY THIS PIECE OF GROUND HERE'

Plate 5.14: Veneto market-gardener family picnic, Morialta Falls, Adelaide, early 1950s
Note: The Ballestrin, Compostella, Marchioro and Zampin families.
Source: Photo supplied by the Zampin family.

Lina and Teresa negotiated the path between their families and the world beyond using the ritual of confession as their outlet for self-expression at the margins of their independence. The act of adornment through applying make-up enabled them to assume a brief sensual identity although constrained by the confession box and the contradiction of the observance of a religious practice. Lina was compassionate towards herself as a naive young woman in a first-generation Italian family in the 1940s, testing boundaries and appropriating religious observance that allowed her and her friend to experiment innocently with their sexuality and family expectations. In contrast, the Catholic Church dictated patriarchal standards and roles that were clearly defined and accepted by the *paese* at Lockleys.

Cohesion of the *paese*

The cluster of market-gardener families from the Veneto region formed the basis of the neighbourhood that evolved as a *paese* at Lockleys for the first generation. The community provided the benefits of support, care and social life. The cohesion reduced the need for the Veneto market gardeners to interact more broadly with the Anglo-Australian community. The group maintained its sense of identity and the inclination to turn inward was rewarded with security and stability achieved through the bonds that transformed neighbours into *paesani* and kin. The ambition to achieve *sistemazione* in the safety of their *paese* at Lockleys countered the harshness of the White Australia policy, which had impacted them since their arrival in the 1920s. However, the insulation could not endure comfortably during World War II, which resulted in troubled times for the Veneto market gardeners.

6
Community in times of crisis

When we arrived—we could go anywhere. That's how Dad went up to the mica mines up there, like that. But four months after we arrived, when Italy entered the War, we became aliens—with restrictions. We were aliens, we were not naturalised, you had to be in Australia for five years before you could apply for naturalisation. We were not allowed … to buy property or buy a house unless you were naturalised. And during the War years that we lived in Waymouth Street, to go down to my Auntie Giovanna, in Frogmore Road, Lockleys, we were not allowed to move outside the square mile of Adelaide. Now there, we got a permit from the police station. So, if ever we wanted to go and visit Auntie, we had to get, me, even twelve years old, we had to go to the police station, and we were finger-printed, and that permit was only allowed for that day.

—Johnny Tormena, 2012[1]

Johnny Tormena recalls an aspect of his experience as a 12-year-old after his family's arrival in Adelaide in February 1940. When Italy joined the war in June 1940, the Australian Government introduced measures to control the lives of Italians and other 'enemy aliens'. Interviewed as an 84-year-old, Johnny recalled the abrupt changes in circumstances and the discomfort of their new negative identity in Australia. Regulations dominated everyday life for his family, other members of the Italian community and other

---

1 Johnny Tormena interviewed by Madeleine Regan, Transcript, J.D. Somerville Oral History Collection, State Library of South Australia, Adelaide, OH 872/18, 6 July 2012: 35.

'I BUY THIS PIECE OF GROUND HERE'

nationalities whose governments were at war with the Allies. The regulations created adverse conditions for enemy aliens and increased hostility and longstanding racial prejudices in the Anglo-Australian press and wider community during World War II.

As an easily discernible group of Italians, the Veneto market gardeners became a target for xenophobic behaviour in the Lockleys area. The racism was not new; it built on attitudes exhibited as the number of Italians had increased and their presence became more visible. These attitudes had become progressively more hostile and deepened with the crisis of unemployment during the Depression and after Mussolini's invasion of Abyssinia (Ethiopia) in 1935.[2] As a consequence of these events, Italians were in a more vulnerable position and, like Johnny, they became more conscious of their exposure.

Plate 6.1: The Tormena family: Johnny and Maria Rosa, at back, with Severina and Galliano, Adelaide, 1940s
Source: Photo supplied by Maria Rosa Tormena.

---

2   The reaction to Italy's invasion of Abyssinia was influenced by Australia's role in the League of Nations as administrator of New Guinea, a mandated territory, and negative opinions about Mussolini. See Tito Cecilia, *We Didn't Arrive Yesterday: Outline of the History of the Italian Migration into Australia from Discovery to the Second World War*, trans. and ed. Moira Furey (Red Cliffs, Vic.: Scalabrinians, 1987), 90. Cecilia notes that the Italian invasion of Abyssinia was viewed with concern in Australia, which, as a member of the League of Nations, imposed sanctions on Italy.

Since the 1920s, the Italian community had witnessed the growth of organisations in Adelaide promoted and supported by the fascist government in Italy.[3] Some narrators in the 1.5 generation spoke of the hardship caused by the regulations and other constraints imposed by the government on enemy aliens. On the other hand, few in the second generation could recall details of the war or political conflict in the lives of their parents or within the Veneto market-gardener community because most were too young. However, several second-generation members remembered what their parents had told them about the impact of the war and spoke of injustices and threats to their family homes and safety at Lockleys. The war years interrupted the progress of *sistemazione* and the security of the Veneto community.

Despite regulations that restricted the leasing of land to enemy aliens, the first-generation Veneto market gardeners retained their leaseholds. With government contracts for their produce, most participated in the war effort by growing vegetables for the armed services. In Pietro Berno's application for naturalisation in 1946, a government official reported that Berno had been a 'gardener for some years, [and] supplied vegetables for troops in large quantities'.[4] With the announcement of war in 1939, restrictions imposed by the Australian Government reshaped the everyday lives of enemy aliens through mechanisms such as compulsory registration and weekly reporting to the local police station, control of travel away from their homes and prohibitions against leasing and purchasing land. These regulations enabled the government to monitor the movement and associations of enemy aliens. In South Australia, the police commissioner had for some time singled out Italians as potential troublemakers, commenting on the perceived difficulty of surveillance because, in his view, it was not possible 'to identify one Italian from another'.[5]

Families endured the affront of the requirement to report weekly to alien registration officers at police stations. Adrian Tonellato, a member of the second generation, acknowledged that the impact on his parents and

---

3   For a detailed account of the development of fascist groups, or *fasci*, in South Australia from the mid-1920s, see O'Connor, *No Need to be Afraid*, 143–62.
4   Department of the Interior [II], Central Office, A435, Class 4 correspondence files relating to naturalisation, 26 April 1939 – 13 July 1945, 1946/4//510, Berno Vittorio Pietro—born 18 July 1909 —Italian, NAA: 4.
5   See Desmond O'Connor, 'Declared Black: Confrontation between Italian and Anglo-Celtic Workers in Port Adelaide 1928–1932', in *Australian Labour History Reconsidered*, eds David Palmer, Ross Shanahan, and Martin Shanahan (Adelaide: Australian Humanities Press, 1999), 204.

grandparents was 'a big stigma for them'.[6] Many market gardeners had been controlled by *padroni* and other structures of serfdom in the Veneto region. Their new-found freedom and opportunities for independence as self-employed business owners were challenged by the wartime climate of surveillance and animosity. In response, the community withdrew further into the *paese* at Lockleys, consolidating it but increasing its isolation.

Enemy aliens faced fines and convictions for breaching national security regulations when they were unable to produce their certificate of registration or did not obtain written permission to travel outside their suburb of residence. In 1943, Isidoro Ballestrin was convicted of failing to produce both documents and received a fine of £13 with £1 costs. At that time the average weekly wage was £4/14/0 for a man in South Australia.[7] In the wider Veneto community, some found ways to resist the regulations that limited even the enjoyment of leisure activities. For example, Oscar Mattiazzo, a 1.5-generation youth who later married into a market-gardener family, was a keen cyclist and, before the war, had competed in cycling events in Adelaide. Prevented under national security regulations from obtaining permission to travel to competitions around the city, Oscar solved the problem by providing false names:

> See, I would have had to have permits, and they wouldn't supply permits for that, so I got used to go just the same and race under a different name, things like that. Peter Peters, I remember one name a lot.[8]

In general, the reaction to the presence of Italians in Anglo-Australia during the war was negative because, as a group, they were perceived as a threat to national security. The reaction was particularly strong where Italians lived in concentrated groups like the Veneto market gardeners at Lockleys. Although the restrictive regulations disturbed the wellbeing of the Veneto community (and other enemy aliens), the threat of internment was even more intimidating.

---

6 Adrian Tonellato, OH 872/35, 30 January 2016: 56.
7 Australian Bureau of Statistics, 'Labour, Wages and Prices', in *1301.0—Year Book Australia*, No. 37 (Canberra: ABS, 1946–47), 435–512, www.ausstats.abs.gov.au/ausstats/free.nsf/0/4030A3460E588633 CA2573AD00200501/$File/13010_1946-47%20section%2012.pdf, at 483.
8 Oscar Mattiazzo, OH 872/13, 25 May 2011: 63.

The fear of internment

By the time Italy allied itself with Germany in June 1940, Australian authorities had prepared for the rapid detention of individuals.[9] The fear of internment increased for enemy aliens when they realised that naturalisation was not a guarantee against it. The Veneto market gardeners, their extended families and the wider Italian community in Adelaide were afraid. Interviewed at 86 years of age, Anna Santin nee Mattiazzo gave an immediate response to a question about the war years. She recalled the general agitation about internment in the Italian community. At the beginning of the war, Anna was a student and aware of the vulnerability of her father—a butcher in the city who served the Italian community:

> You were always frightened because they interned a few people around, and Dad was always frightened they were going to pick him up, but he was never questioned or anything, so we just lived it out till the end of the war … It was always frightening, it was always somebody around to be frightened of, calling 'dirty dago' and all that, though my Dad never had any trouble with anybody.[10]

Anna's repeated use of 'frightened' reveals a level of distress that was also apparent in the memories of other narrators who were old enough to remember the impact of the war on the community. The situation for Italians and other enemy aliens at that time replicated the experience of the German community in Australia during World War I. The similarities of the restrictions, internment and loss of freedom are apparent, including the internment of naturalised British subjects.

Domenico Rossetto, who was brother and brother-in-law to Veneto market gardeners, was interned the day after Italy declared war against the Allies in June 1940. A grocer who served many Italians in the west end of the City of Adelaide, Domenico had been under surveillance by the Commonwealth Investigation Branch for some time. Ironically, he and seven other members of his family had emigrated before the war because of their opposition to Mussolini. In his interview, Domenico's nephew Johnny Tormena reported that two of his uncles had fled to France to avoid the violence of fascism before they migrated to Australia in 1927. In interviews with representatives

---

9   Ilma Martinuzzi O'Brien, 'The Internment of Australia Born and Naturalized British Subjects of Italian Origin', in *War, Internment and Mass Migration: The Italo-Australian Experience 1940–1990*, eds Richard Bosworth and Romano Ugolini (Rome: Gruppo Editoriale Internazionale, 1992), 105–16.
10 Anna Santin nee Mattiazzo, OH 872/24, 3 April 2013: 7.

of the Rossetto family, it is evident that they, including their elderly father, had been identified as anti-fascist and were victims of violence perpetrated by local fascist militia in the village of Bigolino in the Veneto.

The presence of pro-fascist Italian men and women in Australia was a concern for the security services in the late 1930s and dossiers on suspect individuals were prepared at the state level. It appears that Italians were approached to provide information about fascist activity within the community. In late 1939, in a routine interview for his naturalisation application, an Italian man identified Domenico Rossetto among a group of eight who were thought to be fascists, and a dossier was duly prepared.[11]

In Domenico's case, the suspicion of being a fascist sympathiser was unsubstantiated and, after three months, he was released and allowed to return to his family and grocery shop with restrictions that included reporting to the nearest police station twice weekly.[12] However, his internment served as a warning to others in the community and relatives who were interviewed remembered the situation. For example, Johnny Tormena was an adolescent at that time and remembered details of his uncle's experience. In his interview, he hesitated before he spoke for the first time, using the term 'fascist sympathisers' to describe the Italians who used to meet in the building that housed his uncle's shop:

> And we found out afterwards that he was interned purely because there was—fascist sympathisers that used to have meetings and because Uncle had a big house and a big storeroom, they used to ask him, can they use the storeroom to have the meeting. And it didn't worry him: 'Have the meeting.' But because of that, they thought he was a sympathiser which he wasn't because the reason of him coming to Australia was to get away from fascism because they were quite against it, the four brothers were against it … I remember … the first day … [it was reported] in the newspapers that Italy entered the War and the police went around to all, apparently the police were aware of the fascist sympathisers that existed and they went around picking all these people up and interned them down at Keswick [army barracks in Adelaide] … and Uncle Domenico was one of them.[13]

---

11   Department of the Army, Central Office, MP508/1, General correspondence files, Multiple number series, 01 Jan 1898 – 27 July 1974, 4/703/530, Revocation of Detention Order Domenico Rossetto, 1939–1940, NAA.
12   ibid.
13   Johnny Tormena, OH 872/18, 6 July 202: 36.

–5–

FASCIST   ANNEXURE I.

COMMONWEALTH INVESTIGATION BRANCH

Adelaide.

Surname title: ROSSETTO

   and Christian names: Domenico

Alias, and surname at birth, if different: ---

Nationality: Naturalised British subject

Date and place of birth: 29/10/1896, Italy.

Occupation: Grocer

Married or single: Married

If married, wife's name: Sesta Carmela Rossetto

Date and port of arrival in Australia: 7/2/26 at Adelaide.

Employer: In business on own behalf

Address: (a) Business - 264 Hindley Street, Adelaide.
            (b) Private - 264 Hindley Street, Adelaide.

Personal description: Height 5' 8", heavy build, dark
                         complexion, brown hair, brown eyes.

Passport particulars and other official records: Passport No.49
                         issued in Italy on 1/4/26.

Remarks: Naturalised 24/2/33. It is alleged that in the past
            his shop has been used as a meeting place by the
            Fascist Party.

            It is reported also by the Police that he is alleged
            to be an active Fascist.

                                           R. WILLIAMS.
                                                 Inspector.

20/3/40.

Plate 6.2: Excerpt from 'Report from Commonwealth Attorney-General's Department in Recommendation for Ministerial Warrant for Restriction or Detention under Regulations 25 & 26 of National Security (General) Regulations'
Source: MP508/1, 4/703/530, NAA.

While none of the market gardeners at Lockleys were interned, relatives and family friends were taken into custody and two narrators recalled visiting Loveday Internment Camp in South Australia. Oscar Mattiazzo saw Loveday as 'a concentration camp … a vast compound of barbed wire'.[14] These were the kinds of opinions that circulated and increased the anxiety about internment in the Italian community. Italians in fisher communities were deprived of their livelihood because of the possible threat on the sea and large numbers of wage-earners were 'let go' by employers because they were considered a risk during the war.

Assisting the war effort in the market gardens

The livelihoods of the market gardeners were supposedly protected from the impact of the war because of their essential occupation as primary producers, although there were exceptions. From December 1941 after the outbreak of war in the Pacific, market gardeners in several states grew vegetables to meet the increased demand as Australia became a base for Allied forces in the South-West Pacific.[15] Guaranteed fixed prices, they were told which crops to grow. In this way, the Veneto market gardeners were incorporated into the Australian war effort. However, Italian market gardeners were interned in different parts of Australia; in response to the escalating needs of the armed services, some were released. For example, in Western Australia, Italian market gardeners who grew tomatoes and had been interned were released after three months because their role as primary producers was deemed essential.[16]

At Lockleys, some young 1.5-generation men, naturalised as children under the auspices of their fathers, were old enough to serve in the Australian Army but were exempted because of their occupation as market gardeners. Lino Tonellato explained what happened when he registered at army headquarters in Adelaide:

---

14   Oscar Mattiazzo, OH 872/13, 25 May 2011: 67–69.
15   Australian Bureau of Statistics, 'Agricultural Production', in *1301.0—Year Book, Australia*, No. 36 (Canberra: ABS, 1944–45), 777–854, www.ausstats.abs.gov.au/ausstats/free.nsf/0/19AD09393BAD4E22 CA2573AD0020052A/$File/13010_1944-45%20section%2020.pdf, at 838–39.
16   Kay Saunders, 'A Difficult Reconciliation: Civil Liberties and Internment Policy in Australia during World War Two', in *Alien Justice: Wartime Internment in Australia and North America*, eds Kay Saunders and Roger Daniels (Brisbane: University of Queensland Press, 2000), 135.

I was called up. When you come of age, eighteen, you go for the examination, and they say: 'What do you do?' 'I'm a market gardener.' I said: 'We've got contract with the Army, cabbages, caulis, and potatoes.' We had a contract for the Army at Keswick, and then they go: 'Oh,' they looked that up. We were there … 'No, we don't need you, you go home and feed the Army.'[17]

The impact of the civilian manpower initiative

Most of the group remained on their market gardens, earned a secure income through army contracts for growing specific vegetables and experienced the relative security and stability provided within the *paese*. This stability was disrupted when enemy alien men were conscripted into the civilian manpower initiative known as the Allied Works Council. This body was established in March 1942 by the Commonwealth War Cabinet to address labour shortages. The idea was to provide a workforce to support non-combat initiatives in remote locations building infrastructure such as roads, aircraft buildings and landing strips, maintenance of railways, timber-felling in forests and creation of salt pans for the war effort.[18] Despite vegetable growing being identified as an essential occupation, the market gardeners at Lockleys experienced another form of wartime control through conscription into the civilian labour force.

In October 1942, male enemy aliens and refugee aliens were registered by the Allied Works Council in each state but, because of administrative issues in government departments, the men were not required to physically join the civilian labour force until late 1943. Four of the first-generation Veneto men and three close relatives who also worked gardens in the Lockleys area were conscripted to either the Civil Constructional Corps or the Civil Aliens Corps, both of which were constituted under the Allied Works Council. Two others in the Veneto group were exempt because of poor health and three received deferrals.[19] The Allied Works Council program was disbanded in 1945. Today, it seems arbitrary that only some Veneto market gardeners were selected to serve in the corps. The life of a conscript was challenging

---
17   Lino Tonellato, OH 872/10, 16 July 2010: 19.
18   Paul Hasluck, *Australia in the War of 1939–1945. Series 4, Civil. Volume 1: The Government and the People, 1939–1941* (Canberra: Australian War Memorial, 1952), 595–97.
19   Even after analysis of archival records, it is not clear why some in the Veneto market-gardener group had to leave their families and serve in the civilian corps while others were not called up.

in conditions that were like the discipline of army camps. Although there was a small payment, which was allocated relative to one's skill level, men had to apply for leave and faced penalties and the threat of prosecution for infringements of rules.

The case for the conscription of any men from the Veneto community is difficult to understand in the context of their occupation as market gardeners. In the period between registration in the Allied Works Council in October 1942 and being called up the following year, it is likely all Veneto market gardeners had grown vegetables for the armed services. While some men used this period to arrange exemptions, such strategies were not effective for Gelindo Rossetto, who was called up to serve in the Civil Constructional Corps in 1943 even though he had a 4-hectare market garden at Lockleys. Exemptions were also denied for Antonio Ballestrin (who had 3.2 hectares), Giuseppe Ballestrin (1.2 hectares) and Vittorio Marchioro (1.6 hectares), all of whom served with the Civil Aliens Corps from early 1944 to different dates before it was disbanded in August 1945. The following two examples illustrate the impact on families after the men were conscripted.

Gelindo Rossetto: A market gardener balancing roles

Gelindo Rossetto's experience during the war differs from that of the rest of the Veneto market-gardener group because he merged three roles: market gardener, mica miner and political activist. Gelindo had grown vegetables on leased land at Lockleys for several years, which he managed with the assistance of his brother Giuseppe between periods of work on the Northern Territory mica mine in which he had a share.

Unlike others in the Veneto community, Gelindo, his wife, Lina, and their three children had moved their place of residence to the City of Adelaide in the late 1930s and he cycled 8 kilometres to work his market garden in Lockleys. In June 1943, Gelindo was assigned work in the Northern Territory with the Civil Constructional Corps and, because of his market garden, he applied for an exemption.[20] A letter from his lawyer in July 1943 states that Gelindo had 17 glasshouses and a tomato crop worth £500 and confirmed that he supplied vegetables for 'the military authorities'.[21] The lawyer gave two grounds for the

---

20 It is not clear why Gelindo was the only Veneto market gardener who served with the Civil Constructional Corps rather than the Civil Aliens Corps.
21 Personal files for members of the CCC [Civil Constructional Corps] enlisted in South Australia who served in the Northern Territory 1942, 91261, Rossetto Gelindo, 1942–1945, MP14/2, 91261, NAA: 117–18.

request for exemption: Gelindo's wife was seven months pregnant and he had responsibilities to oversee the tomato crop because his brother was unable to speak English and could not transact sales at the market. After initial rejection, he was granted periods of leave without pay to remain with his wife.

Plate 6.3: Lina and Gelindo Rossetto with three of their children, from left, Aldo, Romeo and Lena, Adelaide, c. 1937
Source: Photo supplied by Lena Moscheni nee Rossetto.

Gelindo took liberties with the instructions from the Civil Constructional Corps and was prosecuted and fined for absence without leave. During this time, in addition to staying with his wife and children, Gelindo participated in political activities with the Italia Libera (or Free Italy) movement in South Australia. Italia Libera was founded in Melbourne in 1943 as an anti-fascist organisation to support Allied countries and restore democracy in Italy and it had links to groups of Italian migrants in other countries. In Australia, the movement was also associated with obtaining rights for Italians who were in internment camps or had been conscripted into the civilian corps. Members of Italia Libera distributed political materials such as the fortnightly newspaper *Risveglio* ('Awakening') to members in the civilian labour camps and campaigned on issues such as parity of pay for work undertaken by conscripts. The Australian Government assumed that it was a pro-communist organisation and the South Australian Investigation Branch identified Gelindo as one of five Italians involved in the movement in the state.[22]

Although the reason for Gelindo's discharge was because of his agricultural work, he began official duties as secretary of the state branch of Italia Libera in November 1944 when there was an estimated membership of 60, including internees and conscripted civilians. Living in the city may have made it easier to engage in political discourse but it also exposed him to more surveillance than he would have experienced at Lockleys. Others who remained on their land during the war were singularly focused on their livelihoods, more interested in their occupation and family than in political participation. In contrast, the Molfettese fisher community at Port Pirie generally supported fascism and the initial membership of the local *fascio* or fascist group was more than 100.[23] The case of Gelindo Rossetto illuminates a trajectory that diverges from that of his peers in the *paese* at Lockleys. As far as I can ascertain from archival research, Gelindo was the only openly political activist in the Veneto market gardener community.

Vittorio Marchioro: A foundational family story

Two brothers recounted separately in their interviews a 'foundational family story' about their father, Vittorio Marchioro, who served with the Civil Aliens Corps during the war. In the context of oral history, narrators may tell foundational stories that focus on the same event or theme and

---

22 Investigation Branch, South Australia, D1915, Investigation case files, single number series with 'SA' (South Australia) prefix, 01 Jan 1910 – 31 Dec 1987, SA20480, Free Italy Movement and Anti-Fascist Movement, 1941–1945, NAA.
23 O'Connor, *No Need to be Afraid*, 147–49.

may be interpreted differently by different family members, especially in subsequent generations.[24] In his interview, Vittorio recounted the reason for his conscription to the Civil Aliens Corps, which he believed was the consequence of not being naturalised. He began by responding to a question about his experience in the war:

> VM: Oh, yes. I be up in Northern Territory in the war time … I got the garden here, got two boys … [but] because I not have naturalisations, and Italy [was] with the Germans in the war. They sent me up to the Northern Territory.
> OH: How long?
> VM: One year, three months I worked for the government, after I go and work in the mica fields.[25]

Forty years after his conscription, Vittorio remembered the challenge of being separated by thousands of kilometres from his wife and two young sons. He continued to question why he was conscripted, and his ordeal had been folded into the family story, highlighting the precarious situation for Italians during the war years.

Johnny and Romano received the family narrative about their father, who had not submitted papers for naturalisation before 1940, and they believed this was the reason for Vittorio's conscription to the Civil Aliens Corps.[26] However, archival records show that Vittorio had applied for naturalisation in September 1939 and had completed all the requirements of the administrative processes; he had officially renounced his Italian nationality and taken the oath of allegiance to King George VI. The Department of the Interior in Canberra declined his application 'in view of the international situation' in July 1940, a few weeks after Italy allied itself with Germany.[27] Nonetheless, decades later, Vittorio misremembered and said that his failure to submit his application led to his removal from the family to serve in the Northern Territory for Australia's war effort. This understanding of circumstances has been inscribed in the story of the family's experience of World War II. Perhaps it was easier for Vittorio to think he had made a mistake than to accept that he was one of the few men in the Veneto group randomly conscripted at a time when market gardeners were considered essential workers.

---

24 Alexander Freund, 'A Canadian Family Talks about Oma's Life in Nazi Germany: Three Generational Interviews and Communicative Memory', *Oral History Forum d'histoire orale* 29 (2009): 2, 25–26.
25 Vittorio Marchioro, OH 12/1, 13 March 1984: 12.
26 See Giancarlo Marchioro OH 872/1, 21 July 2008: 3; Romano Marchioro, OH 872/20, 11 June 2012: 1.
27 Department of Immigration, Central Office, A435, Class 4 correspondence files relating to naturalisation, 01 Jan 1944 – 31 Dec 1950, 1946/4/6303, Marchioro Vittorio, NAA.

'I BUY THIS PIECE OF GROUND HERE'

Plate 6.4: Angelina (holding Romano), Vittorio and Johnny Marchioro, Frogmore Road, late 1942
Source: Photo supplied by Giancarlo Marchioro.

Vittorio and other conscripts waited for instructions for more than a year after they were registered with the Allied Works Council in October 1942. For 15 months, the market gardeners continued to grow and sell their vegetables without certainty about their livelihood or security for their families at Lockleys. In his interview, Johnny Marchioro added to the family foundational story and reflected on the challenge for his mother when Vittorio was called up to serve in the Northern Territory in January 1944. Johnny considered the way his mother managed her role on the market gardens:

> The garden, what she could—she had to do it by herself because we were only little. Yes, I don't know how she did it, but she must have got a little bit of help … when she had to sell her tomatoes, to get somebody to pick it up and sell for her.[28]

Angelina Marchioro looked after her children—one aged three and the other 16 months—and cared for the market gardens as best she could with her other responsibilities: a milking cow, chickens and a horse. When she became incapacitated in March 1944 with a serious hand injury that required surgery and constant medical attention, she had several advocates. Her Anglo-Australian neighbour Irene Destro corresponded with the administrators of the Allied Works Council asking for Vittorio to be released to care for his wife. The local police officer, who knew the circumstances of the *veneti* because of the requirement for them to report regularly, also wrote to the council when he was made aware of the difficulties for Angelina to seek leave for Vittorio. He reported that she had been hospitalised for two weeks, needed dressings changed twice a day for some weeks and had to support her arm in a sling. These requests did not influence the state manager of the council, who declared that Vittorio was required for 'essential' work, adding that there were 'no urgent and exceptional circumstances'.[29]

When Vittorio requested a travel permit in October 1944, a legal officer acting for the Allied Works Council declared that his reasons were false and referred to a previous application described as 'the alleged ill-health of his wife'. Both the Adelaide and the northern offices opposed his application because 'the real basis … is his desire to pick his tomato crop'. Vittorio's request was refused despite his 'essential' role as a market gardener.

---

28 Giancarlo Marchioro, OH 872/1, 21 July 2008: 30.
29 Allied Works Council, South Australian Office, MP 14/1, Personal files for members of the CAC [Civil Alien Corps] enlisted in South Australia, by 1942 – circa 1948, NN, Marchioro Vittorio 1942–1945, NAA.

In his interview, Johnny reflected on the difficult experience of his family and his father's failed attempt to submit his application for naturalisation. He also recognised that Angelina could have managed on the market garden only with assistance from the community in the *paese*:

> I can remember Mum going there [visiting neighbours] after tea and talking with the ladies, because at that time Dad was in Alice Springs. And on our way walking to these houses, she'd say: 'The moon'll see Dad in a couple of hours' time', she used to tell us, 'The same moon.' So not every night, but we used to walk over, there used to be, say, half a kilometre of a night-time.[30]

The image of Angelina alone with her young children evokes the migrant narrative of the separation of families. Angelina visualises the location of her husband and suggests a delayed but shared experience of moonlight that links her and the children to Vittorio. Johnny poignantly remembers the setting and the emotion in his mother's words.

Between policy and enactment in the Civil Aliens Corps

The separation from family and their livelihood as market gardeners motivated cousins Antonio and Giuseppe Ballestrin to make repeated attempts to evade conscription. They believed in their rights to live and work with their wives and families, maintain their market gardens and contribute to the family household. In a plaintive letter to the deputy director of manpower, Antonio outlined the extent of his role as a grower with seven glasshouses and several crops.[31]

In Antonio's case, administrative matters kept alive for two years the possibility that he would be called up to serve in the Civil Aliens Corps. In October 1942, Antonio submitted a certificate confirming that he was medically unfit to serve in the corps. Yet, he was called up and threatened with prosecution because he had breached the National Security (Aliens Service) Regulations by not following instructions to report for service and travel to a labour camp in Alice Springs in January 1944. After a subsequent government doctor reported that he was unfit to serve, the charges against Antonio were quashed in November 1944 and he remained on his market garden.

---

30 Giancarlo Marchioro, OH 872/1, 21 July 2008: 4.
31 Allied Works Council, South Australian Office, MP 14/1, Personal files for members of the CAC [Civil Alien Corps] enlisted in South Australia, by 1942 – circa 1948, NN, Antonio Bembenato, 1942–1944, NAA.

6. COMMUNITY IN TIMES OF CRISIS

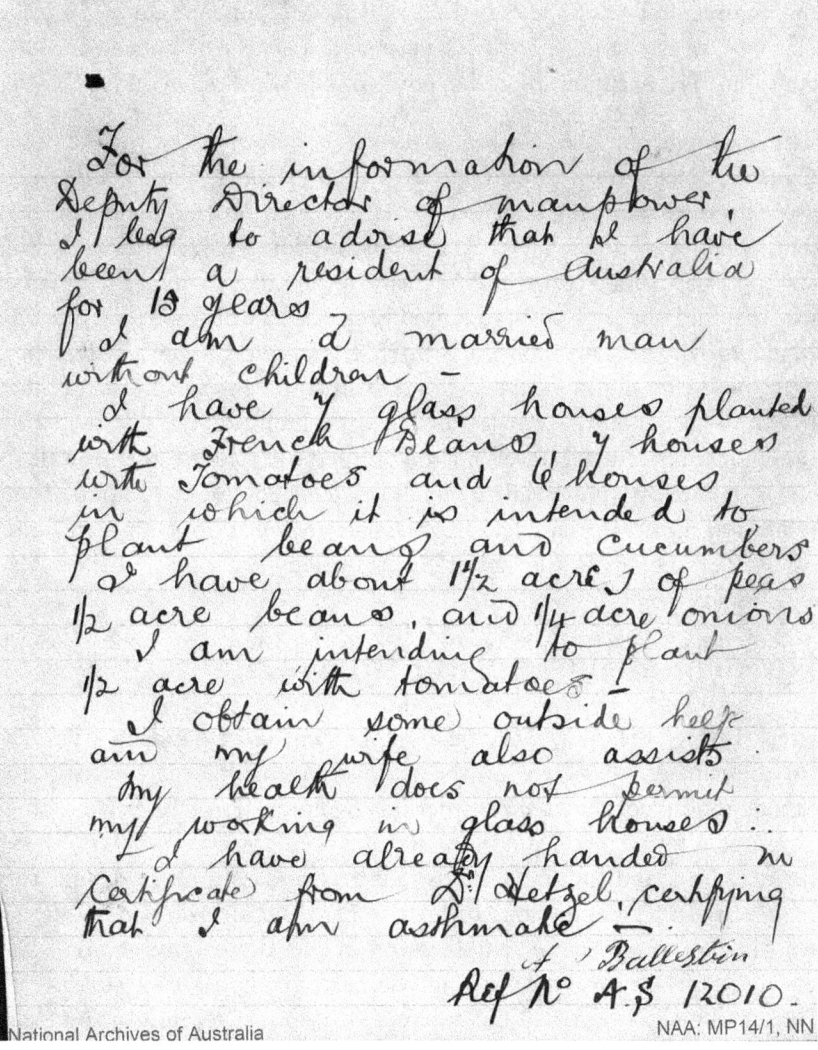

Plate 6.5: Letter written by Antonio Ballestrin to explain his reasons for not serving with the Civil Aliens Corps in 1944
Source: MP14/1, NN, Antonio Bembenato Ballestrin, NAA.

Giuseppe Ballestrin served in five different remote locations in the Northern Territory and South Australia during 18 months of service. He pursued several strategies, including obtaining medical certificates for various ailments, to obtain release and return to his wife, two small children and their extensive market garden. The corps' medical officer was suspicious of the medical certificates and reported that Giuseppe was an 'unmitigated liar', making 'the most flagrant attempt to evade service that I have encountered. He is most emphatically fit for any work.'³² Undeterred, Giuseppe engaged a range of advocates including doctors, lawyers and a state parliamentarian, who contributed to documentation that resulted in his final release in June 1945.

The examples of the market gardeners who served with the Civil Constructional Corps and the Civil Aliens Corps demonstrate their aspirations to maintain their lives as family men on the market gardens with their peers at Lockleys. The differentiation between the men who served in the civilian corps and the majority who remained on their market gardens does not seem to have caused bitterness. In his interview, Vittorio Marchioro did not convey any negative reflections or contrast his experience with those who did not serve in the civilian corps. In the absence of other firsthand accounts, the impact on the community of the differentiation cannot be fully tested. However, if anything, the experience as enemy aliens seems to have drawn the Veneto market gardener community into itself and reinforced the bonds that identified them as *paesani* at Lockleys—the home where they saw their future as settlers in Australia.

Naturalisation during the war

Even before the war, investigation branch correspondence pointed to government suspicion of the motivation of Italians applying for naturalisation. For the market gardeners, the motivation was related to their attachment to their land and livelihood and their origins as *contadini*. Their desire to own land and settle in Australia permanently aroused the mistrust of the authorities and the consequences were serious for six market gardeners who had first applied for naturalisation before 1940. Naturalisation had become a prerequisite for entering contracts for the lease or purchase of land, although it provided no guarantee for Italians wanting to purchase property during the war, as discussed in Chapter 3 in the case of Gelindo Rossetto. Oscar Mattiazzo summarised the situation, making the point that the benefits of naturalisation could be lost during the war because of one's ethnic origin: 'People were in upheaval of all sorts, but that applied to both Italians who were naturalised or not naturalised, they were picking them out like that.'³³

---

32   Allied Works Council, South Australian Office, MP 14/1, Personal files for members of the CAC [Civil Alien Corps] enlisted in South Australia, 03 May 1942 – by 16 Feb 1945, NN, Ballestrin Guiseppe [*sic*], CAS12011, 1942–1945, NAA.
33   Oscar Mattiazzo, OH 872/13, 25 May 2011: 62.

Unless the Veneto market gardeners already owned properties, they were not guaranteed their livelihood on the land because of the National Security (Land Transfer) Regulations, which came into effect in July 1940. Under these regulations enemy aliens were prevented from signing leases for more than five years and the purchase of land required the approval of the attorney-general. In effect, market gardeners were prevented from planning their future on their market gardens, which represented a family's livelihood and accommodation, and the future of the *paese* at Lockleys. The fact that not one Veneto family was evicted during the war suggests that the landowners accepted their presence at Lockleys as satisfactory long-term lessees.

While more than half the Veneto group at Lockleys was naturalised by 1939, some of the market gardeners made attempts to become British subjects during the war years. The government used additional security checks to assess Italians who applied for naturalisation during this time. Investigations of character, questions about loyalty to Britain and intentions to remain in Australia were criteria used against an enemy alien in the approval process. As the war progressed, national security became another test. Antonio Ballestrin, like Vittorio Marchioro, had fulfilled all the security checks for his naturalisation. He had taken the oath of allegiance in March 1940 but, four months later, was informed that the minister had withheld his certificate of naturalisation because of the war. His application was not successful until 1945.

In three other cases, men applied three separate times before finally becoming naturalised after the war. In a show of resourcefulness and evidence of their serious intentions, the Berno brothers sought assistance from lawyers and members of parliament to further their applications after they had been rejected or delayed. Pietro Berno gained the support of Arthur Calwell, minister for immigration, who instructed the department to grant naturalisation in July 1946.[34] Although their identity as market gardeners was putatively secure in the context of the war effort, the right to lease and own land was withheld and the opportunity to become British subjects was denied to some of the market gardeners during the war.

---

34 Department of Immigration, Central Office, MP14/1, Class 4 correspondence files relating to naturalisation, 01 Jan 1944 – 31 Dec 1950, 1946/4/510, Vittorio Pietro Berno—born 18 July 1909—Italian, 1939–1946, NAA.

'I BUY THIS PIECE OF GROUND HERE'

Outsider status and the shadow of war

By the middle of 1943, the Veneto group had negotiated three years of living as enemy aliens in the Anglo-Australian community. The *veneti* adapted to the constraints on daily life and their contribution to the war effort as primary producers afforded some degree of status although their presence in the wider community was controversial. Some local Anglo-Australian farmers resented their proximity and the experience of the war translated at times to localised conflict and distress that could have been orchestrated by fear and uncertainty and the threat of invasion triggered by the Japanese bombing of Darwin in early 1942. In the case of Giosue Zoanetti, a market gardener from the north of Italy well known to the *veneti* at Lockleys, the hostility had fatal consequences.

Giosue had arrived in Australia in 1927 from a small village in Trentino-Alto Adige (South Tyrol) adjoining the Veneto region in the north-east of Italy. The Veneto group at Lockleys accepted his family as part of the small Italian market gardener community in Adelaide. Giosue lived with his wife, Metilde, and daughter, Mary, in a neighbouring suburb on 3.4 hectares of land, close to the Bulgarian community settlement about 2 kilometres from the Veneto market gardeners. The family had leased the property in 1941–42 from landlord Walter Reid, who became unhappy about reduced access to water on the part of the land that he operated. In June 1943, Reid was sufficiently convinced about his rights to the water source on the land he had leased that he took Giosue to court to uphold what he alleged was a verbal agreement to allow him access as the landlord to the bore on the land that the Zoanettis leased for their market garden.

When the court dismissed Reid's claim, he took two further actions against the Italian lessees. The first was to take his case to the Civil Alien Corps, which had registered Giosue in the same way that the Veneto men had been processed in 1942 for the civilian labour corps. In Plate 6.6, a handwritten record of an interview with a military official reveals a list of six grievances Reid made against Zoanetti. For example, Reid accused him of mismanagement of the land and animals and claimed Zoanetti did not understand how to work the soil or how to water appropriately because he flooded rather than saturated vegetables and he tied farm animals to trees.[35]

---

35 Allied Works Council, South Australian Office, MP 14/1, Personal files for members of the CAC [Civil Aliens Corps] enlisted in South Australia, 03 May 1942 – by 16 Feb 1945, NN, Zoanetti, Giosue, 1942–1943, NAA.

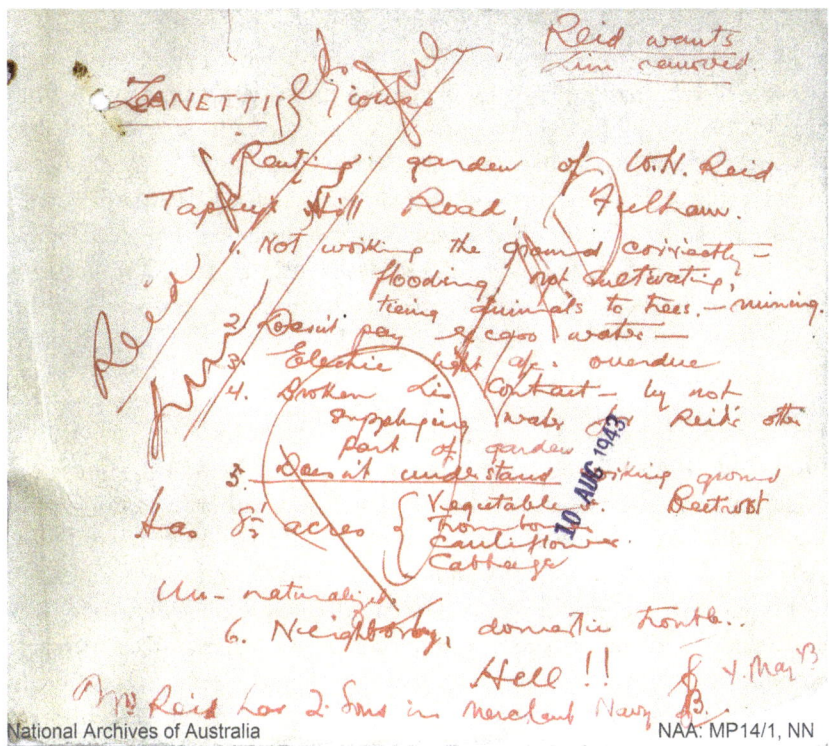

Plate 6.6: Report by a military official in Adelaide of an interview with Walter Reid about Giosue Zoanetti, 4 May 1943
Source: MP 14/1, NN, Giosue Zoanetti, NAA.

Reid's complaints reflected a contemporary reading of the differences in farming practices between southern Europeans and Anglo-Australians. Zoanetti had adapted practices he knew from his experience in a *contadino* family in northern Italy and from 16 years of working land in the Adelaide Hills for an Anglo-Australian grower. Reid added to his list of grievances in his interview with the military officer that there was 'domestic trouble' in the Zoanetti household without providing evidence. Although Reid assumed his accusations would influence the outcome of Zoanetti's case, a note on Giosue's files indicates he had been exempted from conscription on medical grounds. In any case, the Civil Aliens Corps had no jurisdiction to act on Reid's report, which is reflected in the exclamation 'Hell' at the bottom of the page.

Through the actions of Reid, Zoanetti was drawn into a public conflict at a time when Italians across Australia did not want to be visible because of possible discrimination, injustice or the threat of internment.[36] Apart from access to water rights, Reid's reports to the military authority extended to other matters that would have resonated with wider hostility to enemy aliens. For example, Reid stated that Giosue was not naturalised, did not pay excess water rates and was behind with payments for electricity, although there was no evidence for these claims. Reid also declared in a nationalist emphasis that two of his own sons served in the merchant navy. Clearly, he saw this detail as evidence of his family's loyalty to the war effort while he directed his antagonism towards Giosue, an enemy alien.

Unsuccessful in the courts, Reid took the matter into his own hands. On 17 July 1943, Giosue Zoanetti was murdered by Reid, who committed suicide shortly after. Giosue had gone to Lockleys to borrow a horse from one of the Veneto market gardeners and, as Giosue neared his property, Reid stepped out into the road and shot him. Reid's body was found later in his garden. The impact of Giosue's murder was felt deeply in the *paese* at Lockleys and remembered by second-generation narrators in personal conversations rather than in interviews. The family death notice did not provide any detail about the cause of death. It seems that it was a difficult matter to talk about more than six decades later. In her interview, Giosue's daughter, Mary, spoke of the unexpected death of her father but did not specify the cause. However, in later conversations, Mary and I discussed the incident and she was interested to read newspaper reports. The murder remains a traumatic event that does not fit easily into personal and community narratives.

At the time, the implications of the situation were serious for Italians because of their precarious status during the war years. Although it was not possible for her to take a murder charge to court, Zoanetti's widow, Metilde, gained legal assistance to challenge a decision that the public trustee, the executor of Reid's estate, would not have to pay full compensation to her. The ruling had dismissed Metilde's right to an additional reparation because of personal suffering resulting from her husband's murder. The case was heard in the Supreme Court of South Australia, which ruled that Metilde was eligible to receive a payment, *solatium*, for the suffering caused by the wrongful death of her husband in addition to compensation for the loss

---

36   Jenkins, *Power of the Land*, 141–47.

of potential family income due to Giosue's murder.³⁷ The Supreme Court ruling referred to the 1940 legislation of the Parliament of South Australia that required a perpetrator to pay *solatium* for the suffering of the spouse of a person who died as a result of a wrongful act.

The public trustee contested the decision, stating that the *solatium* should be deducted from the damages. The case progressed to the High Court in Melbourne—an indication that Metilde received extensive support from the law firm that acted on her behalf against the public trustee. She was unable to speak English and public opinion would have backed the case against her, given the hostility to Italians at that time. Nevertheless, Metilde's appeal was successful in the High Court and the appeal made by the public trustee was dismissed more than two years after Giosue was killed. The ruling meant that Metilde received two payments, one to compensate for economic loss in the family and the other as reparation for the emotional injury caused by the murder of her husband.³⁸

The security service branch in South Australia was aware of Zoanetti's murder when a report was written a week later after Mussolini was voted out of power on 25 July 1943. An officer reported on the reactions of the largest groups of Italians in Adelaide, and it was noted that the 'Little Italy' market gardeners at Lockleys 'have been very quiet since Zoanette [*sic*] was murdered'.³⁹ Within a short time, Metilde and her daughter were incorporated into the Veneto group when a Veneto market gardener allocated some of his land for the Zoanetti's six glasshouses, and another man in the *paese* lent them a temporary corrugated iron house that was erected on the property. The community assisted the widow and her daughter in selling their vegetables at the market. While not revealing the circumstances of the need for the new accommodation, Mary recalled the support provided by the community:

---

37 *Solatium* is a term used for compensation or damages awarded by a court for the benefit of a spouse or immediate family member for emotional harm and loss rather than physical or financial injury. The legislation relating to *solatium* was included in the *Wrongs Act Amendment Act 1940. No. 48 of 1940* (SA), www.legislation.sa.gov.au/__legislation/lz/c/a/civil%20liability%20act%201936/1998.07.05/1936.2267.pdf.
38 Public Trustee v. Zoanetti [1945] HCA 26, 70 CLR 266, eresources.hcourt.gov.au/showby Handle/1/14882.
39 'Free Italy Movement and Anti-Fascist Movement', D1915, SA20480, NAA: 239.

> Most of the people used to live in sheds ... and they used to split it up and build dividers and sleep in the sheds. Well, there was a friend that lent us his shed that he had because he went overseas, so he said we can use it, and they pulled that shed over where we had the land so we can live in it.[40]

Mary and her mother became neighbours of three Veneto families and, four years after her father was murdered, she married Albert, the son of first-generation couple Secondo and Elisabetta Tonellato. Metilde lived with her daughter and son-in-law and family until she died in 1995.[41] The effects of the murder were surely impressed on other Italian market gardener communities who knew the dependence on a reliable source of water for their livelihoods and who were already subject to enmity in their everyday lives. Like the threat of internment, this single event resonated with the community, as it reinforced fears about their status as Italians during the war years.

American soldiers in Lockleys

When two of the Veneto families encountered American soldiers on their market gardens, the interactions were friendly and neighbourly, in contrast with their relationships with Anglo-Australian ex-servicemen and government authorities. Some narrators provided insight into the affinity they had with the soldiers who were camped in the Lockleys area for periods during the war. For example, Lina Rismondo nee Marchioro remembered her father inviting a group of American soldiers to the family home:

> I don't know what they were doing ... while they were there, but they used to come and see Dad at night-time because at night-time they were free, and they mixed with the Italians and ... I remember them coming to see Dad—I remember it was about three or four of them one night—and Dad was giving them like his home-made wine, and maybe Mum cooked a meal of spaghetti, I don't know, but they had a good time. Dad loved it.[42]

---

40   Mary Tonellato nee Zoanetti interviewed by Madeleine Regan, Transcript, J.D. Somerville Oral History Collection, State Library of South Australia, Adelaide, OH 872/3, 3 October 2008: 5–6.
41   Albert Tonellato, OH 872/4, 3 October 2008: 7, 11–12.
42   Lina Rismondo nee Marchioro, OH 872/9, 15 November 2010: 73–74.

Lina recalled the hospitality her parents extended to the American soldiers at a time when it would have been impossible to interact with Australian soldiers in their home. In their interviews, members of the Zampin family remembered the respect and openness of the soldiers who exchanged food and gave small gifts to the children. Italians in other parts of Australia also mixed with American soldiers and their presence was benign.[43] Images of Veneto market gardeners offering hospitality to American soldiers and trusting their friendly interactions with children contrast with the local military and authorities whose interactions were focused on control. These positive interactions contradicted the popular Anglo-Australian view of Italians as a menace and a threat to national security and the safety of ordinary citizens.

The war years had other impacts on the Veneto group who were cut off from their families in Italy. The Italians in Australia had limited knowledge of the extent of campaigns fought in their homeland, especially in the Veneto region, which was the site of extensive Allied bombing in 1942 and 1943. Communication through letters was prohibited and the migrants were left not knowing how their families were affected by the air attacks and battles in Italy. Lina Rismondo nee Marchioro recalled her father's strategies to learn about the war in Italy:

> Dad had his ears glued to the little tiny radio, listened to the shortwave, heard the Italian news about Mussolini and, and then they'd buy the paper and Dad wanted me to read the paper to him and I couldn't understand what these—[laughs] were about the war. And he'd say: 'Oh, you're in Grade 3 … and you don't, can't understand.' I used to get upset because I couldn't explain the war situation.[44]

Later in the interview, Lina reflected on her father's motivation to know about the war in Italy: 'Well, I think it's only natural, I mean they came from Italy, I think you never forget your homeland, do you?'[45] The concept of 'home' for the *veneti* became even more ambiguous during the war. At the same time as they were prevented from communicating with their

---

43 Rino A. Baggio, *The Shoe in My Cheese: An Immigrant Family Experience* (Melbourne: Department of Humanities, Footscray Institute of Technology, 1989), 50–52; Jenkins, *Power of the Land*, 157–58; Pascoe, *Buongiorno Australia*, 222.
44 Lina Rismondo nee Marchioro, OH 872/9, 9 June 2010: 15.
45 ibid., 67.

families who were living with the threat of destruction in the Veneto, their goal to achieve *sistemazione* on the land that provided their livelihood was threatened by their status as enemy aliens.

Although their identity as market gardeners was strengthened because of their role as primary producers involved in the war effort, the war destabilised the *veneti* at Lockleys. They became marginalised through the restrictions imposed on their daily lives and the conscription of some members to the civilian corps and, at the policy level, as enemy aliens, they were prevented from becoming citizens. The first generation and their families created the *paese* at Lockleys and identified it as their home. Inside the group, the market gardeners had built 'micro-structures' that strengthened the community. These were applied when Giosue Zoanetti was murdered, increasing self-reliance within the *paese*.[46] The Veneto market gardeners continued to work their land, raise families and reinforce the bonds that gave them assurance about their decision to settle in Australia even in a time of crisis and persecution. Families supported one another and continued to celebrate weddings and the birth of children and engage in other social customs that allowed the community to endure the uncertainty of the war years.

After the war, the market gardeners began to reap the benefits of development in South Australia. They saw the rewards for hard work, frugality and community security after the uncertainties of their position as enemy aliens. The processes of *sistemazione* took new directions as other adjustments occurred in the *paese*. The 1.5 generation was making progress: buying their own market gardens, marrying and raising families. The market gardeners took on a new role to support postwar Veneto migrants, who were incorporated into the community. Older sons and daughters in the second generation were finding their own paths to independence. The scene was set for a transformation of the lives of the three generations in the *paese* at Lockleys.

---

46   Castles and Miller, *The Age of Migration*, 23.

7

Pathways: The 1.5 and second generations

> There wasn't a lot [of sons] that went on with the market gardens ... So, it was only Johnny and Frankie, you could say, in that group were the only ones ... Bruno never, he was an engineer so he never, oh, he used to grow a few tomatoes but Bruno's brothers went into the market garden but they ended up giving it away. So, out of the group of that time, not a lot of the boys carried on with the market gardens ... No, they all went different ways, different directions.
>
> —Romano Marchioro, 2012[1]

In his assessment of second-generation sons within the Veneto community at Lockleys born in the late 1930s and early 1940s, Romano Marchioro identified just two who elected to work as self-employed market gardeners like their parents. Romano also named sons in three Veneto market-gardener families who were born in Australia and chose occupations other than market gardening. Most of the second generation withdrew from the market gardens as employment, disrupting the *contadino* culture of families working the land. Sons and daughters in that tradition were expected to acquire the skills of their parents, which, for sons, meant that they took over management of the family land while daughters were prepared for marriage and domestic life.[2]

---

1 Romano Marchioro interviewed by Madeleine Regan, Transcript, J.D. Somerville Collection, State Library of South Australia, Adelaide, OH 872/20, 11 June 2012: 12–13.
2 Bridget Rachel Carlson, 'Immigrant Placemaking in Colonial Australia: The Italian Speaking Settlers of Daylesford' (PhD diss., Victoria University, Melbourne, 1997), 443.

Plate 7.1: Romano Marchioro, Lake Eppalock, Victoria, 2013
Source: Photo supplied by Mirjana Marchioro.

Romano cited his brother Johnny and contemporary Francesco Ballestrin as the only second-generation representatives who followed the occupation of their parents as market gardeners through their working lives. Johnny was the sole member of the second generation to work a market garden with his wife until retirement, cultivating vegetables and selling them at the market, like the first generation of the Veneto market gardeners. The profile was different in the 1.5 generation. Thirteen 1.5-generation sons and daughters had arrived with their mothers in the 1930s: nine males and four females. Of these, eight men worked as market gardeners into adulthood while the ninth established a poultry farm with his wife north of the city after injury prevented him from working market gardens. Two brothers worked the family market gardens for some years before purchasing a grocery shop in the Lockleys area. One woman married into a Veneto market-gardener family and worked with her husband's family. Two women in the 1.5 generation who were intellectually disabled worked on the gardens with their parents. A fourth woman, born in Italy, worked on the family market garden before marrying a Veneto man outside the market-gardener community.

Romano referred to the 'different directions' or new occupational choices available in the second generation and illustrated the transformation in families whose parents had migrated as *contadini*. A study of Veneto farmers in Griffith, New South Wales, found significant changes in families between the 1930s and 1960s and that one-quarter of the men were employed outside family farms, in contrast with the previous generation, of whom less than 10 per cent were in outside occupations.[3] The second-generation sons of the Veneto market gardeners who changed direction entered paid employment across a range of trades and manufacturing work, and a few took white-collar positions. Nearly all daughters chose occupations outside the family business.

In the early years, the first-generation men and women relied on the collaboration of children in the 1.5 generation for the success of the family business. The 1.5 generation embodied the 'translocated migrant tradition' of market gardening brought from the country of origin—both an occupation and a way of being in the world.[4] Unlike some family enterprises in other migrant-family communities, the Veneto market gardeners in the first and 1.5 generations never attained dynasty status. The Veneto families worked industriously and achieved substantial prosperity but did not expand into large, entrepreneurial commercial operations. They remained small family business market gardeners even after some increased their landholdings and bought properties north of Adelaide.

---

3   Price, *Southern Europeans in Australia*, 193–96.
4   James, *Farming on the Fringe*, Ch. 5.

Nearly all in the second generation sought other means of earning a livelihood away from the land, mostly as wage earners. They entered employment with assured income, mostly after completing the compulsory years of education, for which they knew there would be fewer risks than if they were small business owners on the land. The second generation had witnessed the strain of endless physical work on their parents' daily lives, the challenges of self-employment, long hours of physical labour and reliance on seasons, the weather and variable market conditions.[5] They recognised the demands of managing production, labour and sales in the operation of family market gardens. The divergence of pathways between the 1.5 and the second generations was shaped by economic factors, the life cycle of families, gender and differing educational opportunities and social experiences outside the Veneto community, which led to different trajectories in the working lives of the two cohorts. By the time the second generation had completed their compulsory schooling in the early to mid-1950s, postwar economic conditions had generated new employment opportunities.

Other external factors impacted the Veneto group such as when commercial markets expanded in South Australia and reduced the profitability of small-scale family holdings.[6] Whereas previously market-gardener families had grown a variety of crops that they knew would be sold at market and to shopkeepers, methods of production and the economy were changing. New technology increased growers' capacity and created opportunities for growing vegetables on a much larger scale, while supermarket chains contracted market gardeners to grow single crops. Family market gardeners did not have the same control of demand and supply. A new cohort of growers in South Australia, including Italian family businesses, responded to the presence of supermarkets and changes in the demand for fresh vegetables. The second-generation Italians in the new businesses differed from their parents and their vision enabled them to respond to changes in the industry that required investment in larger landholdings, technology and equipment enabling them to compete in primary production in a wider and more complex market.[7]

---

5   Rosario Lampugnani and Robert J. Holton, 'Ethnic Business in South Australia: A Sociological Profile of the Italian Business Community', *Journal of Intercultural Studies* 13, no. 2 (1992): 1–18, doi.org/10.1080/07256868.1992.9963387, at 6.
6   Sara Sophie King, 'Agriculture in South Australia: The Italian Contribution' (PhD diss., Flinders University, Adelaide, 2007), 225.
7   ibid., 320–29.

Settlement, location and community

During interviews, narrators described the management of the family market gardens and the different paths taken by the 1.5 and second generations. However, their stories suggest that the decision to detach from the *contadino* heritage in the second generation had an emotional impact on families. After retirement, many in the first and 1.5 generations preserved their connection to the land and their heritage by selecting a section on the property on which to build their own home and some gifted blocks to their sons and daughters when they married. In this way, the different generations maintained continuity with the physical sites of the market gardens and closeness to the *paesani* who had sustained their community life since the 1930s. Lockleys was a settlement that signified both the physical place and the group of Veneto families in the same way that Veneto farmers in Griffith, New South Wales, identified their location as both their *paese* and a community of *paesani*.[8]

The development of the Veneto group was based on shared origins and work on the market gardens whereas the coherence of some other migrant groups was created through shared origins, culture and religion. The concentrated Lockleys settlement of *veneti* from eight different areas in the Veneto region contrasts with initiatives to support community wellbeing in three other ethnic group settlements in South Australia before World War II. The German community in the Barossa Valley was established from the 1860s largely by a group who migrated together, and their settlement was underpinned by a common language and the traditions of the Lutheran faith.[9]

Greek migrants in South Australia—another significant ethnic group connected by religious practice—had founded a formal Greek Orthodox community by 1930. They began settling in the state in the 1890s through three levels: formal communities who participated in religious practices and taught Greek language to children, regional groups who maintained a sense of belonging and pan-Hellenic groups who supported wider social networks.[10] The experience of the small Bulgarian community who had arrived at a similar time to the *veneti* and lived in a nearby suburb also contrasted with that of the Veneto group at Lockleys. The Bulgarian market

---

8   Huber, *From Pasta to Pavlova*, 122.
9   Borrie, *Italians and Germans in Australia*, 167, 172.
10   Michale P. Tsounis, 'Greek Communities in Australia', in *Greeks in Australia*, ed. Charles A. Price (Canberra: Australian National University Press, 1975), 30–31.

gardeners had contributed to the establishment of a community centre in 1949 partly funded by donations from families. At that time there were 54 members who formally adopted a constitution for their association.[11] The Veneto market gardeners at Lockleys did not rely on formal structures and the welfare of the group emerged through the informal networks within the *paese*.

Place of origin, livelihood and change

The meaning of land and livelihood transformed for the Veneto group from establishment in the 1930s to the late 1970s, by which time most of the market gardens had been sold. The significance of land had steadily evolved between the first, 1.5 and second generations. The first and 1.5 generations knew land almost as a birthright in the Veneto *contadino* tradition, whether families were tenant farmers or owned property. In Australia the meaning of attachment to land and tradition changed in the family networks at Lockleys because property provided income and prosperity, yet cultivating vegetables was not the only livelihood available to the second generation. In addition, the monetary value of land brought changes in the lives of the Veneto families and created conditions for financial security and other opportunities beyond the market gardens. Many in the first generation used their prosperity to build new homes, assist their children to establish themselves when they married and to fund travel to Italy and other destinations outside Australia after retirement.

The *veneti* recognised new meanings of land and landownership at Lockleys. In the Veneto region, land was not a commodity to buy or sell. In Australia, landownership was the apex of self-sufficiency and status—a belief maintained by the 1.5 generation, who, as proprietors, remained at Lockleys, strengthening the stability of the *paese*. When the first generation purchased their properties from the late 1940s, they did not expect the dramatic increase in the value of their land as a result of urbanisation. Changes to land use and ownership in the area began in the late 1950s when land was subdivided for urban development. By the mid-1960s, the Lockleys locality was fast becoming a more densely populated inner western suburb, which created problems with using the land for market

---

11 'Speech of Vice-President, John Bennet', in The Bulgarians' Educational and Friendly Society, *50th Jubilee Book*, 37.

gardens. Horticultural activity such as glasshouse cultivation and the use of pesticides and other farm chemicals to combat weeds, insects and disease were incompatible with urban living and forced changes in land use.[12] As Francesco Ballestrin pointed out:

> And then of course the homes started closing in—you know, they start selling from Grange Road; individual people there sold their little bit and they put homes in. And of course, here, with glasshouses, it got to the stage where they had to fumigate the soil because they had all nematodes and different things in the soil, and they couldn't grow tomatoes successfully, so that they had to fumigate … [T]hey were using chloropicrin that they used during the trenches in the War, so people started complaining because of the smell and eventually they drove the glasshouses away from all this area … They had to get out of there because the gas smelt so much, and people were getting ill about it and they had to move.[13]

Changes to land use created new opportunities for market-gardener families. Some families with adult sons who worked with their parents took advantage of cheaper land about 20 kilometres north of Adelaide. They chose to purchase properties near one another at Bolivar—a re-creation of the *paese* at Lockleys. Members of six original families and four other relatives bought land at Bolivar from the late 1950s.[14] Diana Panazzolo nee Santin recalled that her father and his two brothers had plans at Bolivar. The brothers were in partnership and worked with their wives and planned to expand the family market-garden business based on the assumption that the next generation would continue in the occupation:

> In 1960, they purchased thirty-seven acres [15 hectares] at Bolivar. I remember talking to my Dad and he was saying things are getting a bit tougher with three families and everyone had children, so they bought other land. The twelve and half acres [5 hectares] [at Lockleys] wasn't sufficient enough to maintain the three families. And there were quite a few people from around Kidman Park that were buying land up there at Bolivar.[15]

---

12   The Bulgarian market gardeners in nearby Fulham Gardens experienced the same conditions and also subdivided their land. See Wilkins, *Bulgarian Migration and Market Gardens*, 16.
13   Francesco Ballestrin, OH 872/7, 12 December 2008: 7.
14   Angelo Piovesan, Personal communication, 26 November 2020.
15   Diana Panazzolo nee Santin, OH 872/27, 13 December 2013: 42.

'I BUY THIS PIECE OF GROUND HERE'

Plate 7.2: Three generations of the Santin family, Bolivar, 1985: Alan and his father, Romildo, and Aaron, son of Dean Santin, and Dean Santin
Source: Oscar Mattiazzo.

Oscar Mattiazzo, a 1.5-generation Veneto man who arrived in Australia in the 1930s and married into the Santin family in the early 1950s, also bought land at Bolivar. Oscar identified the life cycle of the Veneto community from its initial good fortune in finding and leasing land to changes in land use and value in suburban Adelaide, which created wealth for families:

> They started off in the market garden there and they worked hard. They bought land, they leased it first and they bought the land while still working there, and when the land became available or became so expensive because of the house development, a lot of them bought these lands up in Bolivar and Virginia … [A]nd they got a double whammy, they got good money for their land which they bought in the first place, and then they got good money for the land that they sold up in Bolivar and other places … When they sold their land, they kept some blocks for themselves to build their own homes, then build the homes for the children … [T]hey worked hard and they deserve every bit of it, but they were lucky to find not one, but two, ways of making money without … working for it because of this development.[16]

---

16   Oscar Mattiazzo, OH 872/13, 6 June 2012: 183.

Oscar's observations explain the economic and social foundations of the Veneto market-gardener group, who, within a generation, benefited from selling their properties as urban development in Adelaide expanded. The *contadino* experience of the contraction and fragmentation of family land in the Veneto region was transformed. At Lockleys, the land that had been the basis of livelihoods became a commodity that built a new future for families.

The case study of the Santin family illustrates ways in which intergenerational perceptions of land changed from its meaning for *contadini* to its value as an asset. After arriving in 1927, Giovanni Santin worked for a Bulgarian farmer in rural South Australia for several years and learned about the cultivation of land in Australia. He continued in this role for a time after his wife and four children joined him in 1935. When the family moved to Adelaide, they leased land and began working as market gardeners not far from the Veneto group at Lockleys. Then the Santins leased from another Veneto man, Gino Berno, on Valetta Road and, after about 10 years, in 1950, they bought a 5-hectare property on Frogmore Road close to other Veneto market gardeners. At that time, Giovanni was 65 years of age and contributed funds for the purchase, which enabled his sons to be among the first in the 1.5 generation to own land. His two eldest sons became business partners and the third son, Romildo, who worked for a time as a wage-earner, was formally brought into the partnership and added to the land title as 'tenant in common' in 1957.[17] The three sons' wives were paid an annual income for their full-time work on the market gardens.[18]

The Santin parents, Giovanni and Costantina, were involved in the market gardens in small ways and Costantina contributed to the family business by caring for grandchildren, maintaining the chicken run and preparing some meals for the three couples. The intergenerational arrangements were reminiscent of the large *contadino* households in the Veneto. However, had the Santin family remained in their village in Italy, the brothers could never have contemplated being joint proprietors of a business or relied on the full-time contribution of their wives to working on the land.

---

17   South Australian Certificate of Title, Vol. 2086, Folio 112, 14 August 1957.
18   Diana Panazzolo nee Santin, OH 872/27, 13 September 2013: 14.

Plate 7.3: Costantina Santin and grandson Alan, Frogmore Road, c. 1961
Source: Photo supplied by Diana Panazzolo nee Santin.

By the early 1960s, changes in land use in the local council area began to influence the Santin family operations.[19] Subdivision for housing in the western suburbs like the Lockleys area was expanding because of its proximity to the city. New regulations for suburban land also impacted on fumigation practices associated with market gardening. When the Santins purchased their new property at Bolivar, they increased and diversified production. The Santin families continued to work the land at Lockleys at the same time as they developed their property at Bolivar without having to move from their homes. Continuing the family tradition, sons in two families worked with their parents, aunts and uncles into the 1980s.

The Santin family attempted to subdivide the Frogmore Road property in 1961 but encountered some difficulties when the local council appropriated eight blocks for a reserve. Anna Santin nee Mattiazzo remembered the loss of land without compensation.[20] When the three families sold the property

---

19 Helen Mattiazzo, 'Development of a Market Garden in an Urban Area and Its Implications', 1973. A granddaughter of the first-generation Santins wrote this report about the consequences of developing a market garden in a residential area for her Year 12 geography course. It provides substantial details about the impact of increased urbanisation on a family market-garden business.
20 Anna Santin nee Mattiazzo, OH 872/24, 3 April 2013: 33.

to a developer in 1973, they allocated themselves adjoining house blocks on the former market-garden property on Frogmore Road. The tradition of working the land passed through three generations until the land at Bolivar was compulsorily acquired by the local government for urban expansion in the 1980s and the family business concluded its market-gardening operations. Changes to land use were a factor outside the control of the Santin group whereas previously, like other Veneto market gardeners, they could regulate local factors that affected the family business. For example, market gardeners determined methods of cultivation, selection of crops, use of chemicals, the need for additional labour and methods of selling vegetables.

By the late 1970s, both the first and the 1.5 generations were ageing or had died and the second generation had re-evaluated market gardening as a viable occupation. A 1966 study of changing trends in market gardening in the wider Adelaide area found that the demise of smaller suburban family market gardens was inevitable because of increasing land values and the proliferation of subdivisions in previously peri-agricultural areas like Lockleys.[21]

Land, mobility and the community at Lockleys

While other studies of Italian migration have documented 'upward mobility' in examining successive generations who expand the boundaries of family through new status in employment and changes in residential location, this group biography focuses on different aspects of mobility.[22] In the first-generation cohort, three kinds of mobility reflected the progressive stages of settlement of the Veneto community: financial, employment and social/residential. The first generation had required a financial base that enabled them to progress from being itinerant labourers to the stability of self-employment in market gardens with their wives and children. However, their aspiration to belong to the *paese* kept them together at Lockleys even after families achieved economic stability and sold their market gardens. The first generation did not move away or seek upward mobility in more

---

21 Derek L. Smith, 'Market Gardening at Adelaide's Urban Fringe', *Economic Geography* 42, no. 1 (1966): 19–36, doi.org/10.2307/141830, at 33–35.
22 Ricatti, *Italians in Australia*, 37–41; Baldassar and Pesman, *From Paesani to Global Citizens*, 23–26, 60–62.

prestigious suburbs—a characteristic identified in postwar Italian migrants who aspired to purchase and/or build grander homes as part of the process of *sistemazione*.[23]

Following their parents, the 1.5 generation, with one exception, worked as market gardeners with their wives and children and continued to live in the Lockleys area even after retirement, maintaining the close connections of the *paese*.[24] The second generation—as in many instances of the settlement pattern of migrant communities—marked the real point of change and mobility in the Veneto market-gardener families through access to education and selection of occupations. However, more than half of the second generation continued to live in the Lockleys area. At the time of their interviews, 17 of the 33 second-generation narrators lived in, or near, the market garden area in which they had grown up.[25]

First generation: Custodians

The different profiles of the generations illustrate the transition in the attachment to land and new pathways. The first-generation men and women acknowledged themselves as *contadini* and embodied their Veneto heritage as custodians of land. This identity underscored their aspirations through the Depression years and led them to become leaseholders in the Lockleys area. The opportunity to establish a market garden generated the conditions for Vittorio Marchioro, in older age, to declare emphatically: 'I buy this piece of ground here.'[26]

The transformation of their role as custodians involved two stages, progressing from being tenant-custodians in the feudal land system in Italy. At Lockleys for the first two or so decades, the Veneto market gardeners were lessee-custodians who were able to improve and expand their production for the commercial market. When the market gardeners bought the land, they acquired a new status as owner-custodians. The properties at Lockleys became a place of residence, a source of livelihood and the foundation of their identity as market gardeners.

---

23 Ricatti, *Italians in Australia*, 35–40.
24 The one exception was Lino Tonellato, who left the family market gardens after sustaining a back injury that prevented him from working in the glasshouses.
25 Of the 13 1.5-generation men and women who became market gardeners, all but one remained living on their property after the gardens were sold. By the time I began interviews, nine of them had died.
26 Vittorio Marchioro, OH 12/1, 13 March 1984: 11.

Even after the first generation retired, many continued the *contadino* tradition of using their property to grow vegetables and fruit trees for their own use. For example, Norma Camozzato nee Ballestrin remembered that her father, Giuseppe Ballestrin, maintained a vegetable garden applying the same methods he had used on a larger scale in his market garden. She compared Giuseppe's approach to preparing the ground with her own practices, which she suggested did not reflect the methods of the first generation:

> Dad had a beautiful garden. I mean, he treated that back garden as a market garden. He'd dig the earth two or three times before you planted anything in that. He'd put the manure in and dig it in, not like us and just plant things here and expect them to grow. No, he really looked after that.[27]

'Like his father …'

The customary expectation for sons to follow their father in the *contadino* working life was a feature of the pre-Australian Veneto family order. First-generation market gardeners Angelina and Vittorio Marchioro were satisfied that their elder son, who was born in Adelaide in 1940, continued the tradition of working the land. Asked what work their sons undertook after they left school, Angelina outlined the employment pathway that led Johnny back to the family market garden, while Vittorio added, laughing, that Johnny chose that work:

> AM: The first, he worked for somebody in their shop, bring all the things to their house. And after he come back, go to work like his father. He worked in the garden.
> OH: Did he become a gardener too?
> VM: Yeah [laughs] he become a gardener too.[28]

Angelina declared that her son had 'come back' to work on the land, emphasising the value of the occupation within the family. Vittorio's laughter and repetition of the phrase 'become a gardener' indicate a mix of feelings: satisfaction, pride and a sense that owning and working a market garden is an honourable vocation. The sentiments highlight the significance of the market gardens for the first generation, whose goal of achieving *sistemazione* and prosperity for their family also included ownership of land and continuity of the occupation in the next generation.

---

27   Norma Camozzato nee Ballestrin, OH 872/37, 21 September 2016: 26.
28   Vittorio Marchioro, OH 12/1, 13 March 1984: 14.

'I BUY THIS PIECE OF GROUND HERE'

Plate 7.4: Vittorio Marchioro on his lettuce block, Lockleys, mid-1960s
Source: Photo supplied by Johnny Marchioro.

1.5 generation: From witness to market gardener

The children who arrived with their mothers in the 1930s witnessed the customs of inheritance of landownership and labour in the Veneto *contadino* households.[29] Sons in the 1.5 generation served their 'apprenticeship' learning about the occupation of market gardener in the 1930s as they attended the compulsory years of schooling. The children of this generation were a valuable resource because their arrival in Adelaide coincided with the early years of the market gardens. The 1.5 generation was especially important when there were several sons and daughters in a family. At

---

29 Six of the 10 narrators in the 1.5-generation cohort were not from the Lockleys group but were closely connected through aunts, uncles, cousins and in-laws who were market gardeners. They developed their own career pathways outside market gardening. However, 12 members of the 1.5 generation worked market gardens with parents in the first years.

Lockleys, the patriarchal family structures of the Veneto household were transformed when sons and fathers could work as peers and wives and daughters could work alongside the men.

Within the small, bounded community of the Veneto market gardeners, the 1.5 generation worked closely with their parents until the mid-1940s when they began marrying and establishing their own gardens with their wives. Generally, they leased land close to their parents' in a replication of structures in the Veneto *paese*. They were then able to purchase land at the same time as their parents were buying their properties—a testament to the successful *sistemazione* of both generations.

The experience of the Tonellato family is evidence of the adaptation of land acquisition. Two of the sons, interviewed when they were in their eighties, provided details about their family labour unit on the market gardens. In 1935, five Tonellato children and their mother, Elisabetta, were reunited with their father and her husband, Secondo, who had arrived in Adelaide eight years earlier. At the time, Secondo was 42 years old and grew vegetables including cauliflowers, cabbages and potatoes on 2.4 hectares. Initially, he worked the land with Angelo Piovesan, who had arrived on the same ship as him and lived on an adjoining property at Lockleys. The five Tonellato children, aged from eight to 13 on arrival, contributed to the family's livelihood while attending school and after they had completed the compulsory years.

The two eldest sons worked for wages for a short time and returned to assist their parents, who were growing vegetables for the army during the war.[30] Albert's statement that '[w]e were always in with Dad' emphasises Secondo Tonellato's strategy to work with his sons to expand production and the family's income. Their assistance was essential when he responded to market demand and began growing tomatoes in glasshouses—a more labour-intensive enterprise than cultivating the 'outside' crops that he had previously produced. In the first years, the full family labour unit of seven, including Secondo's wife and daughter, worked on the market gardens—an example of the three orientations of a traditional *contadino* household: land, physical labour and close family.[31]

---

30 See Albert Tonellato OH 872/4, 3 October 2008, 6–7; Lino Tonellato, OH 872/10, 16 July 2010: 18–19.
31 Pascoe, *Buongiorno Australia*, 141.

Plate 7.5: The Tonellato family, Adelaide, c. 1947. Back: Lui, Orlando, Rosina, Lino and Albert. Front: Secondo, Assunta and Elisabetta

Source: Photo supplied by Assunta Giovannini nee Tonellato.

In their approach to managing the market gardens as a family business, Secondo and Elisabetta set up their sons for the future as a step in the process of *sistemazione* in Australia. Secondo's move to establish a partnership with his two youngest sons to own land as 'tenants-in-common' in 1949 was a change to the original land title made in the previous year. At that time, Lino and Orlando were in their early twenties and had witnessed their older brothers becoming independent landowners after marriage. In a partnership as 'tenants-in-common', each partner had a separate interest in the property and the arrangement reduced financial risk. The intergenerational business partnership illustrates the capacity of the Veneto families to adapt to new circumstances of land, work and intrafamily control in Australia. Similarly, the *veneti* in Griffith, New South Wales, who established themselves on rural properties in the same period were also forging new pathways for owning land in partnerships between fathers and sons, in contrast to the strict lineal structures of the Veneto patriarchy in *contadino* families.[32]

---

32 Huber, *From Pasta to Pavlova*, 208–9.

Marriage, land and *sistemazione* in the 1.5 generation

Sistemazione in the community at Lockleys was furthered when 1.5-generation sons and daughters married. They established nuclear family households, as exemplified by members of the Tonellato family. In 1945, Rosina Tonellato and Lui Santin—both members of first-generation families—married and began a 30-year stint working in the Santin family business on Frogmore Road. By 1947, the two eldest Tonellato sons had married and, with their wives, established market gardens within walking distance of the Tonellato family household. This arrangement re-created the experience of the physical and social proximity of families in the *paese* in the Veneto region.

Landownership and working lives assumed a new significance because of the opportunities to develop intergenerational partnerships. For example, Secondo's partnership with his two youngest sons continued for some years and created a financial base when his sons married. In families with both sons and daughters, the focus was directed more to the *sistemazione* of sons than daughters because it was an expectation that daughters would be taken care of by their future husbands. This was the case for Rosina Tonellato, who married into the Santin family and worked for several decades with her husband, two brothers-in-law and their wives on the market gardens.

Plate 7.6: Three generations of the Tonellato family, Frogmore Road, 1962
Source: Photo supplied by Lino Tonellato.

The aspiration to facilitate better lives for their children was part of the settlement process for first-generation migrants, who endured the challenges of the early years to see that their children could achieve success through marriage, owning a home and raising their own family. The Veneto group at Lockleys was no exception, as illustrated by Albert Tonellato's reference to his mother's views about the consequences of migration for her children: 'She was so happy she said, "At least I've seen my kids doing something for themselves".'[33] Elisabetta Tonellato nee Gatto had known the challenges for large families in the Veneto and experienced the patriarchal and hierarchical structures and limited land availability for one family. She had endured eight years raising five young children by herself in poverty after her husband migrated in 1927. In contrast, once in Australia, Elisabetta observed success in the lives of all her children. Her youngest daughter, Assunta, was brought into the family as a baby after the death of her mother, who was Secondo's sister. Assunta married in 1968 and, with her husband, continued to live in the family home for two years before they bought a house close by. She did not work in the market gardens and had a long working life in retail.

Like the Tonellato sons, other men of the 1.5 generation progressed from working with their parents beyond the experience of subsistence, adapted to the market and participated in the South Australian economy as commercial growers.

Second generation: From family labourers to wage-earners

Occupational profiles diverged markedly in the 1.5 and second-generation cohorts although both were children of the first-generation Veneto market gardeners. External influences including schooling, social life, involvement in sport and even the influence of radio programs led to the pursuit of work and leisure beyond the market gardens. This sometimes resulted in tension within families who held to traditional values of Veneto culture. The decision for most of the second generation to disconnect from the family occupation indicates the new opportunities that were possible for young people from the 1950s when employment increased with the postwar industrial and manufacturing expansion that also accommodated

---

33 Albert Tonellato, OH 872/4, 3 October 2008: 20.

new Italian migrants.³⁴ The following examples illustrate the differences in participation of members of three second-generation market-gardener families.

When Angelo Piovesan died unexpectedly in 1949, his sons Nillo, Dino and Bruno were still at school. Angelo's wife, Rosalia, enlisted the assistance of her brother-in-law, who relocated from a mica mine in the Northern Territory. He worked with Rosalia and her sons to cultivate and sell vegetables at market. Bruno, the youngest son, reflected on the consequences of his father's death and emphasised the reliance on family as the only solution to survive the loss of the head of the family in a market-garden business:

> It would have been pretty hard on my mother, it would have been tough with 11, 12 and 13 year-olds on her own and that was it. No real help from the government in those years, you had to work all the time and that was it.³⁵

After leaving school, the eldest son, Nillo, contributed income to the family through work in a grocery shop owned by a member of the Veneto community. Although the middle son had imagined a different life, Dino's destiny was to take over the family market gardens with the assistance of his uncle. He recalled his experience after his father's death:

> He died in March of 1949, and I knew that at the end of that year I would have had to stay home with my uncle, who came to look after the market garden, and that was my life essentially cut out for me there, from that point on. I always wanted to be a motor mechanic, and naturally if Dad still had been around, he may have steered me towards taking over the garden, but I always wanted to be a motor mechanic, but that never eventuated … From schoolboy to worker, yes, virtually overnight when I left school, that was it, full-time home in the garden.³⁶

---

34   See Dino Ruzzene and Simone Battiston, *Italian-Australians: From Migrant Workers to Upwardly Mobile Middle Class—A Study of Occupational Mobility among Australians of Italian Background, 1971–2001* (Melbourne: Italian Australian Institute, La Trobe University, 2006), 15, 33.
35   Bruno Piovesan, OH 872/5, 4 October 2008: 4.
36   Dino Piovesan, OH 872/17, 25 September 2011: 31.

'I BUY THIS PIECE OF GROUND HERE'

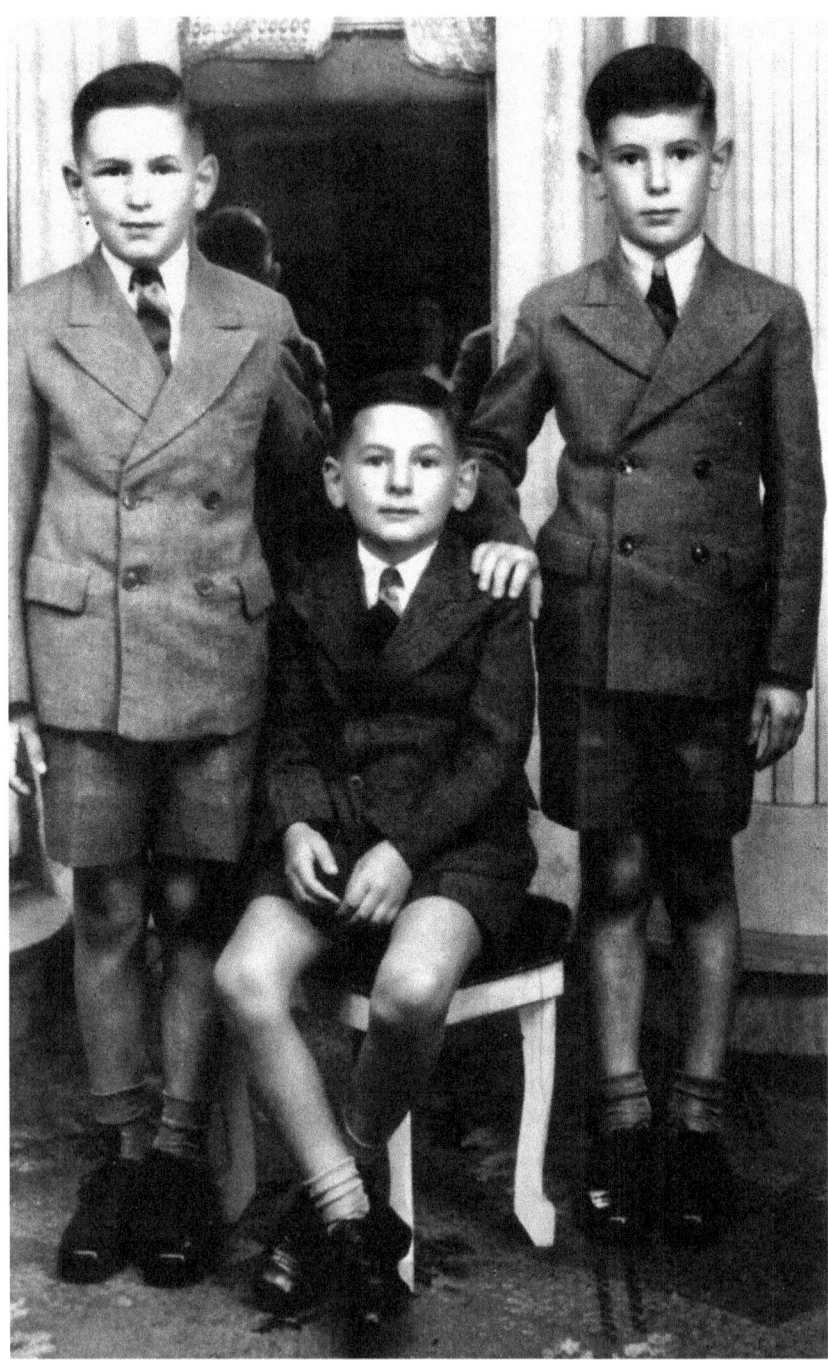

Plate 7.7: The Piovesan brothers, Nillo, Bruno and Dino, Adelaide, c. 1945
Source: Photo supplied by the Piovesan family.

Dino's ambivalence is tempered with the knowledge that had his father not died, there may still have been a moral imperative for him to work in the family's market gardens. Although he had the support of his uncle, he spoke with emotion about taking responsibility for working in the gardens at a young age: 'I cannot remember other young ones like myself, for example, having lost their father and having to take over the business of market gardening, I was on my own in that respect.'[37]

After their mother subdivided her property on Frogmore Road in the 1960s, Dino and his older brother worked land at Bolivar, north of Adelaide, which the family purchased for market gardens. While there was some success, the business lasted only four or five years before the brothers agreed that it would be 'easier to go and earn a wage, from there'.[38] The decision to sell the land, forced by financial problems, was a departure from the working lives of the first and 1.5 generations who persisted with the goal of gaining a livelihood from the land as self-employed business owners. The older two Piovesan brothers took different occupational pathways: Nillo became a police officer and Dino took several jobs before he became a self-employed driving instructor—a job he held for 24 years.

The third brother, Bruno, made what he said was an easy decision to turn his back on working the land when he was first employed as an apprentice toolmaker:

> I didn't want to work in the garden. No, no, no. I had had enough of shifting glasshouses. And I remember going to work there at fifteen and sixteen and have to get up early, and we used to have to hand-dig the glasshouses because we had to dig them properly ... And the hand-digging, that wasn't easy, and I did that a couple of times and then I felt a bit sick at going to work after that and I said, 'Look, I'm not digging glasshouses any more, that's it.' [Laughs].[39]

Bruno's repetition of 'no' emphasises the clarity of his choice for a future disconnected from the market gardens. Unlike the first and 1.5 generations whose only livelihood was from the gardens, Bruno's apprenticeship and work as a toolmaker enabled him to establish a successful small business. He designed and constructed tools and agricultural equipment such as reversible ploughs that he sold to market gardeners and extended to an

---

37   ibid., 36.
38   ibid., 38.
39   Bruno Piovesan, OH 872/5, 4 October 2008: 11.

overseas market.[40] Bruno adapted the mentality of independence and hard work as a son of a Veneto market gardener and used his connection to the land to become a small business owner in the *paese* at Lockleys.

Gender was an important factor in the kind of work undertaken by children in the second generation of the Veneto families. While only two of the 25 sons worked their market gardens, and one carried on his parents' model of growing and selling crops at market until retirement, a study of Italian families who owned agricultural businesses in South Australia found that just over one-third of the second generation remained in that area of work.[41] Several sons in the Veneto families worked for finite periods in family market gardens before becoming wage-earners. Three sons completed secondary education, two became public servants and another became an accountant. Others worked in various trades, construction and small business such as retail and a trucking company.

The 34 daughters in the second generation also took different occupational paths, mostly after completing compulsory schooling. Their participation in the workforce before marriage was a clear departure from *contadino* family culture. Although a few first-generation women had worked in domestic service in Italy, the contractual arrangements for this were made through their fathers and they had to leave the household to live in the homes of the wealthy families who employed them. In Adelaide, however, some daughters began their working lives as employees after leaving school at 14 years of age.

Daughters in just two families, Noemi Zalunardo and Sandra Zampin, undertook what was an unusual post-school path for young women in Australia in the 1960s and worked full-time with their parents in the market gardens until they married. After marriage, although Sandra continued to provide some assistance to her father in the market garden, there was no option of becoming a business partner with him. The occupations of other second-generation women reflected a wider distribution, including office, administrative, nursing, retail and factory work. In one family, three daughters worked in professions after completing tertiary education and, in another, one became a public servant.

---

40   For more details of his manufacturing business, see ibid., 16–18.
41   King, 'Agriculture in South Australia', 316.

Plate 7.8: Noemi, Renato and Eugenio Zalunardo and Amalia Bernardi, Grange Road, c. 1965
Source: Photo supplied by Noemi Campagnolo nee Zalunardo.

In contrast to women who, at marriage, left their parents' household, young men had the opportunity to remain connected to the market gardens and assume a quasi-partner role. For example, Adrian Tonellato, a second-generation son born in 1948, accepted that he would join his parents and work full-time on the family market garden. He had watched his grandfather, parents, uncles and aunts do the same thing. When he left at the end of the second year of high school, it was his trajectory: 'All I know, I stayed with Dad, he wanted me to work with him.'[42] Adrian worked with his parents in 20 glasshouses on Frogmore Road and, later, on the family's land north of Adelaide. When he finished working with his parents, he was the last member of the second generation to work on land in the Lockleys area.

---

42 Adrian Tonellato, OH 872/35, 30 January 2016: 46.

Plate 7.9: Italia and Lui Tonellato with children Luciana and Adrian, Frogmore Road, 1962
Source: Photo supplied by the Tonellato family.

As a young man, Adrian's desire for a social life conflicted with the demands of working on his parents' market garden. Adrian recalled the challenge of meeting his father's expectations:

> Sometimes we used to work seven days a week when it was time for the potatoes … Yeah, we never knew about weekends, never. I never knew about weekends. I always used to argue with Dad because I wanted to go out on Sundays.[43]

Adrian's repetition that he 'never knew about weekends' provides a point of reflection about what he saw as his lack of freedom and suggests the 'cultural ambivalence' identified in studies of second-generation Italians.[44] Adrian experienced the challenge that was evident for sons and daughters who grew up in households with different values from those they observed in the Anglo-Australian environment in which they were educated and in their engagement with peers from families outside the Veneto community. Adrian contrasted his circumstances with those of young men who earned wages as apprentices and did not have to work the extensive hours required by the demanding seasonal cycles in a market garden. When he was 30 years old, Adrian asserted his independence and refused to continue working in the market gardens because of his concern about his mother's allergy to chemicals used in the glasshouses. Although his father wanted to maintain the family market gardens at Lockleys with his son's assistance, Adrian argued against risking his mother's health.

The situation was resolved when his father subdivided the property at Lockleys and bought land at Bolivar like several other Veneto market-gardener families:

> And we bought land out at Bolivar too … Because that's what the idea was because people were starting to build up around here, and the developers wanted the land so the Santins sold the land here and they kept the blocks in the front like we did, for the houses, all the houses in front … So, they sold all the land at the back and shifted all the glasshouses out to Bolivar.[45]

---

43 ibid., 47.
44 Vasta, 'The Second Generation', 155–56.
45 Adrian Tonellato, OH 872/35, 19 November 2015: 53.

Adrian's parents subsidised a partnership that enabled him and his brother-in-law to grow potatoes for a few years—an arrangement that was like an extension of working on the family market gardens. After the land at Bolivar was sold, Adrian pursued other occupations before establishing a successful trucking enterprise, which he maintained even after turning 70 years of age.

Marriages in the second generation

Narrators in the second generation indicated that they had much wider social contact and their leisure time was more varied than the 1.5-generation cohort. However, the young men were more likely to attend dances organised by Anglo-Australian establishments while young women mostly went to dances hosted by the Catholic Church in Adelaide that were introduced to provide social opportunities for young male migrants who arrived after the war. This explains the incidence of four second-generation sons marrying Anglo-Australian women while a high proportion of daughters married newly arrived Veneto migrants. Of 17 second-generation women narrators, 11 married Veneto men, three married Italians from other regions and three married Eastern European men.

Second-generation marriages also tell a story about maintaining transnational connections to Italy. Ten narrators whose parents were market gardeners married spouses born in the Veneto, including seven sisters in one family. All the men had arrived after World War II, many of them welcomed at social occasions held in sheds on family market gardens. Bruna Semola nee Zampin remembered meeting her husband at one of these events:

> After the War everybody nominated somebody to come out and when someone arrived, well, there was always a bit of a welcome party. So, I think I met him … [at one of the Ballestrins'] welcome parties and he—well, we just sort of met. There were two or three that arrived … and everybody was there to meet them because when somebody came from overseas, they usually knew someone who was already here and we'd all go there and you have a bit of a chat, they'd buy a barrel of beer and put something in to eat so we'd stay there for a while and then off we'd go home.[46]

---

46 Bruna Semola nee Zampin, OH 872/39, 8 November 2016: 17.

Nine second-generation male descendants of the Veneto pioneers married spouses born in other regions of Italy. Of the five who married non-Italians, four were Anglo-Australian and one was from Eastern Europe.

Second-generation children often lived near their parents, as was the case explained by Egidio Ballestrin:

> We'd never ever lived very far from my parents … We actually lived on land that was owned by my father … I built a house in 1964 there, and always very close to my parents, and brother and sisters … [I]t was never ever an issue that we weren't close because, like most Italian families, they like to keep theirs very close to each other, especially seeing that they had to leave their own when they left Italy, and I think that they realised how close they needed to be to their offspring, and the offspring to them as well.[47]

Keeping a hand on the vegetables

Johnny Marchioro, one of the two second-generation members who worked full-time as a market gardener with his wife, Eleonora, retired from selling vegetables at market in about 2005 or 2006. However, the couple retained a section of land at Bolivar and continued to grow vegetables including artichokes—a much-prized crop harvested in late winter. They also maintained smaller crops in their home garden. When Johnny spoke about retiring and moving house, he was proud about continuing to grow vegetables at their home:

> Front and back yards, so don't want to lose the idea of growing my own vegies. We had a few plants of zucchini, I planted them in about August last year, and we had all zucchinis until February/March, so I've still got me hand on the vegetables.[48]

---

47 Egidio Ballestrin, OH 872/15, 6 June 2011: 10.
48 Johnny Marchioro, OH 872/1, 11 August 2008: 60.

Plate 7.10: Johnny Marchioro tending tomatoes in his backyard, Nailsworth, Adelaide, March 2023
Source: Madeleine Regan.

Transformations in the three generations

The second generation faced challenges including changes in the market, urbanisation, dynamic circumstances within families, the influence of education and wide occupational choices. Egidio Ballestrin stated that one of the reasons that he did not join his parents in the market garden because they only owned 1.2 hectares in Flinders Park, which was not enough to provide a living for two families and they had not purchased land in Bolivar at the time some other families made that decision.[49]

The original frame of reference, the *contadino* model and patriarchal aspiration for economic interdependence of family on the land, receded as the first generation adapted their cultivation practices. Their ownership of land enabled continuity of the family identity as market gardeners and was replicated by the 1.5 generation. However, the opportunities afforded by selling land brought a new experience: land had become a lucrative asset. Turning away from the hard physical labour and long hours of work on the land, most of the second generation embraced new pathways. They received regular wages and knew a division between home and occupation. Within two generations, Veneto families experienced the transition from agrarian labour to employment and varied socioeconomic status. The line of succession was broken with the second generation. They did not feel constrained by heritage and it was even possible to cross boundaries, including gender roles, which enabled daughters to take different trajectories.

The transformation of the *contadino* heritage and attachment to land illustrates the differences that occurred between the three generations in the market-gardener families at Lockleys in achieving *sistemazione*. The first generation remained on the land that had been their market gardens even after the subdivision and most of the 1.5 generation also built new homes on their properties at Lockleys. The second generation realised that work and earning a livelihood had a new meaning in the Veneto family household. However, the considerable number of the second generation who continued to live in the area indicates an enduring attachment to the market gardens, the land and the community and *paese* at Lockleys.

---

49 Egidio Ballestrin, Personal communication, 13 March 2020.

8

Transforming the *paese*

They were all very close to each other. They [the Santin and Tonellato families] came from Caselle which is close to Riese so they probably felt that they were almost like, how we say *paesani*, which means from the same country [town] and they probably helped each other and that was fairly common, like I can remember the other Italians coming to our place—if a certain job had to be done or when they were doing refurbishing or whatever was needed maybe, in the shed. I can remember many people coming. And probably Dad and Uncle did the same for them. And that's why they helped each other. Surely being able to live close to each other was one way of keeping contact, of whenever needed. I would have said there was probably, you know, mutual support, lending or whatever, borrowing money or whatever it was … a stage when they were very well settled families, okay. There were young people arriving, I can remember them because we used to have young people coming to our place.

—Remo Berno, 2017[1]

Remo Berno was born in Adelaide in 1953 to a Veneto market-gardener family that returned to live in Italy when he was 18 years old. Although more than 40 decades had passed since he left his life in Australia, Remo remembered and identified geographic and relational spaces of the market gardens at Lockleys. In his interview, he recalled a settled community that operated through the proximity of families able to assist with physical tasks

---

1   Remo Berno, OH 872/46, 27 June 2017: 12.

associated with the market gardens. He referred to the close interactions and networks that included other forms of reciprocity such as financial and social support within the community that were part of the culture of the *paese* in his parents' generation.

In another study of the settlement of Veneto migrants between the wars, such initiatives of care, protection and support were identified as 'invisible networks'.[2] Remo remembered that large numbers of migrants who arrived after the war were supported by networks in the *paese* at Lockleys. He provided insight into his family's contribution to supporting *paesani* in the day-to-day interactions of market gardeners in the Lockleys community. His memories illustrate the value of oral history in enabling narrators to remember the past and find subjective meaning in speaking about it from the present.[3]

Plate 8.1: Berno siblings: Diana, Remo and Robert, Valetta Road, c. 1964
Source: Photo supplied by the Berno family.

---

2   Davine, *Vegnimo da Conco Ma Simo Veneti*, 88–89.
3   Alessandro Portelli, 'Living Voices: The Oral History Interview as Dialogue and Experience', *The Oral History Review* 45, no. 2 (2018): 239–48, doi.org/10.1093/ohr/ohy030, at 245–47.

The first generation of men and women adjusted their sense of identity in the *paese* over time. They modified *contadino* values and practices associated with the cultivation of land and conceded to changes within the community in response to external influences that led most of the second generation to withdraw from their family market gardens. The boundaries became more permeable as they incorporated the postwar Veneto migrants into their close community. Other transitions occurred after they sold their market gardens. For example, some in the first and 1.5 generations became members of a pan-Italian association in the mid-1960s that provided a range of social events in Adelaide.[4] When the Veneto Club was established in the western suburbs in 1972, some in the market-gardener group extended their social lives beyond the *paese* at Lockleys into a wider social framework of Veneto people living in Adelaide. Despite the dislocation from the soil and work of the market gardens, the social network developed by the first generation lived on through the 1.5 generation into the second generation, and now even extends to the third generation in some families.

Denise Doyban nee Santin, a second-generation narrator, acknowledged links back to the 'old people', who, in her case, were her Santin and Tonellato grandparents and her own parents. They continued to live on Frogmore Road after their market gardens were sold. Denise also reflected on the continuing community connections in the area that was the *paese*:

> Well, the old people have certainly gone, but the young ones this time around, we still keep in touch with a lot of the ones that are around. Again, most of my relatives still live close to me. Some friends have moved interstate or whatever, but as I said, the older ones have gone, passed on, but we're still there, and I think there's still a few, even though they might have moved a few streets away. You know, their children are still there and we still see each other [but] not as often. But I think the community's still there.[5]

The connections between the *paesani* in the 1.5 and second generations have been maintained over many years through formal and informal gatherings involving extended families that echo the experience of the first-generation market gardeners when they attended celebrations within the community. People like Remo who were brought up in Adelaide and now live in the Veneto region have maintained transnational connections with

---
4   Cosmini and Glenn, *La Seconda Casa*, 51–61.
5   Denise Doyban nee Santin interviewed by Madeleine Regan, Transcript, J.D. Somerville Oral History Collection, State Library of South Australia, Adelaide, OH 872/62, 8 December 2021: 48.

relatives and *paesani*. New strands in the network have emerged through the Veneto market gardeners' oral history project, which has created opportunities for descendants to document their family history and the life of the community—a narrative that now spans nearly 100 years in Australia. The 1.5 and the second generations participate in a relational or virtual *paese* in the form of a dedicated website that archives the memories and history of the Veneto market-gardener families and friends at Lockleys. The collective memories of this community illuminate the role of family in the history of migrant groups and provide context and new approaches to historical study and themes to include in national narratives.[6]

The narratives of the first generation of Veneto market gardeners contain the unfolding experience of migration that has evolved beyond the act of emigration from the Veneto to Adelaide made by the first generation in the late 1920s. When members of the first and 1.5 generations made return visits to their places of origin, they gained a broader perspective of their identity as *veneti* and Veneto Australians.[7] Many in the second generation have also realised their origins through visits to Italy and satisfied some of the longing to understand their heritage. Most narrators have nurtured their transnational links and claim both Australian and Italian, if not Veneto, identities. The high incidence of narrators citing their Veneto identity reflects an attachment to the place of family origin and the significant role of forebears. For example, Romano Marchioro declared:

> I'd class myself as an Italian. Yeah, well, what can you say? They say: 'Where are you from?' I say: 'I was born here but my parents are Italian, that's what I am, Italian' … We were brought up speaking Italian and you never lose that, you never forget that, and you never forget if you've been there, you never forget your cousins, your aunties, and your uncles. Surely, why not? You're Italian, you're Italian.[8]

Romano repeats the word 'Italian' and reflects on his connection to his parents and relatives whom he had visited twice in the province of Vicenza as an adult. His repetition of 'you never forget' is compelling in emphasising his attachment to his ancestry and the memory preserved in migrant families despite the separation of generations and distance. His links to relatives

---

6   Katie Barclay and Nina Javette Koefoed, 'Family, Memory, and Identity: An Introduction', *Journal of Family History* 46, no. 1 (January 2021): 3–12, doi.org/10.1177/0363199020967297.
7   Baldassar, *Visits Home*, 332–38; Baldassar and Pesman, *From Paesani to Global Italians*, 184–85.
8   Romano Marchioro, OH 872/20, 11 June 2012: 19.

illustrate his position as a second-generation Italian Australian who wants to maintain living bonds with his parents' history and relatives in Malo, Italy, although his father had left the family nearly a century ago. Although Romano was second generation, his visits embodied a 'transformation of identity', consciousness of his Italian-ness and his wish to actively maintain intergenerational relationships in the Veneto.[9] Romano's Aunty Angelina made three visits to her brother and sister-in-law, nephews and their families in Adelaide in the 1970s and 1980s. While she was in Adelaide, she helped her nephew Johnny and his wife, Eleonora, with their market garden at Bolivar—an indication of the continuity of the family identity as *contadini*.

Interpreting the *paese*

The distinctive feature of the settlement of the Veneto market gardeners at Lockleys, discussed in previous chapters, was the development of a *paese* as an intraregional community of *veneti* in the interwar years rather than a group formed through chain migration. The image of the *paese* is an element in the foundation story of the Veneto market-gardener community and the first, 1.5- and second-generation accounts offer individual and shared collective memories. The two representatives of the first generation interviewed in 1984 referred to the enduring support of the early community, which Angelina Marchioro expressed simply as: 'All the time, stick together.'[10] The companionship of *paesani*—close neighbours with the same cultural origins—and everyday interactions on their market gardens ameliorated the challenges of settlement, which were also a feature in the Veneto settlement in Gippsland in Victoria.[11]

The physical location of settlement and the formation of community are often elements of analysis in migration studies. At times, the concepts overlap and can be examined simultaneously to understand the processes of migration and settlement. The discussion of location may include references to the development of defined communities separated from the rest of the population as a place of first residence for families who arrive through chain

---

9 Baldassar, *Visits Home*, 287.
10 Angelina Marchioro, OH 12, 13 March 1984: 15.
11 Davine, *Vegnimo da Conco Ma Simo Veneti*, 51–53.

migration.¹² Although the two concepts are similar, it is possible to separate and identify various components of culture that the *veneti* maintained and the adaptations they made to inhabit and shape their network of relationships and physical place of settlement. The families at Lockleys were attached to their *paese* in two ways: physically and relationally, through their community interconnections. Both attachments were emotional but also practical and created opportunities for *sistemazione* and the formation of the Veneto market-gardener identity at Lockleys.

The Italian language has a word that incorporates the two elements of attachment to place, encompassing both meanings: *campanilismo*. It is used to describe a physical locality and a sense of belonging to a community manifested in the emotional attachment a man or woman has to his or her home village through the tall church belltower, or *campanile*, that dominates the sightline in a *paese*.¹³ Adjoining the church, the tower is usually in a central location on the *piazza* (village square). The *campanile* is also a feature because the sound of its bell can be heard throughout the village, calling people to religious ceremonies or to mark significant events such as a funeral. It is a personal and communal reference point for migrants, especially in the first generation and some in the 1.5 generation who retain memories of life in their home village. At Lockleys, the sight lines were dominated by the endless rows of glasshouses, which could be considered a unifying landmark in the landscape—a proxy for the bell tower. Instead of the village *piazza*, at Lockleys, some packing sheds became community spaces for celebrations. The Veneto group created a distinctive sense of *campanilismo* and *paese* at Lockleys as they did not share the single focus of having originated from the same village or *comune*.

The attachment to Lockleys runs deep into the second generation. For example, Diana Panazzolo nee Santin, from the second generation, explained her memory of the land her family farmed on Frogmore Road for more than 40 years. While the market gardens had been sold more than 30 years before her interview, she reflected on her attachment to the family

---

12   John S. MacDonald and Leatrice D. MacDonald, 'Chain Migration Ethnic Neighbourhood Formation and Social Networks', *The Millbank Memorial Fund Quarterly* 42, no. 1 (1964): 82–97, doi.org/10.2307/3348581, at 90–91; Donna Gabaccia, 'Global Geography of "Little Italy": Italian Neighbourhoods in Comparative Perspective', *Modern Italy* 11, no. 1 (2006): 9–24, doi.org/10.1080/13532940500489510.
13   Baldassar, *Visits Home*, 185–208; Rudolph M. Bell, *Fate, Honor, Family and Village: Demographic and Cultural Change in Rural Italy since 1800* (New York: Routledge, 2017), 151–53.

property and visualised physical features drawn from her memory. She began by explaining the route she took to travel away from her home at the time of the interview and the need to change direction because Frogmore Road was being upgraded:

> Frogmore Road's been closed for quite a few months and like yesterday ... I had to go the back streets and I was saying, 'Oh, this is where the house was. Oh, this is where the tank was. Oh, I'm running over, going over where the well was.' [Laughs] ... I was going down Santin Avenue and I was picturing the glasshouses and the tanks because the road was right on the edge of the property, and now there's houses and, along here [indicating on a map], I can still see it.[14]

After the land was subdivided, the local council allocated names to streets in the area of the market-gardener families. Streets were named after the Santin, Piovesan, Tonellato and Ballestrin families and indicate the location of those families' market gardens before subdivision.

When the 1.5- and second-generation narrators reminisce about the market gardens that no longer exist, they convey memories of an idealised place associated with security, productive working lives and the companionship of *paesani*. The narrators' affection for both place and community at Lockleys is a memory of the *paese*, bounded and separated from the Anglo-Australian world. The *paese* was both a place and a community that existed in a particular time with a coherence that allowed the inclusion of some non-*veneti*. For example, when the Recchi family moved onto their market gardens at Lockleys in the late 1930s, the parents and two children were integrated into the Veneto community as neighbours and friends although they were from another region in Italy.[15] The close relationships were evident when their daughter married in 1956 and chose the daughter of a neighbouring Veneto family as one of her bridesmaids

---

14 Diana Panazzolo nee Santin, OH 872/27, 13 December 2013: 52.
15 See Mel Recchi interviewed by Madeleine Regan, Transcript, J.D. Somerville Oral History Collection, State Library of South Australia, Adelaide, OH 872/31; and Aida Valentini nee Recchi interviewed by Madeleine Regan, Transcript, J.D. Somerville Oral History Collection, State Library of South Australia, Adelaide, OH 872/39.

'I BUY THIS PIECE OF GROUND HERE'

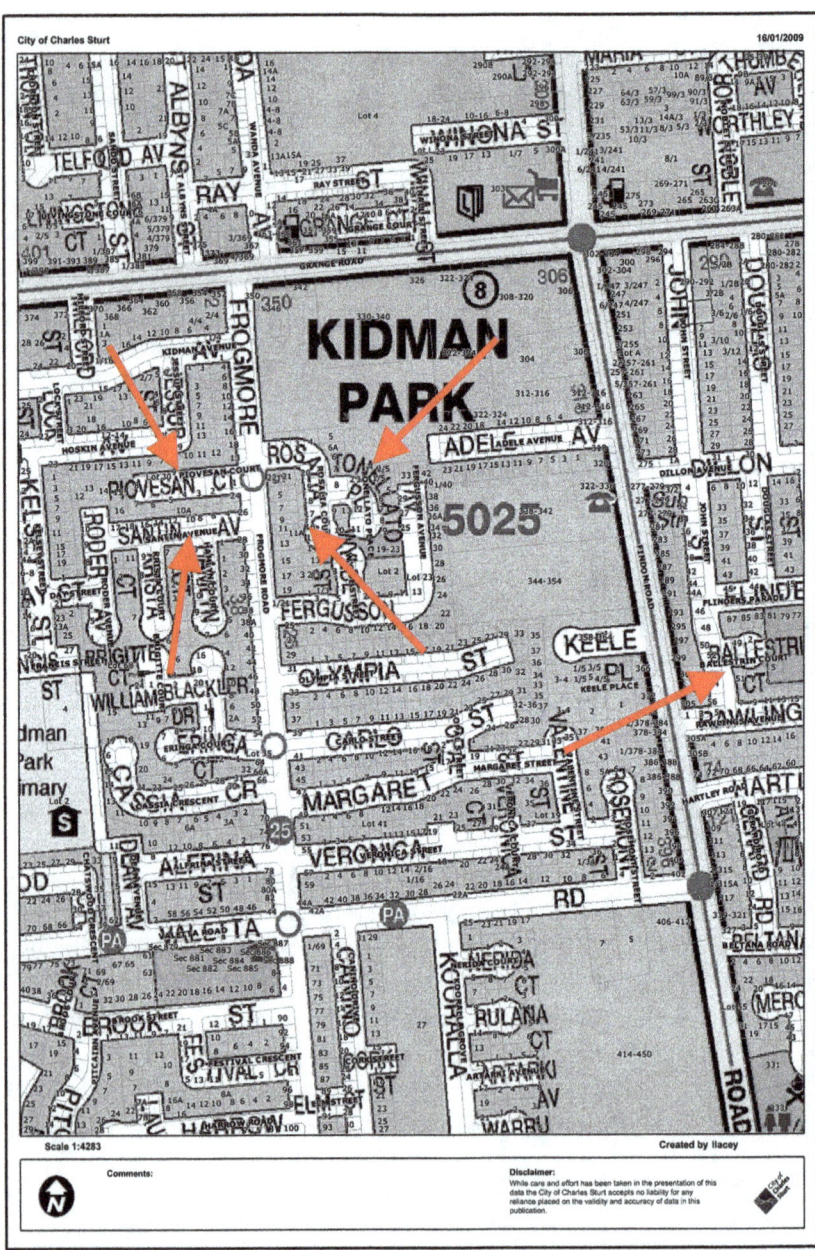

Map 8.1: Detail of street directory marked with names of some Veneto market gardeners

Note: From left: Piovesan, Santin, Rosalia (Piovesan), Tonellato and Ballestrin.

Source: City of Charles Sturt, 2009, reproduced with permission.

Community: Family and friends

At Lockleys, the Veneto group developed a distinctive coupled identity as *veneti* and as commercial market gardeners. Daily interactions through shared language, heritage and occupation created familiarity within a secluded community, evolving on the margins of Anglo-Australian society for three successive generations. The proximity of the market gardens facilitated social interactions and created new opportunities in the Lockleys community.

In 1947, Mary Zoanetti, a 1.5-generation woman whose parents came from another northern region of Italy, was 23 years old and living with her widowed mother, both of them working as market gardeners, with Veneto families as neighbours. Mary married Albert Tonellato, a 1.5-generation man whose parents were Veneto market gardeners. In her interview, Mary referred to the physical and social connections between families at Lockleys:

> It was a community that we were all close together. His [Albert's] father used to live next-door to Bruno's father [Angelo Piovesan] … [I]t was all connected … We were bordering where they had their land and then there was … Ballestrin, Zalunardo, Piovesan, Laio and Tonellato. We were all not far from one another … [P]eople were very helpful then with one another.[16]

Mary's description of the first-generation community—physically close, available to collaborate in everyday social interactions—paints an image of intimacy and a context for understanding the Veneto community, particularly in the first years at Lockleys. Mary was interviewed at the age of 84 and her reference to the community 'then' suggests her nostalgia for the connections forged in the past. Another narrator, a postwar migrant from the Veneto and relative of a market gardener, spoke of the challenges of settlement processes for the first generation and explained the necessity to form strong relationships as *paesani* because their own families were not in Australia.[17]

The concept of 'family' takes on significance and gains symbolic status in narratives of migration and emphasises the complexities of intergenerational responsibilities to pass on and preserve culture and identity.[18] Many narrators

---

16 Mary Tonellato nee Zoanetti, OH 872/3, 3 October 2008: 7.
17 Armida Mattiazzo nee Biasetto, Personal communication, 30 May 2020.
18 Fortier, *Migrant Belongings*, 97–98.

used the word 'family' in recalling their parents' participation in the community of Veneto market gardeners. For example, Milva Rebuli nee Zampin said: 'You know, it was just … a great big family.'[19] Aida Valentini nee Recchi, whose parents were market gardeners from another Italian region, recalled that her family was considered members of the Veneto community at Lockleys: 'We got on as one family with all the neighbours that we had around.'[20] The attribution of 'family' was even more emphatic when Christine Zampin reflected on the way her Irish-Australian mother was respected as a member of the *paese* at Lockleys: 'It was really important to her to feel … wanted and belonging to this family of *veneti*.'[21]

The narrators elevate the idea of family within the *paese* at Lockleys and their nostalgia supports an interpretation of it as a model of a utopian community. The Veneto community at Lockleys experienced a transformation of the concept of belonging to a family. The first generation had imparted the designation of 'community as family' to the 1.5 and second generations in the absence of their own extended family relationships. However, the first generation also expanded the image by being open to new ways of interpreting the construction and meaning of family. They formed nuclear families, integrated godparents as proxy family members, accepted men who married outside the community and incorporated the presence of single men and women within the wider Veneto community.

Changes in the composition of the community that occurred with the arrival of postwar migrants from the Veneto were unforeseen. Some, like the Ballestrins and Bernos in the first generation, sponsored 'new Australians' who were *paesani*—mostly young single men escaping the poverty and hardship brought about by the war. Some families guaranteed accommodation and employment for the arrivals on the market gardens for two years under conditions set by the government. In some cases, the first generation responded to the new arrivals in a manner that echoed the *padrone* relationship of the Veneto region, where bosses organised the conditions of accommodation and labour. For example, some families erected basic accommodation on their properties and rented out rooms to young men (and some couples) who either worked on the market gardens or were employed in factories in nearby suburbs. The transformation occurred

---

19 Milva Rebuli nee Zampin, OH 872/36, 27 March 2016: 8.
20 Aida Valentini nee Recchi, OH 872/39, 28 September 2016: 16.
21 Christine Zampin, OH 872/42, 26 September 2017: 26.

in the *paese* at Lockleys through the initiatives undertaken by the first generation and some in the 1.5 group to support the *sistemazione* of the new Veneto migrants.

A new *sistemazione*

After enduring the challenges of World War II, a new stage in *sistemazione* occurred in the *paese* at Lockleys at the same time as postwar social and economic forces and local circumstances impacted on the Veneto market-gardener community. The families incorporated the new migrants as they began to reap the benefits of their hard work, frugality and the security of the community. Market gardeners met the demand for fresh vegetables generated by the increase in the state's population in the years after the war.[22] While they may have had the support and solidarity of the Lockleys *paese*, those postwar Italian migrants gained employment in factories and interacted with the public domain in Adelaide beyond the safety of the Veneto community. The young migrants benefited from the network of older *paesani* who had lived in Australia for more than 20 years, although there were gaps in the perspectives of the two cohorts of first-generation Italians. The initiatives of the first generation to support the new arrivals also brought some assessments of the relative ease postwar migrants enjoyed in adapting to life in Australia. The older Veneto market gardeners provided support for the new arrivals—a resource that had not been available to them in the 1920s. Vittorio Marchioro compared the simpler and accelerated path to economic success for the postwar migrants with the situation that he and his generation had faced in the interwar years:

> Before the war, the gardens, work and work and no money too. Start after the war, start better, price got better and go up … All different now than before. Now, everybody got a car, before nobody got a car, nothing, take a horse and trolley to market … The people … coming after the war, come here, started work, making money quick.[23]

While Vittorio acknowledged the postwar economic growth that created conditions for increased prosperity, his observations suggested some reservations about the differences in the opportunities for the two generations of Veneto migrants. He observed that postwar Italians obtained

---

22   Sendziuk and Foster (*A History of South Australia*, 153) make the point that between 1947 and 1954 South Australia had 'the nation's highest proportional increase in population due to migration'.
23   Vittorio Marchioro, OH 12, 13 March 1984: 14, 15, 18.

employment, purchased houses and cars and established themselves within a few years of arrival. The younger generation achieved *sistemazione* much more quickly than those who had arrived in the late 1920s in a difficult economic and political period in Australian history.

As the market gardeners extended the social boundaries of their *paese* to the Veneto migrants who arrived after the war, the older *veneti* confronted what it meant to 'belong' to the community at Lockleys. There were some limits to the inclusion of others, at least for one first-generation man, Isidoro Ballestrin, who held Sunday afternoon gatherings for Veneto men in his packing shed. Isidoro had hosted the events for some time and his guests had contributed to the cost of a keg of beer. Because of the limited opportunities for the new migrants to socialise, numbers escalated and changed the nature of the gatherings. His son Francesco explained the situation:

> When Dad was doing it, it was just basic, old friends who were here in those early years. And of course, he dropped it after a while, when it got too big and they started getting people, strangers—although they were Italians—but they weren't of the group that was here years ago. When it got too big, they decided to drop that, otherwise it would have been a circus then, wouldn't it? It wouldn't have been a friendly gathering anymore.[24]

Francesco emphasised that his father's original aim was for the older generation to share precious leisure time in the company of other men they knew. Others also offered social occasions such as *bocce* games on courts built on their market gardens and a range of Veneto men, from the first generation to the newly arrived, socialised at the weekly events.

The boundaries of the *paese* also changed after second-generation daughters married young men who had emigrated from the Veneto in the 1950s and 1960s. New transnational connections developed within families at Lockleys. The sense of identity was intensified as the newly formed Australian families made visits to the Veneto region. The women born in Australia met their in-laws and gained a new perspective as members of a transnational Veneto family.

---

24 Francesco Ballestrin, OH 872/7, 5 January 2009: 39.

Plate 8.2: Sunday afternoon *bocce* group, Santin market garden, Frogmore Road, 1962
Source: Oscar Mattiazzo.

Interactions with Anglo-Australians and Chinese

The first generation of Veneto market gardeners did not mix much with the Anglo-Australian market gardeners—a situation confirmed by Rae Ballantyne, the son of a returned serviceman who had been allocated a soldier-settler block after World War I. The Ballantyne property was close to some of the Veneto families. He recalled that his father sold or gave to an Italian man a number of olive trees that grew on his property.[25] While Rae was able to name some of the Italian and Veneto families, he acknowledged that his family did not interact much with the Italians especially because of the situation during the war years when Italians were regarded with

---

25 Rae Ballatyne, OH 872/21, 25 August 2012: 13.

suspicion: 'Those days, you knew there was Italians there but you didn't mix with them much. No, we were not allowed.'[26] However, as a child, Rae mixed with the son of Gino and Jean Berno, who lived on Valetta Road.

There were at least three Chinese men, two with families, who had market gardens close to some of the Veneto families. Lina Campagnaro nee Ballestrin, from the second generation, spoke about visiting almost daily Yick Kee, a Chinese man who lived on a small neighbouring property where he had ducks and vegetables that he sold at the market. Lina recalled where he lived:

> It was like a shed converted to his kitchen … And he would invite us [in]. My brother would eat everything but I just ate the fried rice … a wonderful sauce and still to this day, I do not know what it was, but it was beautiful.[27]

Lina said she did not know what vegetables Yick Kee grew: 'And I don't think Mum or Dad ever mentioned it.' It appears that children were more comfortable than their parents interacting with the Chinese market gardeners. This is confirmed by Mel Recchi, from the second generation, who recalled some contact and knew enough about their food traditions to say: 'Chinese food didn't suit the Italian food … They were always very friendly and always very, very polite.'[28]

A different perspective of relationships with Chinese who lived in the area is evident in the example of a first-generation man, Angelo Innocente, who arrived in 1950 from the Veneto. Angelo lived on the southern side of the river where there was a half-case factory owned by a Chinese-Australian man, Harold Dare, who employed Angelo for seven years during which time he was made foreman.[29] In a sign of trust and goodwill, Harold lent Angelo money to buy a truck for his new business when Angelo decided to start his own half-case factory. Angelo had his half-case factory for 22 years and served the needs of the Veneto market gardeners at Lockleys.[30]

---

26 ibid., 25.
27 Lina Campagnaro nee Ballestrin, OH 872/28, 13 March 2014: 6.
28 Mel Recchi, OH 872/31, 18 June 2014: 18.
29 The half-case was the object that generated the group biography of the Veneto market gardeners.
30 Angelo Innocente, OH 872/8, 5 January 2009: 10–11.

Identity and place

Between the wars, the Veneto market-gardener community maintained two geographical reference points that preserved their identity and gave a sense of belonging. The connection to their place of origin in the Veneto region was emotional and nostalgic for many in the first and 1.5 generations, while the market gardens at Lockleys were a site with social and economic significance that marked their *sistemazione*. In interviews, narrators from the 1.5 generation remembered both places whereas the second-generation women and men identified the second, the market gardens, as the site of the foundation of the family in Australia. The connection between the two ideas of place and community is evident in the narrators' accounts of the history of their family as migrants from the Veneto or the village from which the family originated. Second-generation narrators who had visited relatives in the Veneto indicated that they felt a deeper sense of belonging to the ancestral *paese* and had increased their knowledge of family history—a new consciousness of their identity attached to the village of their parents and forebears and a new sense of pride in their Italian ancestry.[31]

Attachment to the ancestral *paese*

Those who left their *paese* in the Veneto as children associated the attachment to place with relatives and the family household and expressed a strong emotional relationship. For example, Lino Tonellato, born in 1926, recalled the poignant wrench of leaving the village of Caselle di Altivole, where he had spent the first nine years of his life. With his mother and four siblings, Lino left the village and his relatives in 1935 to join his father in Adelaide:

> LT: We were all happy about it but at the same time you don't like to leave your great-grandfather … I still remember him … my mother's father. He had to be home by himself.
>
> OH: It must have been hard for your mother to leave him?
>
> LT: Oh, it was very hard.[32]

The prospect of being reunited with his father, who had migrated eight years earlier, and reframing family life in Adelaide contrasted with the sense of loss that Lino communicated nearly 80 years after he left Italy.

---

31 Baldassar, *Visits Home*, 286–91.
32 Lino Tonellato, OH 872/10, 16 July 2010: 15.

He used the term 'great-grandfather' for his grandfather and his memories are part of the family history he embodies in his own role as a great-grandfather. Lino conveyed the experience of migration from a child's perspective, balanced between the hurt of losing the relationship with his grandfather and the embrace of a new life with both his parents in a new place. He communicated three images of disrupted family relations in his narrative of migration: his sense of loss, the loneliness of his grandfather, who was left behind, and his mother's sadness about abandoning her elderly father. Lino's is an intergenerational perspective of male emotions relating to the separation from the intimacy of close relatives in the context of the migration experience.

The second generation imagined the *paese* and relatives in the Veneto region through the lens of their parents, who maintained links to their place of origin. They acknowledge the language and the *contadino* customs their parents preserved that created a distinctive identity. For example, Virginia Rodato nee Zampin, born in 1945, reflected on the rhythm of working life in the family household in the Veneto region and compared it with the experience of the market gardeners at Lockleys. She was familiar with both places because she spent extensive periods in the village where her relatives lived and in her husband's village in the Veneto:

> [S]ix days a week was hard work and seven days … most of them would have had a few hours off. That was more or less in them when they were young. And they would go to church or something when they were back in Italy and come back, have their little sleep in the afternoon and probably go and play bowls in the afternoon if they were in Italy or just catch up with their mates, and that was always the atmosphere here, as well. I suppose some didn't, but those that I knew done that.[33]

Virginia linked the working life of the market gardeners at Lockleys to the *contadino* work ethic in the Veneto region. She identified the tenacity of the men, the domination of work, the allocation of time to religious observance and some leisure activity, which included a siesta on non-working days. She outlined the weekly routine for men in the first generation like her father, who kept some land and continued to work a glasshouse after selling their market garden.

---

33   Virginia Rodato nee Zampin interviewed by Madeleine Regan, Transcript, J.D. Somerville Oral History Collection, State Library of South Australia, Adelaide, OH 872/43, 15 March 2017: 33.

Plate 8.3: Silvano Zampin tending tomatoes, Findon, late 1970s
Source: Photo supplied by the Zampin family.

Links to origins: Visits to the Veneto

Intermediaries facilitated connections between the first generation at Lockleys and their families in the Veneto when travel was infrequent and took several weeks by ship. The people who returned to Italy visited their own families and met with the relatives of other market gardeners and members of the wider Veneto community in Adelaide, reporting back after they returned to Lockleys. Virginia Rodato nee Zampin, a second-generation woman who married a postwar Veneto man, explained how her father preserved his connections with his relatives:

> Well, in those days there was a lot of immigrants out here as well and a lot of times, they would bring him a letter and he would have the latest news, of course. And then, other than that, he would himself write letters and that would take, those days, about a month to arrive there. But, in the meantime, perhaps someone had went to Italy and they came back and they said, 'I've been to see your family. They look good. And your mother, this, or your father, that.' Or, 'They had a good harvest this year.'[34]

Virginia's reference to 'out here' indicates the close association between 'here' as Adelaide and 'there' as the village of Riese Pio X, her father's hometown. The use of the two reference points is similar to the way British people who migrated to Australia considered England as the orientation for the colonial country. Virginia captures the intimate connections in families separated by distance and time although they were able to maintain membership of both households, in their ancestral *paese* and in the home they created with their family in Adelaide. As Virginia indicates, when members of the *paese* at Lockleys visited the Veneto, they assumed roles as conduits between *paesani* in both locations.

Transnational voices and images

Another second-generation narrator outlined her father's active role in strengthening links between *veneti* in Adelaide and their families in the Veneto. Romildo Santin was a member of the 1.5 generation and returned briefly to his village of Caselle di Altivole to get married in 1950. Twelve years later, Romildo and his wife, Clara, and their two eldest children made their first visit together to Italy, where they stayed with Clara's parents for several months. About two years before the family went to Italy, Romildo made a tape recording of Veneto people who lived at Lockleys or nearby and who had originated from the locality of Caselle di Altivole. Romildo had invited people to record messages that could be played to their relatives in Italy.

---

34 ibid., 17.

In 2023 Romildo's daughter Diana unexpectedly discovered the old cassette tape, labelled 'Australia per Italia 1958–59'.[35] Romildo must have devoted weeks to collecting the messages because there were more than 90 voices on the cassette, which was converted from his reel-to-reel tape recorder. The messages are poignant and convey the sense of families fragmented by migration. One man emphasised the transnational context and addressed family members as 'your relatives far away'. Another spoke with a faltering intonation: 'After 22 years, you hear my voice.' One woman who was known as a good singer sang *Ave Maria* accompanied by a friend on an organ. Speakers addressed categories of relatives—brothers, sisters, in-laws, cousins, aunts and uncles—and some ended by sending wishes to the local priest, who had been in the parish for many years. Other *veneti* outside the *paese* in Lockleys were invited to record their messages.[36]

Once in Italy, Romildo repeated his role as go-between, as Diana recalled:

> I remember Dad going over on the ship, [he] bought a movie camera, and … he went around to every family who had children here [in Australia], you know, all their parents and took photos of every family. And when he came back here, he showed them … Oh, and we travelled [in the Veneto] and found all these people. Going over, we, you remember the old tape? The old—before the cassette—a tape recorder, we took. And he'd called people over to come and send their regards and their love to their mother, so they could hear their voice … then Dad would take the film, and brought it back here … Because you know, it was 1962, and you think 50 years, they didn't have all these things and the phone, it was very rare.[37]

Diana uses the word 'photos' to refer to the films her father shot on his Super 8 camera. In 1962, Romildo recorded more than two and a half hours of various families and gatherings, including a wedding, in the Veneto region. Countless scenes of relatives, groups sharing meals, wedding banquets and *contadino* farms convey interactions within families and with *paesani*, which at times are self-conscious because of the camera's presence. In her telling, Diana communicates pride in her father's capacity to connect transnational

---

35 Diana thinks her father made the recordings as a response to a priest who had visited from Caselle di Altivole. She gleaned from listening to the tape that the priest had brought recorded messages from relatives to their kin in Adelaide.
36 The use of the tape recorder and Super 8 camera to record the messages of the *veneti* in Adelaide was an example of the strong regional identity of the migrant group.
37 Diana Panazzolo nee Santin, OH 872/27, 18 October 2013: 21.

families through the intimacy of voice recordings and moving images—an initiative made possible by the technology of the time and Romildo's skills and ingenuity.

Visits to Italy by the second generation

The experience of travelling to Italy, meeting close relatives and being present in family households enabled second-generation narrators to understand their origins and the context of their heritage. The visits became an initiation into the process of connecting with relatives and forming a new appreciation of their ancestry and identity. Baldassar provides case studies of young second-generation Italians for whom a visit to their parents' origin village takes on the status of a 'rite of passage'.[38] Such visits enable the second generation to begin to develop connections with their grandparents and other relatives. This process has three elements—opportunities to: gain knowledge of the family context, engage and spend time with the relatives, and maintain links with family members who previously were only distant figures in the transnational family story.[39] Some of the second generation who grew up in nuclear families at Lockleys and visited Italy with their parents stayed in intergenerational family households with grandparents or aunts and uncles. Through encounters with their transnational family and the experience of being in, and learning about, Italy, they gained a new recognition of their Italian identity.[40]

Diana Panazzolo nee Santin, whose father was the conduit between the two communities of *veneti*, remembered precise details of her first visit to her parents' village when she was 11 years old in 1962. She spent a lot of time with her grandparents and aunts and these connections continued as she grew older.[41] Ten years later, her parents invited Diana to accompany them with her siblings to celebrate the sixtieth wedding anniversary of her maternal grandparents. When her parents offered to pay for her airfare, Diana did not hesitate to go for three months even though she was engaged to be married at the time. The attachment to her *nonni* (grandparents) and other relatives in her father's village outweighed her need to be with her fiancé at a time when young women would typically have focused on planning their

---

38 Baldassar, *Visits Home*, 286–91.
39 ibid., 257.
40 ibid., 287–91.
41 See Maria Chiara Marchetti-Mercer and Anita Virga, *The Italian Diaspora in South Africa: Nostalgia, Identity, and Belonging in the Second and Third Generations* (London: Routledge, 2023), doi.org/10.4324/9781003266884, 75.

wedding. Diana made two further visits to spend time with her relatives. In 2019, Diana and her husband spent time in Caselle di Altivole with her relatives with whom she maintains regular contact. Also included in that trip were her children, their spouses and her grandchildren.[42]

Lockleys: A second place of origin

Narrators ascribe a second meaning of place to the location of the market gardens and the *paese*. Lockleys became a place that signified Veneto-Australian identity. At Lockleys on the market gardens, the community developed a 'place consciousness' over three generations.[43] One 1.5-generation narrator, Maria Mazzarolo nee Compostella, a relative of market gardeners, who married and lived on Frogmore Road for more than 60 years in two different houses, spoke about the benefits of living there. Maria summed up her feelings, beginning by referring to the sense of community among the retired market gardeners:

> It was still there especially when people knew each other … [E]verybody was retired down this area … Well, to me this is like a home, a second home. That's all. I would not shift from here to go anywhere else. No way. No.[44]

Maria's first home was the house in which she lived with her parents and brothers on the south side of the River Torrens. It was a significant home, found by her father, who arrived in Adelaide in 1938 and reunited with his wife and three children nine years later. Before migration, the family had shared accommodation in a large multigenerational household in Caselle di Altivole. Maria lived with her parents until she was married, when she and her husband built a house on Frogmore Road near relatives and *paesani*. After some years, Maria and her husband and children moved to another house on Frogmore Road that had been built by first-generation market gardeners. Maria's affection for Frogmore Road communicates her deep feeling for the place where she married, raised her family and continued to live as a neighbour to other *veneti*, although the composition of the locality changed over the six decades that she lived there.

---

42 Diana Panazzolo nee Santin foreshadowed the visit when she was interviewed some years earlier. OH 872/27, 13 September 2013: 20–21.
43 Shopes, 'Oral History and the Study of Communities', 593–94.
44 Maria Mazzarolo nee Compostella, OH 872/30, 23 April 2014: 18.

Plate 8.4: The Mazzarolo family: Lina, Sonia, Maria and Arsenio, Frogmore Road, c. 1972
Source: Photo supplied by Maria Mazzarolo nee Compostella.

Narrators who were born on family market gardens acknowledged their attachment to the *paese*, where they felt the strength of belonging to a community of other families with the same heritage. Second-generation woman Denise Doyban nee Santin spoke about her attachment to Frogmore Road, where two sets of grandparents, her parents, uncles and aunts had worked their large market gardens:

> [I was b]orn at [number] 40, lived at 36 and then got married and moved to 38 … I'm not going anywhere. No … I think it's just part of me … I've never really wanted to live anywhere else … My oldest daughter, Nicole, she lives at number 36 now … In my Mum's home, yeah, Mum and Dad's home. And we've still got the gate between the two houses.[45]

---

45 Denise Doyban nee Santin, OH 872/62, 8 December 2021: 50.

Denise had earlier referred to the closeness of the community of Veneto market-gardener families who continued to live on Frogmore Road: 'I told you, we're all related here.'[46]

Narrators in both the 1.5 and the second generations attribute meaning to the market gardens, the place of settlement, in a way that implies that Lockleys is the 'second place of origin'.[47] They understand it as the place of settlement for the first generation and the location where families established themselves and achieved *sistemazione*. That place has assumed significance for second-generation narrators because they were born and grew up there. It remains a site of belonging even for those who no longer live there. For example, Sandra Conci nee Santin spoke about the changes that had occurred on Frogmore Road in her lifetime. Sandra was born in 1947 and lived for the first two years of her life on Valetta Road before her parents, uncles and aunts moved to a market garden on Frogmore Road. Sandra spoke about her sense of home although, at the time of the interview, she had not lived there for more than five decades. Her memories linked back to her grandparents to whom she was very close:

> It's changed a lot. I go down there and it still feels as if it's Frogmore Road, the place I knew back all those years ago … And you picture as you go down that my grandfather's house is still there and I can imagine that was their land and I can still visualise that. No, it's still nice down there. It feels [like] home even though I haven't lived there for fifty years, it always feels [like] home there.[48]

Movements away from the *paese*

While the first and 1.5 generations continued to live on house blocks on the properties that had been their market gardens, the community experienced disruptions in the 1960s. Circumstances changed as families sold market gardens and the first and 1.5 generations retired. Changes also came with the deaths and re-migration of some of the first generation. By the end of the 1960s, 13 members of that group had either died or returned to live in the Veneto region, which was enjoying an economic boom. After years of arduous physical labour on the market gardens, the two older generations improved their financial status, gained more leisure time and

---

46 ibid., 22.
47 Fortier, 'Re-Membering Places and the Performance of Belonging(s)', 46–47.
48 Sandra Conci nee Santin, OH 872/47, 25 August 2018: 36.

took opportunities to visit their families in the Veneto or travel more widely. Second-generation sons and daughters finished school, moved away from the market gardens to employment and came of age, undertaking the processes of *sistemazione*: marriage and raising their own families. Some moved outside the family and community boundaries and, consequently, the composition of the *paese* transformed.

For its first three decades, the community of Veneto market gardeners had enjoyed a social life built mostly around the relationships in the *paese*. From the early 1960s, some families had become members of the Casa d'Italia, a pan-Italian social organisation in Adelaide that brought together Italians from different regions and reflected the postwar increase of the Italian population in South Australia. Two first-generation Veneto market gardeners, Giuseppe Ballestrin and Eugenio Zalunardo, were foundation members of the South Australian Italian Association (SAIA).[49] This body was formalised in 1967 'to promote and facilitate activity as an umbrella organisation to connect all Italians in South Australia, and to promote outreach to the wider community'.[50] At the time, Ballestrin and Zalunardo, who had been in Australia for 32 years, undertook a significant commitment to belong to this organisation.

Six men in the 1.5 generation became foundation members of the SAIA in 1967: the three Santin brothers, Lui, Vito and Romildo, and Luigi, Albert and Orlando Tonellato. Lui Santin was also a member of the Building Fund Committee, which suggests he took an even greater responsibility for the establishment of the association. Although the men had received education to compulsory age in Australia and some of them mixed with Anglo-Australians through sporting activities, they were drawn to join an association formed as a 'second home' for the social life and wellbeing of Italians in South Australia. Lui Santin and Luigi Tonellato were identified as volunteers who doorknocked Italian men to ask them to become members and provide funds to establish the centre. The active participation in the establishment of the Casa d'Italia suggests that some in the 1.5-generation families developed a strong affiliation with the wider Italian community in Adelaide.

---

49   Cosmini and Glenn, *La Seconda Casa*, 148–49.
50   ibid., 63–64, 149. The authors outline the genesis of the SAIA in two previous organisations that had supported the wellbeing of Italians in the state: the Catholic Italian Welfare Association (1949–65) and the Italian Australian Centre (1965–67).

The men supported the vision of developing a place of connection for migrants who could feel 'at home' in the company of other Italians even in the period when the Australian Government promoted assimilation.[51] Oscar Mattiazzo, another narrator and brother-in-law of the Santin brothers who had a wider range of friends and business contacts outside the Veneto community, was a member of the first SAIA committee in 1967–68. Oscar explained the reasons for his involvement in the association:

> Yes, I was on the committee of the Italian Association, in Carrington Street, [the] Italian Club, and that's the only club that I joined … because that was, to me, that was Italian, because I feel greatly this way, that when you're in another country like now we're in Australia, when you're in Australia, you're Italian, and when you're in Italy, you're regional, you're Veneto, Calabrese, Molfetta or whatever the case may be, but I feel very strongly that when I'm here that I don't say that I'm a Veneto, I'm an Italian, because I feel that we should all be together as we came out here.[52]

The association opened its new premises in 1972 at a time when multicultural policies created possibilities for ethnic groups to establish their own centres in a more inclusive environment. The centre in Adelaide quickly became a venue for intergenerational groups of Italian Australians to gather in large numbers and participate in social events and regional associations like the Veneto Club began building their own facilities. The Casa d'Italia became a popular venue for all age groups, hosting functions, wedding receptions and providing Italian meals. Young people attended Sunday evening dances with live music that could attract more than 200 people in the 1970s.[53]

By the 1970s, the idea of preserving the *paese* at Lockleys was not the shared priority it had been for the community in the previous 35 or so years. The Australian population had become more diverse through postwar migration initiatives and government policies reflected the need to respond to the increasingly multicultural context. There was bipartisan agreement that multiculturalism must replace earlier policies of assimilation and integration. In July 1976 the Liberal government established the federal Department of Immigration and Ethnic Affairs and the services and programs available to migrants were reviewed in a report published two

---

51   The vision of establishing the Casa d'Italia was finally realised in 1967 by the SAIA Incorporated. Cosmini and Glenn, *La Seconda Casa*, 55.
52   Oscar Mattiazzo, OH 872/13, 13 April 2011: 187.
53   Christine Rebellato nee Mattiazzo, Personal communication, 20 October 2020.

years later. It recommended new approaches to increasing the rights of and opportunities for migrants and improving access to services and programs. It also proposed providing financial support to ethnic groups and associations for special projects.[54] The report prepared the way for ethnic communities with large cohorts of postwar migrants to develop their own organisations and associations. By 1977, nearly 2,000 ethnic organisations and media platforms had been formed, reflecting the multicultural composition of the Australian population.[55] The identity of separate groups in the Italian population was strengthened as different regions established their own clubs and associations across the country.

The Veneto Club in South Australia was officially registered in 1972 and some market gardeners were foundation members. It was established to cater for all people from the Veneto, although, at first, the membership comprised only men and included more postwar migrants than those who had migrated between the wars. A substantial membership fee was required to join the club—something one narrator described as an excessive amount, which he recalled was twice his weekly wage at the time.[56] However, 300 men became members before the foundation stone was laid in 1973.[57] Initially, many in the older generation of market gardeners were not attracted to the idea of the club, relying on familiar ways of socialising and gathering in homes to share hospitality and companionship. Some of those in the first and the 1.5 generations who had joined the SAIA also became foundation members of the Veneto Club. When members of the older generation saw the success of the large social gatherings at the Veneto Club and the opportunities to mix with a larger group of *veneti*, they participated in events such as the large Sunday night dinner dances.[58]

---

54   Frank Galbally, 'Migrant Services and Programs—Summary', in *Review of Post Arrival Programs and Services for Migrants Migrant Services and Programs*, Parliamentary Paper No. 164 (Canberra: Australian Government Publishing Service, 1978), 3–13, 15–28, www.multiculturalaustralia.edu.au/doc/galbally_1.pdf.
55   James Jupp, *From White Australia to Woomera: The Story of Australian Immigration* (Cambridge: Cambridge University Press, 2002), 27–29, doi.org/10.1017/CBO9781139195034.
56   Johnny Tormena, OH 872/18, 7 July 2012: 62.
57   Veneto Club Adelaide Inc., *In 84 Domeniche Nasce il Veneto Club*.
58   Gino Innocente and Rinaldo Secca, Personal communication, 11 August 2021.

Plate 8.5: Amelia and Silvano Zampin celebrate their fiftieth wedding anniversary at the Veneto Club, Beverley, 1981
Note: With their daughters Milva, Bruna, Roma, Angela, Christine, Virginia, Sandra and Cynthia (seated).
Source: Photo supplied by the Zampin family.

Members of the community gave their time, skills and equipment to the construction of the club's facilities over 84 Sundays.[59] Veneto tradesmen contributed their labour; some second-generation Veneto market gardeners used their equipment to level the ground, assisted with erecting steel works and contributed in other practical ways. In 1974, the Veneto Club opened its facilities about 4 kilometres from the market garden area and hosted social events, cultural activities and an extensive sporting program that included first-, second- and third-generation Veneto Australians. Events that market gardeners had held previously in packing sheds such as baptism parties, birthdays, wedding receptions and anniversaries began to be celebrated at the Veneto Club.

Although clubs were not part of cultural practices in Italy, the new generation who had arrived after the war was interested in retaining Veneto culture and mixing with other *veneti* through the social events and other

---

59 See 'About the Veneto Club Adelaide' for a summary of the history of the Veneto Club of Adelaide: www.venetoclubadelaide.com.au/veneti-in-adelaide.

programs of the Veneto Club.⁶⁰ The *veneti* wanted to speak dialect within an environment where they felt at home. Families attended social events, and sporting activities like netball, basketball and *bocce* enabled women to represent the club. In the wider Veneto community, the existence of the club facilitated a sense of ownership and belonging among *veneti* and the growing membership in the 1970s was evidence of the need for a venue where they could speak dialect and identify as a regional group of Italians in South Australia. Although membership of the club diminished as the postwar generation aged and died, it continued to exist, albeit in a different form from the vision of its founders, especially when the venue had to be sold in 2014 because of financial challenges. However, the club realigned itself with new accommodation arrangements and, in November 2024, there were more than 400 members, a small number of whom are descendants of the Veneto market gardeners.

Identity and multiculturalism

Multicultural policies provided scope for migrant communities to form their distinctive clubs and associations in Australia in the 1970s and rejected assimilationist protocols and practices. The multicultural approach created an idealised concept of Australia as a place where people from many cultures could participate equally. However, the Anglo-Australian ideal remained pivotal and multiculturalism became a vehicle for 'inducing pride in people's "ethnic heritage" and in Australia's cultural diversity'.⁶¹ The impact of multiculturalism allowed groups like the *veneti* in South Australia to develop their own cultural centre and place of belonging. Transnational associations such as the Trevisani nel Mondo for people who had roots in the Veneto province of Treviso were significant for supporting provincial identity in Australia. In 1999, 80 Italian Australian associations were active in South Australia, including in regional areas;⁶² most had been established in the 1970s after Australia officially became 'multicultural'.

Some narrators spoke about their sense of identity and growing pride in being Italian as they became older. One notable example is Norma Camozzato nee Ballestrin, who articulated the development of her identity through her life:

---

60   Baldassar and Pesman, *From Paesani to Global Italians*, 121–22.
61   Hsu-Ming Teo, cited in Arapakis, 'Ethnic Compartmentalisation', 145.
62   Antonio Cocchiaro, 'The History and Future of Italo-Australian Associations in South Australia', in *Proceedings: The First Conference on the Impact of Italians in South Australia, 16–17 July 1993*, eds Desmond O'Connor and Antonio Comin (Adelaide: Italian Congress, The Italian Discipline, Flinders University of South Australia, 1993), 67–77.

> Once upon a time, I'd say, 'I'm Australian, definitely Australian.' If somebody asks me, I say, 'I'm Australian but I have Italian parents.' I've changed a bit … Maybe I'm older, maybe the world is different. I like being part of the Trevisani, [I'm] proud of it, I suppose … [O]nce upon a time, I'd say, 'I'm Australian' and then I'd come out and say, 'My parents were Italian.' But now yeah, I'm Italian, yeah, I'm Australian, yeah, I'm half and half, yeah I'm part of this, I'm part of the Italian group. Maybe I'm not ashamed.[63]

Norma clarified her status in relation to her age and with a reference to the times in which she now lives. She can declare proudly that both her parents were born in Italy and she has Italian heritage without feeling the shame she experienced as a young girl when she was one of a very few who had her ears pierced—a feature that made her feel self-conscious and part of a group with a foreign culture in Anglo-Australia. As a woman in her mid-seventies, she had thrown off the stigma of being a 'wog' and perhaps this was an advantage of multicultural Australia for her generation.

Redefining the *paese*

Belonging to the *paese* at Lockleys was always the first choice for the Veneto market gardeners and their families because of the reciprocity within the community and the security of proxy family relationships that contrasted with the lack of interest and early hostility of the Anglo-Australian world. Consequently, there was little incentive for the first generation to move outside the boundaries of the Lockleys market garden area. With the deaths of the first generation and many in the 1.5 generation, the network of families changed, although relationships continued through informal connections. However, a redefinition of the *paese* created new prospects for the 1.5 and second generations, especially through the intervention of two forms of media.

First, narrators recorded their memories of the community from its origins in the 1930s to the loss of the market gardens in the 1970s through the community oral history project. Second, the Veneto market gardeners' website created possibilities for descendants to listen to interviews with members of other families, view photos and documents, write blogs and interact with writers. The sons and daughters who grew up on the

---

63   Norma Camozzato nee Ballestrin, OH 872/37, 21 September 2016: 32.

gardens have participated in the collection of historical evidence about the family market-gardening enterprises that were part of the social and economic history of the area now known as Kidman Park and Flinders Park. The website, launched in 2014, created a virtual *paese* and a site of belonging for the 1.5- and second-generation narrators and descendants of the first generation of market gardeners.[64] The website also embodies the circular connection between the two places of origin for the Veneto market-gardener families.

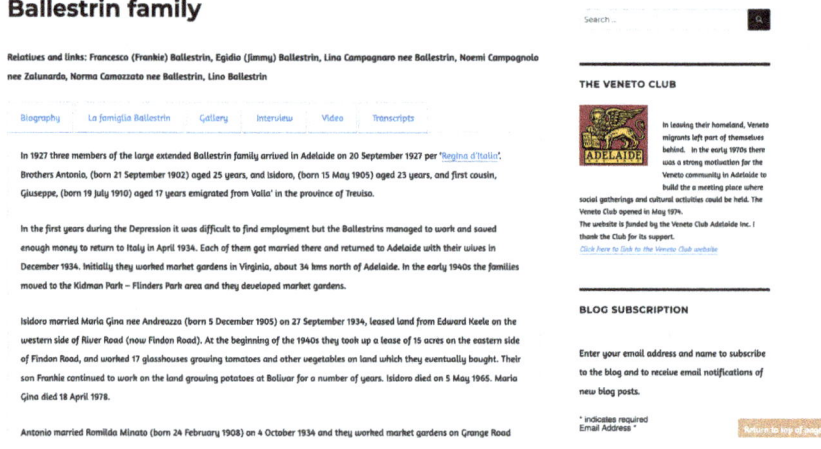

Plate 8.6: Example of a family biography page on the Veneto Market Gardeners 1927 website
Source: venetimarketgardeners1927.net, accessed 2 March 2023.

A regular blog on the website reconstructs the *paese* through the histories of individual families and work on the market gardens, customs related to food, rituals at Christmas and Easter, and the meaning of Australian-Veneto identity. The participation of guest bloggers from Adelaide, Melbourne, the Veneto and Canada reflects local and transnational interest in the history of the market-gardener community and family histories and accounts of migration. In 2022, one-third of the blogs were written by guests.[65] Eulogies

---

64 In 2013, the local council, the City of Charles Sturt, provided a cultural heritage grant to develop the website.
65 See examples of guest blogs on the Veneto Market Gardeners 1927 website: Irene Zampin, 'The Three Simeoni Sisters', 8 March 2020, venetimarketgardeners1927.net/the-three-simeoni-sisters/; Aida Innocente, 'A Child Discovering Italy', 22 May 2022, venetimarketgardeners1927.net/a-child-discovering-italy/; Rosa Parletta, 'Giovanni Ballestrin's Story', 8 May 2022, venetimarketgardeners1927.net/giovanni-ballestrins-story/; Remo Berno and Madeleine Regan, 'The Mezzadria System', 15 September 2019, venetimarketgardeners1927.net/?s=mezzadria+system.

were added at the suggestion of families and provide a permanent record of the story of individuals and their experience as migrants in Australia. Several eulogies were added during the Covid-19 pandemic when restrictions prevented attendance at funerals and their online publication enabled wider access to the stories of people's lives.

In 2015, the National Library of Australia added the website to its PANDORA (Preserving and Accessing Networked Documentary Resources of Australia) archive of web publications and websites that have cultural and research significance. The items are selected in partnership with state libraries. A copy of the website is archived annually, in a national database to ensure its preservation.[66] The website is now formally acknowledged by the wider Veneto community. In 2021, after seven years of the website's existence, the Veneto Club Incorporated Adelaide guaranteed the future of the website by contributing funds to its maintenance costs. Angelo Piovesan, the second-generation relative of an original market-gardener family, advocated for the annual funds and affirmed the role of the website in the context of the community of the previous generation:

> [The] work over the life of this project has been a source of enormous pleasure for the Veneti families and their friends, and will continue to give pleasure to our children, grandchildren—and I hope the many generations that follow us. It has become a source of great pride to not only see our migrant heritage preserved, but it has also become a means for us all to share our stories and to unite us again into a community which closely resembled the spirit shared by our parents and relatives in those early times of migration. I also grew up amongst nearly all of the Pioneering Families and thought I knew a lot about their families ... I became addicted to reading about their family backgrounds!! It allowed me to group together their family members into a structure—much the same [as] I had done many years earlier in drawing up our Family Tree.[67]

As both a source of knowledge and a resource, the website develops an understanding of the ongoing transformation of a migrant community in Australia and the widening circles of interactions with each successive generation. Memories of parents, grandparents and great-grandparents

---

66   See: webarchive.nla.gov.au/awa/20240411140025/https://venetimarketgardeners1927.net/.
67   Angelo Piovesan, email communication to the Veneto Club Adelaide Inc., 19 January 2021. I was copied into the email correspondence and it is reproduced with permission.

accessed on the website are passed down as intimate migration stories and oral testimony that communicate ideas about families in the context of identity, belonging and change.

Opening memories

When they recall the experience of the *paese* and the lives of the market-gardener families, narrators project an image of community as 'common ground … a ground that is material, but also virtual, real and imaginary'.[68] The shared experiences of growing up on a market garden surrounded by other Veneto and Italian families are real for the narrators; they also represent the memories and the mostly idealised stories of the *paese* at Lockleys. The website created a space where memories of the market gardens and belonging to an early migrant community are shared through the voices and images of three generations and it continues to attract new visitors more than a decade after it was first established.

The *paese* has been redefined by recent generations and the emotional attachment to the community has transformed over nine decades. Although the market-gardener families gradually became part of the Veneto community in South Australia and the South Australian community more broadly, descendants have maintained the identity and history that connect them to their parents' *paese* at Lockleys. Attachment to the place of origin in the Veneto region is a continuous thread in the interviews and in the archive of communal memories on the website. However, the market gardens where the *veneti* settled and created their life in Australia have always been the heart of the story now preserved in the memories of the first, 1.5, second and third generations of the community.

---

68 Sara Ahmed and Anne-Marie Fortier, 'Re-Imagining Communities', *International Journal of Cultural Studies* 6, no. 3 (2003): 251–59, doi.org/10.1177/13678779030063001, at 257.

9

Conclusion: Continuity of the *paese*

> It's important that people know what happened in those years, because one thing that I've found lacking in growing up in Australia … is that we don't know what happened just before we were born, or just before the war, or what people—how people lived—Australians lived just before the war in the 1920s and the 1930s. We grew up in a period … [of] abundance, and where everything was readily available, and work was readily available but it hasn't always been that way, and no-one's ever delved into the fact that things do change, things weren't always this way, and even Australians like Italians, like Germans—they all went through this period of poverty where there wasn't a lot of work, and … there was hardships and stuff, but we were never exposed to that at school … And it's important that people realise that it hasn't always been this way.
>
> —Giuseppe Chiumento, 2018[1]

Giuseppe Chiumento, a second-generation relative of a Veneto market-gardener family, speaks about the history of Italian migration in Australia in this extract from his interview.[2] Born in Wollongong, New South Wales, in 1958, he now lives in Italy. Although he grew up in a strong Italian

---

1   Giuseppe Chiumento interviewed by Madeleine Regan, Transcript, J.D. Somerville Oral History Collection, State Library of South Australia, Adelaide, OH872/55, 3 November 2018: 32.
2   Giuseppe Chiumento is married to Monica Urbani, a great niece of Vittorio Marchioro, who migrated from Malo, Italy, in 1927. Giuseppe and Monica live in Monte di Malo in the province of Vicenza in the Veneto. There is a strong link between the Marchioro families in Adelaide, Malo and Monte di Malo.

community, Giuseppe acknowledges that he did not appreciate that there had been different phases of Italian migration to Australia—a realisation that highlights the separation between 'the history of Australia, and people's perception of that history'.³ He speaks from the experience of his own family's migration and his transnational life nine decades after the first generation of Veneto market gardeners arrived in Australia.

Plate 9.1: Giuseppe Chiumento and his wife, Monica Urbani, Malo, Italy, 2018
Source: Madeleine Regan.

---

3   Clark, 'Private Lives, Public History', 121.

Giuseppe contrasts the overarching theme of the hardship of *contadino* life and the earlier period of migration with subsequent periods of abundance in Australia. It is poverty, he asserts, that connected diverse migrant groups such as Italians and Germans in Australia in the interwar years. This study of the Veneto market gardeners at Lockleys examines the development of the community that evolved through the transformation of a *paese* from its roots in the Veneto culture. Through the oral histories, the group biography moves the narrative of the small group of Veneto migrants from a period of transient mobility in the early years of the Depression in Australia, through World War II, to the achievement of *sistemazione* and the pathways taken by the second generation after the market gardens at Lockleys finished. It documents the continuity of the migrant community, intergenerational links and the transnational dimension maintained by descendants.

The first generation formed their identity as market gardeners and provided a future for their children that was the culmination of decisions and opportunities that enabled them to achieve *sistemazione* and create a sense of belonging in their new homeland through adapting their *contadino* experience and adjusting to the social structures in Australia over five decades.[4] The history of the Veneto market-gardener community began in the most difficult of times for Italian and other southern European migrants who arrived early in the Depression. Their existence in that early period was the antithesis of the ordered, if poor, life of the *contadino* family household. Had a functioning chain migration system been in place, an existing nuclear community would likely have welcomed the first generation of *veneti* as new migrants.[5] However, the economic situation and hostility of Anglo-Australia militated against an easy transition. Instead, the new arrivals confronted a prolonged period of itinerant labour caused by the Depression.

The first generation of *veneti* adapted and expanded the model of Veneto men returning to their family household from seasonal migration. After scattering across South Australia and other states for several years seeking work, the men returned to the boarding houses of Adelaide and found land at Lockleys and companionship with other *veneti*. The Veneto men who had arrived alone gradually incorporated their wives and children and created a community. By degrees, a new *paese* came into being as a

---

4   Samuel L. Baily, *Immigrants in the Lands of Promise: Italians in Buenos Aires and New York City, 1870–1914* (Ithaca: Cornell University Press, 2004), 91.
5   Veneto migrants who settled in central and East Gippsland in Victoria between the wars were drawn to the area by family members or men from the same villages through chain migration. See Davine, *Vegnimo da Conco Ma Simo Veneti*, 52–55.

place the first generation could experience as home for family members and *paesani* and, later, for Veneto migrants who arrived after the war. They initiated what became a permanent life as market gardeners and developed the processes of *sistemazione*.

Based on their experience as *contadini*, the initial group adapted ancient cultivation practices to incorporate glasshouses and grow new varieties of vegetables. The first-generation community made another significant modification in adjusting the regulated structures of the patriarchal intergenerational households of the Veneto to accommodate new roles as self-employed market gardeners with wives who worked beside husbands in the *paese* at Lockleys.[6] The formation of the *paese* at Lockleys enabled the initial group to tolerate the separation from the relationships, traditions and culture they had left behind in their Veneto villages as they developed processes of *sistemazione* and raised families on the market gardens. The absence of intergenerational family support was ameliorated by the social networks formed with *paesani*, who became proxy family members.

The flattened hierarchical structures of the *paese* at Lockleys modified the demarcation of roles in the Veneto land system, especially in the early years when individual families set up their market gardens from a similar low economic base. The concentration of the group of families at Lockleys from the 1930s made it possible to develop a community that nurtured Veneto identity even as it encountered a xenophobic Anglo-Australia in which tensions were exacerbated during the Depression and World War II. The group replicated the traditional social networks of extended family in the absence of government, formal religious or other social support structures.

By the 1950s, the Veneto market gardeners had overcome challenges that had threatened the stability of some other Italian communities across Australia including the re-migration of a few families.[7] The first generation not only survived but also evolved into an expanded *paese* that absorbed the postwar wave of Veneto migrants who were integrated into the community at Lockleys. In Australia, the period of postwar economic stimulus with

---

6   Christiane Harzig and Dirk Hoerder, with Donna R. Gabbacia, *What Is Migration History?* (Hoboken: Wiley, 2009), 106. The authors argue that migration and settlement can enable migrants to adopt gender-specific roles in their new country.

7   For example, interwar Italian communities diminished in the rural area of Lismore in New South Wales in the 1960s. See Jenkins, *Power of the Land*, 237–57. The small group of Sicilian market gardeners at Werribee, Victoria, were evicted from their leaseholds in the late 1940s and found separate landholdings. The economic situation had improved in Italy by the mid-1960s, which led to increased re-migration.

increased manufacturing initiatives drew large numbers of Italians who were mostly from rural areas and unskilled.[8] Some in the market-gardener families entered employment in local manufacturing industries. Many new migrants benefited from the sponsorship arrangements provided by the Veneto market gardeners in their first years after arrival and their contribution made it possible for the production increases that the market demanded during the early postwar years in South Australia.

Between 1940 and 1960, on average, the annual population of Adelaide grew by 3 per cent and expanded from 380,000 to 582,100, with large increases in urban areas.[9] The Veneto market gardeners at Lockleys, and those with land at Bolivar, responded to the increased need for fresh vegetables in South Australia in that period. As small landholders, they were subject to the expansion of subdivisions and increasing land prices that changed inner suburban areas like Lockleys and, by the mid-1960s, urban market gardens in Adelaide diminished.[10] Maintaining the viability of family market gardens was a challenge when large-scale vegetable growers entered the market and supermarkets influenced production. By the 1970s, the first generation, and many in the 1.5 generation, had aged or died. Most of those in the second generation did not take up employment in the market gardens, however, the first generation did not take the option to leave the stability of the *paese* at Lockleys.

Belonging to the *paese*

Lockleys was more than the location of a diasporic migrant group. The narrators in their interviews looked back on their parents' market gardens at Lockleys as a place with a personality and identity. The legacy of the *paese* is evident in the accounts of the first, 1.5- and second-generation narrators who acknowledged the role of market gardens as home, family workplace and *paese*—an idealised place.

---

8   Simone Battiston and Bruno Mascitelli, 'Migration, Ethnic Concentration and International Trade Growth: The Case of Italians in Australia', *People and Place* 15, no. 4 (2007): 23–24.
9   Smith, 'Market Gardening at Adelaide's Urban Fringe', 20.
10 The subdivision also affected the group of Bulgarian market gardeners 2 kilometres to the west of the Veneto families at Lockleys. Wilkins, *Bulgarian Migration and Market Gardens*, 16.

Plate 9.2: Children of the Ballestrin, Marchioro, Piovesan and Tonellato families in front of the Tonellato truck, Frogmore Road, c. 1946–47
Note: Six of the seven in this group were interviewed for this study.
Source: Photo supplied by Assunta Giovannini nee Tonellato.

In their interviews, first-generation couple Angelina and Vittorio Marchioro contrasted their life in retirement with the period when they began working their market gardens together in the late 1930s. While they referred to their origins in and links with relatives in the Veneto, the market gardens at Lockleys—the place and the community in which they lived, worked and raised their family—was where they achieved *sistemazione*. They found their bearings, worked in partnership to earn their livelihood, raised their children and enjoyed the network of *paesani* at Lockleys. They made visits to Italy and maintained transnational relationships with their relatives in the Veneto, which continue to be nurtured by their sons and daughters and their families.

Plate 9.3: Group of Veneto families on one of the market gardens, early 1950s
Source: Photo supplied by Terry Mazzarolo nee Zampin.

Although they used the Australian administrative processes to satisfy their ambition to be self-employed on the land and become naturalised, the first generation concentrated on the achievement of *sistemazione* in families and in the *paese* rather than on assimilation to British Australia. Ricatti acknowledges the migrants' need for security in the family unit and home as a mechanism for families to inhabit 'a space relatively protected from the racism and discrimination they experience in the broader society'.[11] The physical boundaries of the *paese* opened as the market gardens began to disappear in the late 1950s and early 1960s as urban subdivisions crept into these suburbs. In addition, generational changes, the demise of the market gardens, the re-migration of a few significant families and the wave of new Italian migrants from the Veneto created new opportunities. The incorporation of these 'new Australians' reinforced intergenerational links with relatives and *paesani* in the Veneto region, deepening the transnational dimension of migration at Lockleys. While the first generation adopted some transcultural strategies and actions, the 1.5 generation developed these further and it was the second generation who took the initiative to move the focus of life in Australia beyond the market gardens.

---

11   Ricatti, *Italians in Australia*, 77.

In the second-generation cohort, most took occupational choices that flowed from increased education and employment options and postwar economic development. Even after land became a commodity and the Veneto market gardeners profited from its sale, they stayed at Lockleys, in contrast to theories that migrants often seek 'geographic and social mobility' after they have established themselves in their new country.[12] The configuration of the market gardens at Lockleys as a *paese* enabled the families to experience a connection, both physical and emotional, that allowed the first-generation men and women—and most of the 1.5 generation—to enjoy the comfort of living close to their *paesani* in old age.

Plate 9.4: Baptism of Remo Berno, Adelaide, 1953
Note: Remo's parents, Pietro and Antonietta Berno, and godparents, Angelina and Vittorio Marchioro, with other *paesani*.
Source: Photo supplied by the Berno family.

---

12   Huber refers to the greater opportunities for migrants in urban areas to move as they gain more prosperity as an example of internal migration. Huber, *From Pasta to Pavlova*, 137. For examination of the mobility of the interwar generation, see Price, *Southern Europeans in Australia*, 190–97. For discussion of employment and the socioeconomic mobility of postwar Italians in Australia, see Lampugnani and Holton, 'Ethnic Business in South Australia'; and Ricatti, *Italians in Australia*, 35–51.

The continuity of the *paese* through the generations

The community did not dissolve with the passing of the first and 1.5 generations. Although the second generation has had access to different educational, employment and social interactions, they retain a form of the networks that assisted the first generation in settling on the market gardens. The children born in Australia to first- and 1.5-generation parents have redefined their attachment to the *paese* and developed an identity as descendants of the Veneto market gardeners. The relational community of the *paese* is a thread that connects the descendants of the market gardeners today long after the disappearance of the physical site of the gardens and the deaths of the first generation.[13]

Geographer Doreen Massey states that place provides meaning and is associated with the formation of 'belonging, identity and security', but it is not static and relies on 'social relations which interact at a particular location'.[14] Although no longer defined by their occupation and the land, the descendants of the Veneto market gardeners have retained an identity characterised by the 'old people' or *paesani* who spoke the Veneto dialect, followed its customs and cultural practices and shared the experience of working market gardens and owning land at Lockleys. The second, and sometimes the third, generation has retained their parents' belief that the community is a proxy family.

The living *paese*

Second-generation man Silvano Ballestrin explained the connections between *paesani* and recalled the family tradition of *fiò* or visiting one another at the end of the working day. Silvano offered a key to understanding the bonds in the market-gardener community as a *paese*:

> We all worked very hard, as did all the Italian families living in the Findon, Flinders Park, Kidman Park and Lockleys area. Every man, woman and child laboured to help their families … [T]he Italians did not have a great need to learn English as they mixed and socialised

---

13 For discussion of the emotional attachment to place and the imaginary boundaries that people can construct around a place that might constitute home, see Peter Read, *Returning to Nothing: The Meaning of Lost Places* (Melbourne: Cambridge University Press, 1996), doi.org/10.1017/CBO9781139085069, 2.
14 Massey, 'A Place Called Home'.

among themselves, helping each other out, as in a community …
This *paese* in the western suburbs was, and *is* alive and well and the
fiòs [regular visits to other Veneto families] promulgated these events
… [T]he various *feste* [festivals] showed how much the Australian
version of the *fiò* informally helped them to bond and form a new
paese, comfortably surrounded by friends and relatives.[15]

Silvano Ballestrin acknowledges that the social customs brought families together and drew on traditions brought from the Veneto region, which the community transformed at Lockleys. For the first three decades, the first and 1.5 generations kept their boundaries at Lockleys tight as they overcame the hurdles of a meagre education and poverty in Italy and xenophobia and marginalisation in Australia and developed their market gardens. Their descendants, like Silvano, acknowledge the continuity of the *paese* even as the families have become part of the wider population and expanded their sense of belonging in Australia.

Plate 9.5: Representatives of first-generation market-gardener families at a gathering, Seaton, South Australia, 22 October 2022
Note: From left: Francesco Ballestrin, Silvano Ballestrin, Alan Santin, Johnny Marchioro, Egidio Ballestrin and Lena Moscheni nee Rossetto.
Source: Alex Bennett.

---

15   Ballestrin, 'Parties and Festivals'.

Angelo Piovesan's parents were relatives of a market gardener and arrived in Australia in 1950, living in a shed on the land of one of the market gardeners. Angelo described the friendships in the group today and confirmed that members of the first generation established the social network of *veneti*:

> I think we were all just friends from birth basically. And you all went to the same schools, went to the same church, saw each other on social outings, generally all got invited to the same weddings.[16]

Many in the second generation have developed connections to their parents' home villages because they have visited and because their parents inculcated their attachment to the place of origin. In a similar custom, Greek Australians in the second and third generations continue to refer to their families' country of origin although they have lived in Australia for much of or all their adulthood.[17] There are strong connections even in the third generation of the Veneto market-gardener families who have visited the villages of their grandparents.

Recognising Veneto traditions

The snapshot of Louis Ballestrin and his family illustrates the transmission of Veneto heritage to the second and third generations in Australia. Louis was born in 1950 in Adelaide, the son of first-generation Veneto market gardeners. In his interview, Louis reflected on how he acquired knowledge of the Veneto villages where his parents were born. When he was 13 years old, Louis visited Italy with his parents and sister and stayed with relatives for nine months, gaining an understanding of the networks of his paternal and maternal families in the province of Treviso. Louis married Janette, an Anglo-Australian woman who died when their three children were adolescents. The children had formed a close relationship with their Veneto grandparents who had lived close by on land that had been part of their market garden. Through this attachment, they observed the customs of a Veneto-Australian household, spent time in the company of their grandparents, who spoke the Veneto dialect, and preserved *contadino* practices of making salami and traditional food, growing vegetables and keeping chickens.

---

16   Angelo Piovesan interviewed by Madeleine Regan, Transcript, J.D. Somerville Oral History Collection, State Library of South Australia, Adelaide, OH 872/66, 28 November 2022: 18.
17   Lütfiye Ali and Christopher C. Sonn, 'Constructing Identity as a Second-Generation Cypriot Turkish in Australia: The Multi-Hyphenated Other', *Culture & Psychology* 16, no. 1 (2010): 416–36, at 419, cited in Pam Papadelos, '"Greeks Are Different to Australians": Understanding Identity Formation among Third-Generation Australians of Greek Heritage', *Ethnic and Racial Studies* 44, no. 11 (2021): 1975–94, doi.org/10.1080/01419870.2020.1813318, at 1976.

'I BUY THIS PIECE OF GROUND HERE'

Plate 9.6: Members of the Ballestrin family: Jacqueline and Simon Ballestrin with Ariana, Louis Ballestrin, Michelle Ballestrin and Fay Ballestrin with Archie Ballestrin-Egan, Castelfranco Veneto, Italy, 2017

Source: Photo provided by Louis Ballestrin.

Louis commented: 'Well, they [my children] knew my Mum and they used to eat down there and stay around there. And they can see the difference between an Australian household and an Italian household. And they liked it [laughs].'[18]

In the past 17 years, Louis has twice spent time in the Veneto region with his second wife, Fay. His children and grandchildren joined them on the visits and, on one occasion, they met relatives, one of whom lived in part of the original Ballestrin house. In response to a question about his identity, Louis acknowledged that he felt more Italian than Australian although it was a feeling of being 'between the two'. He added that he appreciated his heritage, which he sensed strongly on visits to the Veneto:

> Well, it helps me recognise the traditional Veneto customs that you have around the place and you enjoy it and then [that] brings back sort of memories of Italy, you know? When you walk around and everybody talks, some talk Veneto or some talk Italian, having this language around you, it's really nice.[19]

As members of the second and third generations, Louis and his wife and children have formed a physical connection to the homeland that sustains transnational family threads between Australia and the villages in which their ancestors lived and worked.[20]

The feeling of returning home

Elena Rebuli, a granddaughter of first-generation market gardeners, acknowledged her transnational family and sense of attachment to the Veneto region in a blog posted on the Veneto market gardeners' website.[21] Elena has a keen understanding of her grandparents' family history and has had the experience of 'returning' to Italy. She began the blog by providing the context of her father, who migrated as a child and returned to Italy to marry her mother after living in Adelaide for 30 years:

---

18 Louis Ballestrin interviewed by Madeleine Regan, Transcript, J.D. Somerville Oral History Collection, State Library of South Australia, Adelaide, OH 872/61, 2 December 2021: 39.
19 ibid., 39.
20 Loretta Baldassar, 'Migrant Visits over Time: Ethnographic Returning and the Technological Turn', *Global Networks* 23, no. 1 (2023): 160–73, doi.org/10.1111/glob.12393, at 162.
21 Elena Rebuli, 'Returning Home', *Veneto Market Gardeners 1927 Blog*, 10 June 2019, venetimarket gardeners1927.net/returning-home/.

My dad, Vito (Albino) Rebuli left Bigolino, Italy, in 1931, when he was seven, with his mother, sister and brother, to meet up with his father in Adelaide, South Australia. He went back to Italy in 1962 … He met my mother, Antonietta Danieli, during this trip, and they were married in her hometown of Caerano San Marco, Provincia di Treviso, in November of that year. They came to Australia shortly after that with the intention of returning to Italy to live at some time in the near future. My brother was born [in] August 1963 and I was born [in] January 1965. As a family, we left Australia on May 21, 1968 … We ended up staying in Italy for one year. The decision to return [to Adelaide] was mostly because of my Dad's sense of loyalty to his mother and disabled sister who were back in Adelaide. My mother agreed it was the best thing for us despite the fact it meant she had no one at all from her side of the family in Australia and she was leaving all of her family behind … I have been fortunate to return twice as an adult and have always maintained a strong connection with Italy. I have always felt like I was returning home when I was there.[22]

Plate 9.7: Vito Rebuli and Antonietta Danieli, Monte Grappa War Memorial, province of Treviso, Italy, 1962
Source: Photo supplied by Elena Rebuli.

22 ibid.

Elena's description of her connections to the Veneto demonstrates the continuity of transnational family connections maintained by descendants of the Veneto market gardeners. The website provided Elena with the opportunity to document a story of her family, the complexity of the circulatory migration that was embodied in her parents' experiences and the contradictions in the emotions that migrants can feel in the sense that there are moral obligations to family in two countries.[23] She communicates the significance of the lasting relationships with kin and place in the Veneto. Elena also demonstrates the emotional and complex perspective of her identity as a Veneto-Australian that has developed from childhood to adulthood.[24]

A type of nostalgia

Commonly woven into the narratives of migration are feelings of nostalgia—an emotion associated with separation from people and place in the country of origin. Second-generation migrants can also experience nostalgia and idealisation as they look to Italy and the villages from which their forebears migrated. They can also inherit this kind of nostalgia from the first generation.[25] Irene Zampin, who left Adelaide as an adolescent when her parents migrated back to Italy in the late 1960s, identifies with her place of birth as a kind of nostalgia.

Irene was born in Adelaide in 1952 and grew up on a market garden in the Lockleys area with her parents and siblings. In 1967, when her parents re-migrated, Irene was 15 years old and she experienced disruption in her education, language and friendships as the family undertook reorientation in the village of Riese Pio X. Irene's older sister, Teresa, remained in Adelaide because she had already married. Although the family unit was separated, there was a strong continuing affiliation between Adelaide and Riese Pio X, which included her parents making several trips back to Australia to see Teresa and her family.

---

23 Maruška Svašek, 'Who Cares? Families and Feelings in Movement', *Journal of Intercultural Studies* 29, no. 3 (2008): 213–30, doi.org/10.1080/07256860802169170, at 216.
24 Cathrin Vesna Anderson, 'Shame and Pride in Second-Generation German Identity in Melbourne, Australia: Emotions and White Ethnicity', *Journal of Ethnic and Migration Studies* 42, no. 9 (2016): 1439–54, doi.org/10.1080/1369183X.2015.1120660, at 1442, 1451.
25 See Marchetti-Mercer and Virga, *The Italian Diaspora in South Africa*, 83–92.

After 30 years, Irene made her first return visit to Adelaide and it raised emotional questions about her identity and sense of belonging. In her interview, Irene reflected on her nostalgia for Australia and compared her experience of displacement with her father's life as a migrant in Adelaide. She analysed the different kinds of nostalgia her father felt for his home country, his deep roots and the way of life in the Veneto:

> I remember the last time I went there [Adelaide] hoping I will feel better here in Italy. But only when I came back, I felt worse … So, I am afraid that if I go there again, I'll miss it more when I come back … I'm living well here and I used to live well there. My father, when he lived in Italy, he was really poor so he wasn't living very well. When he got there [to Australia] … he worked hard so it wasn't an easy life for him. So, it was another type of nostalgia. Mine is—I don't how to explain it—it's a country nostalgia. Instead, [for] my parents … there was a nostalgia to go back … to where they were born, where they had their *radici*, their roots.[26]

Plate 9.8: Marriage of Teresa Zampin and Lui Mazzarolo, Adelaide, 1965
Note: From left: Irene, Lui, Teresa, Delia and Nico with Dennis.
Source: Photo supplied by Irene Zampin.

---

26   Irene Zampin interviewed by Madeleine Regan, Transcript, J.D. Somerville Oral History Collection, State Library of South Australia, Adelaide, OH 872 /45, 23 June 2017: 56.

Irene explains her parents' nostalgia as born of the desire to return to their roots whereas Irene's feelings of nostalgia reflect an imagined life and identity as an Australian. Although Irene has lived away from Australia for more than 50 years and her husband, children and grandchildren live in the Veneto region, she sees Adelaide as her place of origin and has created memories of attachment and belonging. There is a sense of both continuity and discontinuity as she identifies with Adelaide, her sister, other relatives and the people in the community of Veneto market gardeners with whom she has maintained connections and affinity.

In a complicated narrative of nostalgia, Teresa Mazzarolo nee Zampin (Irene's older sister) spoke in her interview about her experience of separation when her family moved to Italy. Teresa had arrived in Adelaide in 1949 as a two-year-old and she married a year before her parents migrated back to Italy. She was 20 years old and committed to staying in Adelaide with her husband:

> My parents wanted to go back overseas and my Dad said I had to [go] back with them. And I said I was going to get married instead. So that's what I did ... I wouldn't have been happy ... I couldn't speak Italian. Oh, I spoke dialect but you know, it would have been hard for me. I had a job here.[27]

There were strong connections with the family through visits that included Teresa staying with her family in Riese Pio X, where, coincidentally, her husband was born. The emotional ties to family in the Veneto continued over the years although Teresa and her husband had children and grandchildren in Adelaide and were part of a strong social network including some other relatives. The pain of separation was heightened as her parents aged and Teresa was unable to be present for their funerals. The opportunities to communicate with her siblings via social media increased the regular contact and made it possible to feel connected and more involved in knowing about the family and the circumstances of beloved elderly aunts.[28] However, the feeling of being physically apart from her siblings and extended family in

---

27 Teresa Mazzarolo nee Zampin interviewed by Madeleine Regan, Transcript, J.D. Somerville Oral History Collection, State Library of South Australia, Adelaide, OH 872/64, 17 December 2021: 53.
28 Loretta Baldassar, Mihaela Nedelcu, Laura Merla, and Raelene Wilding, 'ICT-Based Co-Presence in Transnational Families and Communities: Challenging the Premise of Face-to-Face Proximity in Sustaining Relationships', *Global Networks* 16, no. 2 [SI] (April 2016), 133–44, doi.org/10.1111/glob.12108; Loretta Baldassar, 'De-Demonizing Distance in Mobile Family Lives: Co-Presence, Care Circulation and Polymedia as Vibrant Matter', *Global Networks* 16, no. 2 [SI] (April 2016): 145–63, doi.org/10.1111/glob.12109.

the Veneto has persisted and Teresa suggested that her desire to visit had increased with age.[29] In a close family that has been separated through migration, decisions made in different generations, the ambiguity of the benefits of migration is carried as a form of nostalgia and questions endure about identity, belonging and where is 'home'.

Love of all things from our culture

The links within Veneto families who were market gardeners in the Lockleys area stretch across three generations in Australia and to the Veneto region. At a gathering for the Veneto market-gardener families and friends in October 2022, Amanda Rossetto gave a presentation about connections to her grandparents, who migrated to Adelaide in 1927 and 1930. Amanda provided context for her attachment to her grandmother, who arrived as a bride after marrying by proxy. Outlining connections with her father's relatives in Adelaide, the *paese* at Lockleys and the Veneto, Amanda demonstrated her familiarity with her family's cultural context:

> I stand here with immense pride as a third-generation Australian-Italian who feels very connected to my Veneto culture and heritage. I have my *nonna* to thank for that—she taught me well about our history, love of family, food and culture. She encouraged my love of all things from our culture. She always told me stories, taught me to speak our *dialetto*, took me to visit all our *parenti* [relatives], took me to the Italian and Veneto clubs whenever she could.
>
> It was never hard, it was fun, and I took every opportunity to be with her, to go and visit all the Rossetto, Tormena, Rebuli and Bernardi families, to go to the parties and weddings, to visit the Frogmore Road families and her dear friends, the Marchioros. She would get me to always write a few lines at the bottom of her letters to our families back in the Veneto—in Bigolino, Biadene, Valdobiaddene, Montebelluna and Castelfranco.[30]

---

29 See Vincent Horn, 'Migrant Family Visits and the Life Course: Interrelationships between Age, Capacity and Desire', *Global Networks* 17, no. 4 (2017): 518–36, doi.org/10.1111/glob.12154.
30 Presentation by Amanda Rossetto, Gathering of Veneto market-gardener families and friends, Seaton, SA, 22 October 2022.

9. CONCLUSION

Plate 9.9: Amanda Rossetto making a presentation at a Veneto market-gardener families and friends gathering, Seaton, South Australia, 22 October 2022
Source: Alex Bennett.

Amanda, who was born in Adelaide in 1960, connects with her family across time and space and the reference points of both Australia and the Veneto region. When Amanda first visited the Veneto as a 12-year-old with her father, she stayed in the large old Rossetto house where her grandfather and his eight siblings had been raised. As an adult, she has made four visits to the home villages of her grandparents and, because of her facility with the Veneto dialect, has developed strong relationships with her relatives. Amanda has also continued regular contact through social media: 'I'm able to stay in touch with them easily—and we do … We probably communicate once a week in one way or another.'[31]

The challenges of geographical distance and the span of time since her grandparents' migrant narrative began have been swept aside for Amanda and others in the community who maintain contact with relatives in the Veneto. Opportunities for face-to-face interaction have been transcended in a way that could not have been imagined by the first generation. Those who left their villages in the interwar years were not certain they would see

---

31 ibid.

their families again. Contact was made through letters, rare phone calls and occasional return visits by some in the first generation after 20 or so years. Today communication between migrant families has been revolutionised by technology and contact with transnational relatives is meaningful, immediate and intimate: it is 'transnational emotional interaction'.[32] Amanda's connections with her grandparents' descendants in the Veneto reflect her sense of Veneto identity, which parallels the experience of third-generation Greek Australians who participated in a study about identity formation. Its findings showed that a significant number identified themselves as Greek and different from 'Australians' even though they had reaped the social and economic benefits of their grandparents' migration.[33]

Plate 9.10: The names of Veneto market gardeners in the *paese* at Lockleys as featured in the design of a commemorative tea towel, 2019
Source: Madeleine Regan.

---

32 Svašek, 'Who Cares?', 220.
33 Papadelos, 'Greeks Are Different to Australians'.

9. CONCLUSION

The history of the Veneto market gardeners at Lockleys is not just a counternarrative to the Anglo-Australian record of migration between the wars; it is a new strand. The group biography of the Veneto community at Lockleys from the 1920s to the 1970s assigns perspective to the history of Anglo-Australia at that time and raises questions about the presence and role of migrant groups. The experiences of southern European migrant communities who, like the Veneto market gardeners, developed initiatives, pursued aspirations and made economic and social contributions were not incorporated into the narrative of the nation. The documentation of the lives of the Veneto market-gardener community in the western suburbs of Adelaide shifts the understanding of the boundaries of the Australian experience of migration and settlement between the wars and illuminates the strategies the families used to achieve *sistemazione* as they formed an intergenerational *paese* that created transnational belonging. This group biography highlights migrant experiences of inclusion and exclusion, agency and courage, belonging and participation, risk and achievement, and the desire for 'home'.

Bibliography

Abrams, Lynn. 2010. *Oral History Theory*. London: Routledge. doi.org/10.4324/9780203849033.

Accarigi, Ilaria Vanni. 2017. 'Transcultural Objects, Transcultural Homes.' In *Reimagining Home in the 21st Century*, edited by Justine Lloyd and Ellie Vasta, 192–206. Cheltenham: Edward Elgar Publishing. doi.org/10.4337/9781786432933.00022.

Ahmed, Sara, and Anne-Marie Fortier. 2003. 'Re-Imagining Communities.' *International Journal of Cultural Studies* 6, no. 3: 251–59. doi.org/10.1177/13678779030063001.

Alessi, Angela A. 2021. 'Reimagining Italian Spaces: *La Fiamma* as a Lens to Explore the Development of the Italian Community in Adelaide, South Australia, between 1947 and 1963.' In *Voices of Challenge in Australia's Migrant and Minority Press*, edited by Catherine Dewhirst and Richard Scully, 107–25. Cham, Switzerland: Palgrave Macmillan. doi.org/10.1007/978-3-030-67330-7_6.

Amadio, Joe. 1997. *An Immigrant's Story*. Adelaide: Self-Published.

Anderson, Cathrin Vesna. 2016. 'Shame and Pride in Second-Generation German Identity in Melbourne, Australia: Emotions and White Ethnicity.' *Journal of Ethnic and Migration Studies* 42, no. 9: 1439–54. doi.org/10.1080/1369183X.2015.1120660.

Andreoni, Helen. 2003. 'Olive or White? The Colour of Italians in Australia.' *Journal of Australian Studies* 27, no. 7: 81–92. doi.org/10.1080/14443050309387853.

Anon. 1986. 'C'era una volta una famiglia che viveva in un vagone … [Once upon a Time There Was a Family Who Lived in a Railway Carriage …].' *Il Messaggero*, [Rome], June: 17.

Arapakis, Daphne. 2023. 'Ethnic Compartmentalisation: Greek Australian (Dis) Associations with White Australia and Indigenous Sovereignty.' *Journal of Intercultural Studies* 44, no. 6: 799–817. doi.org/10.1080/07256868.2023.2192468.

Australian Bureau of Statistics (ABS). 1925. *Official Year Book of the Commonwealth of Australia*. No. 18. Canberra: ABS.

Australian Bureau of Statistics (ABS). 1944–45. 'Agricultural Production.' In *1301.0—Year Book, Australia*. No. 36, 777–854. Canberra: ABS. www.ausstats.abs.gov.au/ausstats/free.nsf/0/19AD09393BAD4E22CA2573AD00 20052A/$File/13010_1944-45%20section%2020.pdf.

Australian Bureau of Statistics (ABS). 1946–47. 'Labour, Wages and Prices.' In *1301.0—Year Book Australia*. No. 37, 435–512. Canberra: ABS. www.ausstats.abs.gov.au/ausstats/free.nsf/0/4030A3460E588633CA2573AD00 200501/$File/13010_1946-47%20section%2012.pdf.

Baggio, Rino A. 1989. *The Shoe in My Cheese: An Immigrant Family Experience*. Melbourne: Department of Humanities, Footscray Institute of Technology.

Baily, Samuel L. 2004. *Immigrants in the Lands of Promise: Italians in Buenos Aires and New York City, 1870–1914*. Ithaca: Cornell University Press.

Baldassar, Loretta. 1999. 'Marias and Marriage: Ethnicity, Gender and Sexuality among Italo-Australian Youth in Perth.' *Journal of Sociology* 35, no. 1: 1–22. doi.org/10.1177/144078339903500101.

Baldassar, Loretta. 2001. *Visits Home: Migration Experiences between Italy and Australia*. Melbourne: Melbourne University Press.

Baldassar, Loretta. 2016. 'De-Demonizing Distance in Mobile Family Lives: Co-Presence, Care Circulation and Polymedia as Vibrant Matter.' *Global Networks* 16, no. 2 [SI] (April): 145–63. doi.org/10.1111/glob.12109.

Baldassar, Loretta. 2023. 'Migrant Visits over Time: Ethnographic Returning and the Technological Turn.' *Global Networks* 23, no. 1: 160–73. doi.org/10.1111/glob.12393.

Baldassar, Loretta, Mihaela Nedelcu, Laura Merla, and Raelene Wilding. 2016. 'ICT-Based Co-Presence in Transnational Families and Communities: Challenging the Premise of Face-to-Face Proximity in Sustaining Relationships.' *Global Networks* 16, no. 2 [SI] (April): 133–44. doi.org/10.1111/glob.12108.

Baldassar, Loretta, and Ros Pesman. 2005. *From Paesani to Global Italians: Veneto Migrants in Australia*. Perth: University of Western Australia Press.

Balint, Ruth, and Zora Simic. 2018. 'Histories of Migrants and Refugees in Australia.' *Australian Historical Studies* 49, no. 3: 378–409. doi.org/10.1080/1031461X.2018.1479438.

Ballestrin, Silvano. 2020a. 'Narciso Ballestrin and Maria Dotto Family.' *Veneto Market Gardeners 1927 Blog*, 12 July. venetimarketgardeners1927.net/narciso-ballestrin-and-maria-dotto-family/.

Ballestrin, Silvano. 2020b. 'Parties and Festivals.' *Veneto Market Gardeners 1927 Blog*, 12 July. venetimarketgardeners1927.net/parties-and-festivals/.

Barclay, Katie, and Nina Javette Koefoed. 2021. 'Family, Memory, and Identity: An Introduction.' *Journal of Family History* 46, no. 1 (January): 3–12. doi.org/10.1177/0363199020967297.

Battiston, Simone, and Bruno Mascitelli. 2007. 'Migration, Ethnic Concentration and International Trade Growth: The Case of Italians in Australia.' *People and Place* 15, no. 4: 23–24.

Bell, Rudolph M. 2017. *Fate, Honor, Family and Village: Demographic and Cultural Change in Rural Italy since 1800*. New York: Routledge.

Berno, Remo. 2019. 'The Mezzadria System.' *Veneto Market Gardeners 1927 Blog*, 15 September. venetimarketgardeners1927.net/the-mezzadria-system/.

Berno, Remo, and Madeleine Regan. 2019. 'The Mezzadria System.' *Veneto Market Gardeners 1927 Blog*, 15 September. venetimarketgardeners1927.net/?s=mezzadria+system.

Boccagni, Paolo. 2014. 'What's in a (Migrant) House? Changing Domestic Spaces, the Negotiation of Belonging and Home-Making in Ecuadorian Migration.' *Housing Theory and Society* 31, no. 3: 277–93. doi.org/10.1080/14036096.2013.867280.

Boileau, Joanna. 2017. *Chinese Market Gardening in Australia and New Zealand: Gardens of Prosperity*. Cham, Switzerland: Palgrave Macmillan. doi.org/10.1007/978-3-319-51871-8.

Bornat, Joanna. 1993. 'Two Oral Histories: Valuing Our Difference.' *The Oral History Review* 21, no. 1: 73–95. doi.org/10.1093/ohr/21.1.73.

Borrie, Wilfrid David. 1954. *Italians and Germans in Australia: A Study of Assimilation*. Melbourne: Cheshire.

Breschi, Danilo. 2022. 'Genealogia E Fenomenologia Do Fascismo: Entre a história E a interpretação [Genealogy and Phenomenology of Fascism: Between History and Interpretation].' *Locus: Revista de História* 28, no. 2: 41–63. doi.org/10.34019/2594-8296.2022.v28.37466.

Bromley, J.E. 1955. 'The Italians of Port Pirie.' MA thesis, The Australian National University, Canberra.

Broomhill, Ray. 1978. *Unemployed Workers: A Social History of the Great Depression in Adelaide*. Brisbane: University of Queensland Press.

Caine, Barbara. 2019. *Biography and History*. 2nd edn. London: Red Globe Press.

Cannistraro, Philip, and Gianfausto Rosoli. 1979. 'Fascist Emigration Policy in the 1920s: An Interpretive Framework.' *International Migration Review* 13, no. 4: 673–92. doi.org/10.1177/019791837901300404.

Carlson, Bridget Rachel. 1997. 'Immigrant Placemaking in Colonial Australia: The Italian Speaking Settlers of Daylesford.' PhD diss., Victoria University, Melbourne.

Castles, Stephen, and Mark J. Miller. 1993. *The Age of Migration: International Population Movements in the Modern World*. 3rd edn. Basingstoke: Macmillan.

Cecilia, Tito. 1987. *We Didn't Arrive Yesterday: Outline of the History of the Italian Migration into Australia from Discovery to the Second World War*. Translated by Moira Furey, Moreno Giovannoni, and Walter Musolino. Red Cliffs: Scalabrinians.

Chanfrault-Duchet, Marie-Françoise. 1991. 'Narrative Structures, Social Models and Symbolic Representation in the Life Story.' In *Women's Words: The Feminist Practice of Oral History*, edited by Sherna Berger Gluck and Daphne Patai. New York: Routledge.

Church, Julia. 2005. *Per l'Australia: The Story of Italian Migration*. Melbourne: Miegunyah Press.

Clark, Anna. 2019. 'Private Lives, Public History: Navigating Australian Historical Consciousness.' In *Contemplating Historical Consciousness: Notes from the Field*, edited by Anna Clark and Carla L. Peck, 113–24. New York: Berghahn Books. doi.org/10.2307/j.ctvw04bhk.13.

Clarke, Sharyn Beth. 2005. 'The Creation of the Torrens: A History of Adelaide's River to 1881.' MA thesis, University of Adelaide, Adelaide.

Cocchiaro, Antonio. 1993. 'The History and Future of Italo-Australian Associations in South Australia.' In *Proceedings: The First Conference on the Impact of Italians in South Australia, 16–17 July 1993*, edited by Desmond O'Connor and Antonio Comin. Adelaide: Italian Congress, The Italian Discipline, Flinders University of South Australia.

Corrieri, Michael Peter. 1992. *Italians of Port Pirie: A Social History*. Port Pirie: Our Lady of Martyrs, Port Pirie Italian Community.

Cosmini, Daniela, and Diana Glenn. 2021. *La Seconda Casa: The Second Home— A History of the South Australian Italian Association*. Adelaide: South Australian Italian Association.

Cosmini, Daniela, Diana Glenn, Maria Palaktsoglou, and Eric Bouvet. 2018. 'The Making of Home in a New Land: A Study of the Significance of Personal Objects and Cultural Practices of Aging Italian and Greek Migrants in a Transnational Context.' *Italian American Review* 8, no. 1: 1–22. doi.org/10.5406/italamerrevi.8.1.0001.

Cosmini-Rose, Daniela, and Desmond O'Connor. 2008. *Caulonia in the Heart: The Settlement in Australia of Migrants from a Southern Italian Town*. Adelaide: Lythrum Press.

Cresciani, Gianfranco. 2003. *The Italians in Australia*. Cambridge: Cambridge University Press.

Cronin, Constance E. 1970. *The Sting of Change: Sicilians in Australia*. Chicago: University of Chicago Press.

Curthoys, Ann. 1999. 'An Uneasy Conversation: Multicultural and Indigenous Discourses.' In *The Future of Australian Multiculturalism: Reflections on the Twentieth Anniversary of Jean Martin's The Migrant Presence*, edited by Ghassan Hage and Rowanne Couch, 277–93. Sydney: Research Institute for Humanities and Social Sciences, University of Sydney.

Davine, Annamaria. 2002. 'Pioneer Veneti in Gippsland and Their Role in the Development of an Italian Farming Community.' *Italian Historical Society Journal* 10, no. 2.

Davine, Annamaria. 2006. *Vegnimo da Conco Ma Simo Veneti: A Study of the Immigration and Settlement of the Veneti in Central and West Gippsland 1925–1970*. Melbourne: Italian Australian Institute, La Trobe University.

De Bolfo, Tony. 2004. *In Search of Kings: What Became of the Passengers of the 'Re d'Italia'*. Melbourne: HarperCollins.

De Francesco, Vincenzo SJ. 2010. *Letters to Naples: A Neapolitan Writes Home about His Work in Melbourne, 1919–1928*. Edited and translated by Aniello Iannuzzi. Ballan: Connor Court.

Del Giudice, Luisa. 2013. 'Italian-American Oral History and Its Digitized Sites.' *Digital Media Review* 3, no. 2: 154–65. doi.org/10.5406/italamerrevi.3.2.0154.

Dellios, Alexandra. 2018. '"It Was Just You and Your Child": Single Migrant Mothers, Generational Storytelling and Australia's Migrant Heritage.' *Memory Studies* 13, no. 4: 586–600. doi.org/10.1177/1750698017750000.

Depasquale, Paul. 2009. *My Path to the Brownlow*. Adelaide: Pioneer Books.

Dewhirst, Catherine. 2008. 'Collaborating on Whiteness: Representing Italians in Early White Australia.' *Journal of Australian Studies* 32, no. 1: 33–49. doi.org/10.1080/14443050801993800.

Dewhirst, Catherine. 2014. 'The "Southern Question" in Australia: The 1925 Royal Commission's Racialisation of Southern Italians.' *Queensland History Journal* 22, no. 4: 316–32.

di Leonardo, Micaela. 1984. *The Varieties of Ethnic Experience: Kinship, Class, and Gender among California Italian-Americans*. Ithaca: Cornell University Press. doi.org/10.7591/9781501721250.

Evans, Robert H. 1976. *Life and Politics in a Venetian Community*. Notre Dame: University of Notre Dame Press.

Ferry, Thomas Arthur. 1925. *Report of the Royal Commission Appointed to Inquire into and Report on the Social and Economic Effect of Increase in Number of Aliens in North Queensland*. Brisbane.

Fobear, Katherine. 2016. 'Do You Understand? Unsettling Authority in Feminist Oral History.' *Journal of Feminist Scholarship* 10, no. 10: 61–77.

Foot, John. 2022. 'A Microhistory of Fascist Violence: Squadristi, Victims and Perpetrators.' *Journal of Modern Italian Studies* 27, no. 4: 528–49. doi.org/10.1080/1354571X.2022.2045454.

Fortier, Anne-Marie. 1999. 'Re-Membering Places and the Performance of Belonging(s).' *Theory, Culture & Society* 16, no. (1999): 41–64. doi.org/10.1177/02632769922050548.

Fortier, Anne-Marie. 2000. *Migrant Belongings: Memory, Space, Identity*. London: Routledge.

Freund, Alexander. 2009. 'A Canadian Family Talks about Oma's Life in Nazi Germany: Three Generational Interviews and Communicative Memory.' *Oral History Forum d'histoire orale* 29: 2, 25–26.

Freund, Alexander. 2014. *Oral History and Ethnic History*. Immigration and Ethnicity in Canada Series Booklet No. 32. Ottawa: Canadian Historical Association.

Frisch, Michael. 1990. *A Shared Authority: Essays on the Craft and Meaning of Oral and Public History*. Albany: State University of New York.

Gabaccia, Donna R. 2005. 'Italian Diaspora.' In *Encyclopedia of Diasporas*, edited by M. Ember, C.R. Ember, and I. Skoggard, 143–52. Boston: Springer. doi.org/10.1007/978-0-387-29904-4_15.

Gabaccia, Donna. 2006. 'Global Geography of "Little Italy": Italian Neighbourhoods in Comparative Perspective.' *Modern Italy* 11, no. 1: 9–24. doi.org/10.1080/13532940500489510.

Galbally, Frank. 1978. 'Migrant Services and Programs—Summary.' In *Review of Post Arrival Programs and Services for Migrants*. Parliamentary Paper No. 164, 3–13, 15–28. Canberra: Australian Government Publishing Service. www.multiculturalaustralia.edu.au/doc/galbally_1.pdf.

Girola, Stefano. 2003. 'Saints in the Suitcase: Italian Popular Catholicism in Australia.' *The Australasian Catholic Record* 80, no. 2: 164–74.

Glenn, Diana. 2013. 'Writing Campanian Lives: Considerations of Transnational Identity and Belonging.' *Forum Italicum* 47, no. 1: 150–66. doi.org/10.1177/0014585813478924.

Gluck, Sherna Berger. 2011. 'Has Feminist Oral History Lost Its Radical/Subversive Edge?' *Oral History* 39, no. 2: 63–72. www.jstor.org/stable/i40061538.

Gluck, Sherna Berger, and Daphne Patai. 1991. *Women's Words: The Feminist Practice of Oral History*. New York: Routledge.

Green, Anna. 2019. 'Intergenerational Family History and Historical Consciousness.' In *Contemplating Historical Consciousness: Notes from the Field*, edited by Anna Clark and Carla L. Peck, 200–11. New York: Berghahn Books. doi.org/10.2307/j.ctvw04bhk.19.

Haebich, Anna. 2008. *Spinning the Dream: Assimilation in Australia 1950–1970*. Fremantle: Fremantle Press.

Hamilton, Olivia. 2017. 'Senses of Home.' In *Reimagining Home in the 21st Century*, edited by Justine Lloyd and Ellie Vasta, 179–91. Cheltenham: Edward Elgar Publishing. doi.org/10.4337/9781786432933.00021.

Harzig, Christiane, and Dirk Hoerder, with Donna R. Gabbacia. 2009. *What Is Migration History?* Hoboken: Wiley.

Hasluck, Paul. 1952. *Australia in the War of 1939–1945. Series 4, Civil. Volume 1: The Government and the People, 1939–1941*. Canberra: Australian War Memorial.

Hirsch, Marianne. 2008. 'The Generation of Postmemory.' *Poetics Today* 29, no. 1: 103–28. doi.org/10.1215/03335372-2007-019.

Hirsch, Marianne. 2012. *The Generation of Postmemory: Writing and Visual Culture after the Holocaust.* New York: Columbia University Press.

Horn, Vincent. 2017. 'Migrant Family Visits and the Life Course: Interrelationships between Age, Capacity and Desire.' *Global Networks* 17, no. 4: 518–36. doi.org/10.1111/glob.12154.

Huber, Rina. 1977. *From Pasta to Pavlova: A Comparative Study of Italian Settlers in Sydney and Griffith.* Brisbane: University of Queensland Press.

Hugo, David Frederick. 1995. 'Mica Mining at Harts Ranges, Central Australia, 1880s–1960: A Study of Ethnicity and the Impact of Isolation.' PhD diss., Northern Territory University, Darwin.

Innocente, Aida. 2022. 'A Child Discovering Italy.' *Veneto Market Gardeners 1927 Blog*, 22 May. venetimarketgardeners1927.net/a-child-discovering-italy/.

Innocente, Aida, Gino Innocente, and Mary Innocente. 2021a. 'Making Salamis—Part 1.' *Veneto Market Gardeners 1927 Blog*, 2 May. venetimarketgardeners1927.net/making-salamis-part-1/.

Innocente, Aida, Gino Innocente, and Mary Innocente. 2021b. 'Making Salamis—Part 2.' *Veneto Market Gardeners 1927 Blog*, 16 May. venetimarketgardeners1927.net/making-salamis-part-2/.

Iuliano, Susanna. 1999. 'Donne Buoi dai Paesi Tuoi [Choose Women and Oxen from Your Home Village]: Italian Proxy Marriages.' *Australian Journal of Social Issues* 34, no. 4: 319–35. doi.org/10.1002/j.1839-4655.1999.tb01083.x.

James, Sarah. 2016. *Farming on the Fringe: Peri-Urban Agriculture, Cultural Diversity and Sustainability in Sydney.* Cham, Switzerland: Springer. doi.org/10.1007/978-3-319-32235-3.

Janover, Michael. 2000. 'Nostalgias.' *Critical Horizons* 1, no. 1: 113–33. doi.org/10.1163/156851600510453.

Jenkins, Lesley. 1993. *Power of the Land: A Social History of Italian Settlement in Lismore.* Mullumbimby: L. Jenkins.

Jupp, James. 2002. *From White Australia to Woomera: The Story of Australian Immigration.* Cambridge: Cambridge University Press. doi.org/10.1017/CBO9781139195034.

King, Sara Sophie. 2007. 'Agriculture in South Australia: The Italian Contribution.' PhD diss., Flinders University, Adelaide.

Laffin, Josephine. 2008. *Matthew Beovich: A Biography.* Adelaide: Wakefield Press.

Lampugnani, Rosario, and Robert J. Holton. 1992. 'Ethnic Business in South Australia: A Sociological Profile of the Italian Business Community.' *Journal of Intercultural Studies* 13, no. 2: 1–18. doi.org/10.1080/07256868.1992.9963387.

Lancaster Jones, Frank. 1964. 'The Territorial Composition of Italian Emigration to Australia, 1876 to 1962.' *International Migration* 2, no. 2: 247–65. doi.org/10.1111/j.1468-2435.1964.tb00632.x.

Lancaster Jones, Frank. 1967. 'Ethnic Concentration and Assimilation: An Australian Case Study.' *Social Forces* 45, no. 3: 412–23. doi.org/10.2307/2575200.

Langfield, Michele. 1991. '"White Aliens": The Control of European Immigration to Australia 1920–1930.' *Journal of Intercultural Studies* 12, no. 2: 1–14. doi.org/10.1080/07256868.1991.9963375.

Lewins, Frank W. 1980. 'The Catholic Church in Australia: An Agent of Assimilation.' *Clearing House on Migration Issues* no. 391: 1–6.

Longo, Don, ed. 2010. *Terra Lasci, Terra Trovi: From Molinara to Adelaide—The History of a Southern Italian Community in South Australia 1927–2007*. Adelaide: Molinara Social and Sports Club Inc. and Lythrum Press.

Lyng, Jens. 1935 [1927]. *Non-Britishers in Australia: Influence on Population and Progress*. Melbourne: Melbourne University Press.

MacDonald, John S., and Leatrice D. MacDonald. 1964. 'Chain Migration Ethnic Neighbourhood Formation and Social Networks.' *The Millbank Memorial Fund Quarterly* 42, no. 1: 82–97. doi.org/10.2307/3348581.

Mantello, Maria. 1981. 'Their Words … My Words … Our Words: A Reflection on Oral History with Reference to Italian Immigrant Identity in the Werribee Community during World War 2.' BA Hons thesis, University of Melbourne, Melbourne.

Mantello, Maria. 1986. *Now and Then: The Sicilian Farming Community at Werribee Park, 1929–1949*. Melbourne: Globe Press.

Marchetti-Mercer, Maria Chiara, and Anita Virga. 2023. *The Italian Diaspora in South Africa: Nostalgia, Identity, and Belonging in the Second and Third Generations*. London: Routledge. doi.org/10.4324/9781003266884.

Marino, Simone. 2020. *Intergenerational Ethnic Identity Construction and Transmission among Italian-Australians: Absence, Ambivalence and Revival*. Cham, Switzerland: Palgrave Macmillan. doi.org/10.1007/978-3-030-48145-2.

Marino, Simone. 2021. 'Thrown into the World: The Shift between Pavlova and Pasta in the Ethnic Identity of Australians Originating from Italy.' *Journal of Sociology* 57, no. 2: 231–48. doi.org/10.1177/1440783319888283.

Marino, Simone. 2022. 'Beyond Authenticity: An Ethnographic Reflection on Italians in Australia and Italians in Italy.' *Journal of Sociology* 58, no. 4: 588–604. doi.org/10.1177/14407833211016090.

Marino, Simone, and Giancarlo Chiro. 2014. 'Family Alliances and "Comparatico" among a Group of Calabrian-Australian Families Living in Adelaide, South Australia.' *Journal of Anthropological Research* 70, no. 1: 107–30. doi.org/10.3998/jar.0521004.0070.105.

Martin, Jean I. 1978. *The Migrant Presence: Australian Responses, 1947–1977*. Sydney: George Allen & Unwin.

Martinuzzi O'Brien, Ilma. 1992. 'The Internment of Australia Born and Naturalized British Subjects of Italian Origin.' In *War, Internment and Mass Migration: The Italo-Australian Experience 1940–1990*, edited by Richard Bosworth and Romano Ugolini. Rome: Gruppo Editoriale Internazionale.

Massey, Doreen. 1995. 'Places and Their Pasts.' *History Workshop Journal* 39, no. 1: 182–92. doi.org/10.1093/hwj/39.1.182.

Massey, Doreen. 2018. 'A Place Called Home.' In *The Doreen Massey Reader*, edited by Brett Christophers, Rebecca Lave, Jamie Peck, and Marion Werner, 1701–172. Newcastle upon Tyne: Agenda Publishing Limited.

McDonald, J.S. 1958. 'Migration from Italy to Australia with Special Reference to Selected Groups.' PhD diss., The Australian National University, Canberra.

Mercurio, Antonio, and Angela Scarino. 2004. *We Left: Narratives of the Sangiorgesi in South Australia = E Partimmo: Narrazioni die Sangiorgesi del Sud Australia*. Adelaide: San Giorgio la Molara Community Centre.

Murphy, Amy Tooth. 2020. 'Listening In, Listening Out: Intersubjectivity and the Impact of Insider and Outsider Status in Oral History Interviews.' *Oral History* 48, no. 1: 35–44.

Norrick, Ned R. 2006. 'Humour in Oral History Interviews.' *Oral History* 34, no. 2 (Autumn): 85–94.

O'Connor, Desmond. 1996. *No Need to be Afraid: Italian Settlers in South Australia between 1839 and the Second World War*. Adelaide: Wakefield Press.

O'Connor, Desmond. 1999. 'Declared Black: Confrontation between Italian and Anglo-Celtic Workers in Port Adelaide 1928–1932.' In *Australian Labour History Reconsidered*, edited by David Palmer, Ross Shanahan, and Martin Shanahan. Adelaide: Australian Humanities Press.

O'Connor, Desmond. 2005. 'Club e Associazioni dei Veneti nel South Australia [Clubs and Associations of the Venetians in South Australia].' In *Veneti d'Australia*, edited by Luciano Segafreddo and Ilma Martinuzzi O'Brien, 177–87. Ravenna, Italy: Angelo Longo Editore.

Oglethorpe, Stuart. 2014. 'The End of Sharecropping in Central Italy after 1945: The Role of Mechanisation in the Changing Relationship between Peasant Families and Land.' *Rural History* 25, no. 2: 243–60. doi.org/10.1017/S0956793314000089.

Orsi, Robert. 1990. 'The Fault of Memory: "Southern Italy" in the Imagination of Immigrants and the Lives of their Children in Italian Harlem, 1920–1945.' *Journal of Family History* 15, no. 2: 133–47. doi.org/10.1177/036319909001500108.

Paganoni, Tony. 2007. 'The Italian Community in Australia: Historical Notes on Pastoral Care, its Development to Date and Future Options.' *The Australasian Catholic Record* 84, no. 2: 185–203.

Papadelos, Pam. 2021. '"Greeks Are Different to Australians": Understanding Identity Formation among Third-Generation Australians of Greek Heritage.' *Ethnic and Racial Studies* 44, no. 11: 1975–94. doi.org/10.1080/01419870.2020.1813318.

Parletta, Rosa. 2022. 'Giovanni Balestrin's Story.' *Veneto Market Gardeners 1927 Blog*, 8 May. venetimarketgardeners1927.net/giovanni-balestrins-story/.

Pascoe, Robert. 1987. *Buongiorno Australia: Our Italian Heritage*. Melbourne: Greenhouse Publications.

Pascoe, Robert. 1990. *Open for Business: Immigrant and Aboriginal Entrepreneurs Tell Their Story*. Canberra: Office for Multicultural Affairs, Department of the Prime Minister and Cabinet.

Pascoe, Robert. 1992. 'Place and Community: The Construction of an Italo-Australian Space.' In *Australia's Italians: Culture and Community in a Changing Society*, edited by Stephen Castles, Caroline Alcorso, Gaetano Rando, and Ellie Vasta, 85–97. Sydney: Allen & Unwin.

Persian, Jayne, and Karen Agutter. 2021. 'European Post-War Migrants and Indigenous Australians: A History in Fragments.' *History Australia* 18, no. 1: 112–29. doi.org/10.1080/14490854.2021.1878912.

Phillips, Daphne Eunice. 1970. 'Italians and Australians in the Ovens Valley Area: A Sociological Study of Interaction between Migrants and the Host Population in a Rural Area of Victoria.' PhD diss., The Australian National University, Canberra.

Philp, Barry. 2012. 'Glasshouse Tomatoes.' In *History of Agriculture in SA*. Adelaide: Department of Primary Industries and Regions, Government of South Australia. www.pir.sa.gov.au/aghistory/industries/horticulture/glasshouse_tomatoes2.

Piovesan, Angelo. 2020. 'Links between the Piovesan and Tonellato Families.' *Veneto Market Gardeners 1927 Blog*, 29 November. venetimarketgardeners1927. net/links-between-the-piovesan-and-tonellato-families/.

Portelli, Alessandro. 2018. 'Living Voices: The Oral History Interview as Dialogue and Experience.' *The Oral History Review* 45, no. 2: 239–48. doi.org/10.1093/ ohr/ohy030.

Price, Charles A. 1963. *Southern Europeans in Australia*. Melbourne: Oxford University Press.

Price, Charles A. 1968. 'Southern Europeans in Australia: Problems of Assimilation.' *The International Migration Review* 2, no. 3: 3–26. doi.org/10.1177/ 019791836800200301.

Pugliese, Joseph. 2002. 'Migrant Heritage in an Indigenous Context: For a Decolonizing Migrant Historiography.' *Journal of Intercultural Studies* 23, no. 1: 5–18. doi.org/10.1080/07256860220122368.

Pulvirenti, Mariastella. 2000. 'The Morality of Immigrant Home Ownership: Gender, Work and Italian Australian *Sistemazione*.' *Australian Geographer* 31, no. 2: 237–49. doi.org/10.1080/713612245.

Pyke, N.O.P. 1946. 'Some Reflections on Italian Immigration into Australia.' *The Australian Quarterly* 18, no. 4: 35–44. doi.org/10.2307/20631402.

Read, Peter. 1996. *Returning to Nothing: The Meaning of Lost Places*. Melbourne: Cambridge University Press. doi.org/10.1017/CBO9781139085069.

Rebellato, Christine. 2020. 'Polenta e Baccalà: More Than a Meal.' *Veneto Market Gardeners 1927 Blog*, 5 April. venetimarketgardeners1927.net/polenta-e-baccala-more-than-a-meal/.

Rebuli, Elena. 2019. 'Returning Home.' *Veneto Market Gardeners 1927 Blog*, 10 June. venetimarketgardeners1927.net/returning-home/.

Regan, Madeleine. 2020. 'The Tormena Family.' *Veneto Market Gardeners 1927 Blog*, 15 November. venetimarketgardeners1927.net/?s=Tormena+family.

Regan, Madeleine. 2021. 'Autumn and Wine-Making.' *Veneto Market Gardeners 1927 Blog*, 21 March. venetimarketgardeners1927.net/autumn-and-wine-making/.

Reid, Annmarie. 2015. 'Ella's Clippy Mat: Progging the Memories of Migrants from England's North East.' PhD diss., University of South Australia, Adelaide.

Ricatti, Francesco. 2013. 'The Emotion of Truth and the Racial Uncanny: Aborigines and Sicilians in Australia.' *Cultural Studies Review* 19, no. 2: 125–49. doi.org/10.5130/csr.v19i2.2839.

Ricatti, Francesco. 2018. *Italians in Australia: History, Memory, Identity*. Cham, Switzerland: Springer International. doi.org/10.1007/978-3-319-78873-9.

Rossetto, Marietta. 1995. *La Pioggia nelle Scarpe: Aneddoti di una protagonista = Rain in These Shoes: Anecdotal Memoirs of Adelina Rossetto*. Adelaide: VIA Magenta.

Rumbaut, Ruben G. 2004. 'Ages, Life Stages, and Generational Cohorts: Decomposing the Immigrant First and Second Generations in the United States.' *International Migration Review* 38, no. 3: 1160–205. doi.org/10.1111/j.1747-7379.2004.tb00232.x.

Ruzzene, Dino, and Simone Battiston. 2006. *Italian-Australians: From Migrant Workers to Upwardly Mobile Middle Class—A Study of Occupational Mobility among Australians of Italian Background, 1971–2001*. Melbourne: Italian Australian Institute, La Trobe University.

Ruzzene Grollo, Diana. 2004. *Cooper's Creek Gippsland: The Trevisani*. Melbourne: Mure.

Ryan, Louise. 2015. 'Inside and Outside of What or Where? Researching Migration through Multi-Positionalities.' *Forum, Qualitative Social Research* 16, no. 2.

Sala, Emanuela, and Loretta Baldassar. 2017. 'Time to Revisit the Family in Italian-Australian Studies: Charting a Way Forward.' *Flinders University Languages Group Online Review* 5, no. 2: 1–15.

Saluppo, Alessandro. 2020. 'Paramilitary Violence and Fascism: Imaginaries and Practices of Squadrismo, 1919–1925.' *Contemporary European History* 29, no. 3: 289–308. doi.org/10.1017/S0960777319000390.

Samuel, Raphael, and Paul Thompson. 1990. 'Introduction.' In *The Myths We Live By*, edited by Raphael Samuel and Paul Thompson. London: Routledge.

Saunders, Kay. 2000. 'A Difficult Reconciliation: Civil Liberties and Internment Policy in Australia during World War Two.' In *Alien Justice: Wartime Internment in Australia and North America*, edited by Kay Saunders and Roger Daniels. Brisbane: University of Queensland Press.

Schech, Susan, and Jane Haggis. 2001. 'Migrancy, Multiculturalism and Whiteness: Recharting Core Identities in Australia.' *Communal/Plural* 9, no. 2: 143–59. doi.org/10.1080/13207870120081460.

Sendziuk, Paul, and Robert Foster. 2018. *A History of South Australia*. Cambridge: Cambridge University Press. doi.org/10.1017/9781139196352.

Shanin, Teodor. 1973. 'The Peasantry as a Political Factor.' In *Peasants and Peasant Societies: Selected Readings*, edited by Teodor Shanin, 240–44. Harmondsworth: Penguin Education.

Shopes, Linda. 2002. 'Oral History and the Study of Communities: Problems, Paradoxes and Possibilities.' *The Journal of American History* 89, no. 2: 588–98. doi.org/10.2307/3092177.

Shopes, Linda. 2014. '"Insights and Oversights": Reflections on the Documentary Traditions and the Theoretical Turn in Oral History.' *The Oral History Review* 41, no. 2: 257–68. doi.org/10.1093/ohr/ohu035.

Skrbis, Zlatko, Loretta Baldassar, and Scott Poynting. 2007. 'Introduction—Negotiating Belonging: Migration and Generations.' *Journal of Intercultural Studies* 28, no. 3: 261–69. doi.org/10.1080/07256860701429691.

Smith, Derek L. 1966. 'Market Gardening at Adelaide's Urban Fringe.' *Economic Geography* 42, no. 1 (1966): 19–36. doi.org/10.2307/141830.

Svašek, Maruška. 2008. 'Who Cares? Families and Feelings in Movement.' *Journal of Intercultural Studies* 29, no. 3: 213–30. doi.org/10.1080/07256860802169170.

Tavan, Gwenda. 2004. 'The Dismantling of the White Australia Policy: Elite Conspiracy or Will of the Australian People.' *Australian Journal of Political Science* 39, no. 1: 109–25. doi.org/10.1080/1036114042000205678.

Tavan, Gwenda. 2005. *The Long, Slow Death of White Australia*. Melbourne: Scribe Publications.

The Bulgarians' Educational and Friendly Society. 2000. *50th Jubilee Book*. Adelaide: The Bulgarians' Educational and Friendly Society Incorporated.

Thompson, Paul, and Joanna Bornat. 2017. *The Voice of the Past: Oral History*. 4th edn. Oxford: Oxford University Press.

Thomson, Alistair. 2008. 'Oral History and Community History in Britain: Persona and Critical Reflections on Twenty-Five Years of Continuity and Change.' *Oral History* 36, no. 1: 95–104.

Tolcvay, Monica. 1999. 'Community and Church: Italians in South Australia in the Early Post-War Years.' *Italian Historical Society Journal* 7, no. 2: 4–8.

Tsounis, Michale P. 1975. 'Greek Communities in Australia.' In *Greeks in Australia*, edited by Charles A. Price. Canberra: Australian National University Press.

Vasta, Ellie. 1992. 'The Second Generation.' In *Australia's Italians: Culture and Community in a Changing Society*, edited by Stephen Castles, Caroline Alcorso, Gaetano Rando, and Ellie Vasta. Sydney: Allen & Unwin.

Veneto Club Adelaide Inc. n.d. *In 84 Domeniche nasce il Veneto Club: Ricordi, Appunti e Riflessioni sugli Eventi dal 1971 al 1974* [*The Veneto Club was Born in 84 Sundays: Memories, Notes and Reflections on Events from 1971 to 1974*]; *Veneto Club 25th Anniversary, 1974–1999*. Adelaide: Veneto Club Adelaide Inc.

Veracini, Lorenzo. 2011. 'On Settlerness.' *Borderlands* 10, no. 1: 1–17.

Wardrop, Susi Bella. 1996. *By Proxy: A Study of Italian Proxy Brides in Australia*. Melbourne: Italian Historical Society, CO.AS.IT.

Wilkins, Kristen. 2012. *Bulgarian Migration and Market Gardens in the Western Suburbs*. Report submitted to the City of Charles Sturt and the Faculty of Humanities and Social Sciences. Adelaide: University of Adelaide.

Wise, Amanda, and Selvaraj Velayutham. 2017. 'Transnational Affect and Emotion in Migration Research.' *International Journal of Sociology* 47, no. 2: 116–30. doi.org/10.1080/00207659.2017.1300468.

Zampin, Irene. 2020. 'The Three Simeoni Sisters.' *Veneto Market Gardeners 1927 Blog*, 8 March. venetimarketgardeners1927.net/the-three-simeoni-sisters/.

Index

*Page numbers in **bold** text indicate images.*

Acquasaliente (Salent), Ampelio 39
Adelaide Hills 146, 191
Adelaide Plains 5
Adelaide, City of 2, **11**, 40, 43, 72, 115, **134**, 163, 166–7, 175, 180
Alice Springs 86, 88, 186
Allied Works Council 179, 180, 185
Altivole 31n.5
Andreazza, Maria Gina (Ballestrin) **105**
Attorney-General's Department 80, 81, 82, **83**, 84, 85, **177**
Australian Government 26, 37–8, 79, 85, 125, 131, 133, 140, 173, 194
   and 'enemy aliens' 171, 173, 179, 189
   and anticommunism 182
   and land allocation 80, 81, 82, 84, 85, 88–9, 144, 173, 189
   and naturalisation 79, 80, 133–4, 144, 173, 188, 189
   assimilation policy 26, 131–4, 160, 164, 251, 254, 265
   education 160, 161
   immigration policy 26, 30, 105, 140, 196
   lack of language programs 140, 141, 160
   lack of support for migrants 131, 140, 215, 262
   multicultural policy 18, 26, 47, 251, 252, 254–5
   sponsorship of migrants 39, 236
   taxation 81, 82, 125, 141, 144
   War Cabinet 179
   see also individual departments, White Australia policy
Australian Labor Party 39

Ballestrin
   Antonio 55, 71, 180, 186, **187**, 189
   Ariana **270**
   Cesira (nee Tieppo) 55, **56**, 92, **93**, **136**
   Dolfina **105**, **159**
   Egidio (Jimmy) 71, 106, **107**, 119, 154, **159**, 223, 225, **268**
   Ermenegildo 92, **93**, **153**
   family 33, 51, 71, 77, **93**, 102, 125, **168**, 233, **234**, 235, **264**, 271
   Fay **270**, 271
   Francesco (Frankie) 43, 44, 45, 47, 119, 150, 158, 198, 203, 238, **268**
   Giuseppe 55, **56**, 92, **93**, **136**, 180, 186, 187–8, 209, 250
   Isidoro 43, **44**, **45**, 55, 71, 91, 125, 148, 174, 238
   Jacqueline **270**
   Lesley **159**
   Lina (Campagnaro) 33, **107**, 121, **159**, 164, 165, 240
   Lino **56**, **78**, **93**, 106, 125, 161
   Louis 56, **136**, 269, **270**, 271

297

    Luigia (Luigina) (Zalunardo) 64, **65**, **105**
    Maria **30**, **107**, **159**
    Maria Gina (nee Andreazza) **105**
    Michelle **270**
    Narciso **107**, **159**
    Norina 92, **107**, **159**
    Norma (Camozzato) 55, **56**, 57, 103, **114**, 115–16, 209, 254–5
    Silvano **107**, 145, **159**, 267, **268**
    Simon **270**
Ballestrin-Egan, Archie **270**
Barossa Valley 201
Battaglia
    Bruna (Rossetto) 88, 167
    family 166
    Guido 166–7
    Maria 166–7
Beovich, Archbishop Matthew 162
Bernardi
    Amalia **219**
    family 276
    Leon 132, 166
    Lina **159**
Berno
    Alberto 50, 57, 79–81, 125, 126, 142, **143**, 144, 189
    Antonietta 138, **266**
    Diana 148, **150**, **228**
    family 33, 50, 57, 81, 138, **147**, 148, 236
    Gino 64, 74, 79–82, 109, **136**, **139**, 205, 240
    Irma **139**
    Jean (nee Dyson) 64, 240
    Lucy **150**
    Maria **150**
    Marisa **150**
    Pietro 50, 57, 79–81, 125, 126, 138, 142, **143**, 144, 173, 189, **266**
    Remo 138, 148, 227, **228**, **266**
    Robert **147**
    Roberto **228**

Berti, Primo **93**
Beverley **253**
Biadene 276
Biasetto, Armida (Mattiazzo) 88n.40
Bigolino **35**, 58, **59**, 158n.55, 176, 272, 276
Bolivar 3, **98**, 203, **204**, 206, 207, 217, 221–2, 223, 225, 231, 263
Bordignon, Emilio **159**
Bordin, Adele (Lina) (Rossetto) 36, 58, **59**, 74, **75**, 82, 85, 157, 180, **181**
Brazzale mica factory 94
Bulgarians 3, 77, 85, 134, 190, 201–2, 203n.12, 205, 263n.10
Butterfield family 79

Caerano San Marco 272
Calabrese 251
Calabrians 7, 17, 18, 74, 106, 132n.4, 136
Calwell, Arthur 189
Camozzato
    Joanne 55, 57
    Norma (nee Ballestrin) 55, **56**, 57, 103, **114**, 115–16, 209, 254–5
Campagnaro
    Lina (nee Ballestrin) 33, **107**, 121, **159**, 164, 165, 240
    Luigi **159**
Campagnolo, Noemi (nee Zalunardo) 102, **105**, 121, 124, 146, **159**, 218, **219**
Campania 74
Canada 35, 38, 108, 256
Canberra 55, 88, 183
Candiotto
    Attillio **159**
    Izetta **159**
    Mario **159**
Capuchin 166n.81
Carignano 72
Carrington Street 251
Casa d'Italia 250, 251

Caselle di Altivole **70**, 108, 166, 227, 241, 244, 245n.35, 247
Castelcucco 31n.4
Castelfranco Veneto **270**, 276
Catholic Church 15, 132–3, 136, 156, 160, 161–3, 164–6, 222
  influence of 25, 166–8
  Irish-Catholic tradition 162, 163, 164
  newspaper (*The Southern Cross*) 149
  schools 122, 161, 165
Catholic Italian Welfare Association 163, 250n.50
Central Australia **46**
  see also Northern Territory
Chiumento, Giuseppe 259, **260**, 261
City of Adelaide 2, **11**, 40, 43, 72, 115, **134**, 163, 166–7, 175, 180
Civil Aliens Corps 179, 180, 182, 183, 186, **187**, 188, 191
Civil Constructional Corps 179, 180, 182, 188
Commonwealth Government, *see* Australian Government
Commonwealth Investigation Branch 80–3, 84, 88, 175, 188
Commonwealth Public Service 161
Commonwealth War Cabinet 179
Compostella
  Angelina **30**
  family **168**
  Maria (Mazzarolo) 147, 247, **248**
Conci, Sandra (nee Santin) 75, 108, 165, 249
court cases 190, 192–3

Danieli, Antonietta **272**
Dare, Harold 240
Darwin 84, 190
De Francesco, Father Vincenzo 162
De Pieri
  Attilio **46**
  Serafina **46**

Department of Education 122
Department of Immigration 189
Department of Immigration and Ethnic Affairs 251
Department of Taxation 144
Department of the Interior 183
Depression, the 2, 7, 21, 24, 26, 29, 30, 42–3, 45, 47, 72, 172, 208, 261, 262
Destro
  Attilio 137
  family 137
  Irene (Rene) **137**, 138, 185
Doyban, Denise (nee Santin) 229, 248–9
Duke and Duchess of York 75
Dyson, Jean (Berno) 64, 240

East End market 101, 145
Eyre Peninsula 43

fascism 7, 18, 26, 36–7, 173, 175–6, 182
Favaro, Maria **159**
Fazzalari, Nina (Quaresima) **14**
Ferry Royal Commission on Increase of Aliens in Queensland 133
Findon **14**, 48n.55, 49, **243**, 267
Findon Road 50, 90
Finke 44
Flinders Park 48, 49, 92, **93**, **107**, **153**, 225, 256, 267
Flinders Park church 133n.8, 163
Frogmore Road 50, 75, **78**, **137**, 171, 232, **239**, **264**, 276
  Marchioro family 5, **184**, **264**
  Mazzarolo family 247, **248**
  Piovesan family 19, 217, **264**
  Rossetto family 82, 84
  Santin family 71n.5, 82, 107, 109, 205, **206**, 207, 213, 229, 232–3, **239**, 248
  Tonellato family **1**, 19, **130**, 151, **213**, 219, **220**, 229, **264**

Fulham 74, 79
Fulham Gardens 77, 203n.12

Gatto, Elisabetta (Tonellato) 34, 36, **76**, **139**, 194, 211, **212**, 214
Geelong 76
German community 175, 201, 259, 261
Germany 34, 79, 175, 183,
Giovannini, Assunta (nee Tonellato) 108, 129, **130**, 131, 138, 151, **212**, 214
Gippsland 76, 142, 231, 261n.5
Glenelg Beach **150**
government, *see* Australian Government
Grange Road 43, **78**, 203, **219**
Greek community 3, 30, 201, 269, 278
Griffith 76, 199, 201, 212

Halidon 43
Hartley Road **114**, **136**
Harts Range 86, 88
High Court of Australia 193
Hobart 151

Innocente
    Aida xv, 3
    Angelo 2, **3**, 6, **14**, 142, 240
    Elsa 2
    family 3, 4
Italia Libera (or Free Italy) 182
Italian Government 37, 173

Kangaroo Island 43, 158n.55
Kaurna 46
Kee, Yick 240
Keswick 176, 179
Kidman Park 203, 256, 267

Laio family 235
Legovich, Connie (nee Marchioro) 92, **113**

Leonardi, Gino **159**
Lismore 262n.7
Loveday Internment Camp 178

Malo **17**, 31n.5, 60, 231, 259n.2, **260**
Marchioro
    Angelina 16, **17**, **30**, 59–60, **61**, 62, 91, 137, 162, **184**, 185–6, 209, 231, 264, **266**
    Connie (Legovich) 92, **113**
    Eleonora (nee Ottanelli) xv, 3, **4**, 6, 62, 223, 231
    family 3, 4, 33, 89n.43, 137, 146, **168**, 259n.2, **264**, 276
    Francesco 38, 40, **41**, 52, **53**
    Giancarlo (Johnny) xv, 3, **4**, **5**–6, 13, 62, 91, 97, **98**, 100–1, 137–8, 151, 152, 183, **184**–6, 197, 198, 209, 223, **224**, 231, **268**
    Lina (Rismondo) 19, 20, 52, **53**, 99, 112–**13**, 141, 167–8, 194–5
    Margherita 38, 52, **53**, 91, 92, 112–13
    Mary 52, **53**, **113**
    Romano 60, 77, 137, 159–60, 183, **184**, 197, **198**, 199, 230–1
    Vittorio 16, **17**, 40, **41**, 42, 52, 59–60, **61**–2, 91, 92, **98**, 137, 141, 180, 182–3, **184**–6, 188, 189, 208, 209, **210**, 237, 259n.2, 264, **266**
Mattiazzo
    Anna (Santin) 102, 108–9, **110**, 111, 148, 149, 175, 206
    Armida (nee Biasetto) 88n.40
    Christine (Rebellato) 154, 157
    Emilio **134**
Mattiazzo family 157
    Oscar 49–50, **155**, 156–7, 174, 178, 188, 204–5, 251
    Virginia 156

Mazzarolo
   Arsenio **248**
   family **248**
   Lina **248**
   Lui **274**
   Maria (nee Compostella) 147, 247, **248**
   Sonia **248**
   Teresa (nee Zampin) 165, 273, **274**, 275–6
Melbourne 39, 42, 102, 182, 193, 256
Molfetta 9, 251
Molfettese 76, 139, 182
Monte di Malo 162, 259n.2
Monte Grappa **272**
Montebelluna 276
Morialta Falls **168**
Moscheni, Lena (nee Rossetto) 88, 157, **181**, 268
Multicultural SA 14
Mussolini, Benito 36, 172, 175, 193, 195

Nailsworth **224**
Naples 162
National Security (Aliens Service) Regulations 186
National Security (Land Transfer) Regulations (1940) 80, 81, 84, 88–9, 144, 173, 189
national security, and Italians 25, 80, 144, 172–3, 174, 176, **177**, 189, 193, 195, 196
naturalisation 43, 48, 79, 80–1, 82, 88, 94, 133–4, 157, 171, 173, 175, 176, 178, 183, 186, 188–9, 192, 265
New South Wales 10, 39, 76, 199, 201, 212, 259, 262n.7
Newton 166n.81
Northern Territory 46, 84, 85, 86, **87**, 180, 183, 185, 187, 215

Ottanelli, Eleonora (Marchioro) xv, 3, **4**, 6, 62, 223, 231
Outer Harbour **159**
Ovens Valley 160

Panazzolo
   Diana (nee Santin) 108, 126–7, 138, 203, 232–3, 245–7
   family **54**
Parliament of South Australia 193
Pastro, Antonietta (Berno) 57
Pietrobon
   Mabile **159**
   Raoul **159**
   Vito **159**
Piovesan
   Angelo 19, 59, 86, 88–9, 103–4, 211, 215, 235, 257, 269
   Bruno 89, 122, 215, **216**, 217–18, 235
   Dino 35, 86, 107, 120, 138, 140, 215, **216**, 217
   family 33, 35, 77, 233, **234**, 235, **264**
   Nillo 215, **216**, 217
police 171, 173, 176, 185
Ponzano Veneto 31n.5
Port of Adelaide 60
Port Pirie 9, 76, 139, 163, 182
Provincia di Treviso, *see* Treviso Province
Puglia 9

Quaresima, Nina (nee Fazzalari) **14**
Queensland 30, 39, 111, 133

Rebellato
   Christine (nee Mattiazzo) 154, 157
   Peter **155**
Rebuli
   Brunone 54
   Elena 158n.55, 271–3
   family 89n.43, 276

Giovanni 111–12
Guido **14**, 142, 151
Milva (nee Zampin) 94–5, 236, 253
Vito (Albino) **272**
Recchi
Aida (Valentini) 236
family 233
Melbourne (Mel) 240
Re d'Italia (ship) 39
Reid, Walter 190, **191**, 192
Reynella 152
Riese Pio X **21**, 31n.5, 57, 227, 244, 273, 275
Rismondo, Lina (nee Marchioro) 19, 20, 52, **53**, 99, 112–**13**, 141, 167–8, 194–5
Risveglio ('Awakening') 182
Riverina 76
River Road 50
   see also Findon Road
River Torrens **5**, 46, 48, **49**, 50, 72, 74, 77, 79, 81, 82, 92, 247
Rodato, Virginia (nee Zampin) **139**, 242, 244, **253**
Rossetto
Adele (Lina) (nee Bordin) 36, 58, **59**, 74, **75**, 82, 85, 157, 180, **181**
Adeodato (Atto) 19, 48
Aldo **14**, 71–2, 151, **181**
Amanda 276, **277**, 278
Bruna (nee Battaglia) 88, 167
Domenico 54, 175, 176
family **35**, 176, 276, 277
Gelindo 58, 74, **75**, 82, **83**, 84–6, **87**, 88–9, 180, **181**–2, 188
Giuseppe 167, 180
Lena (Moscheni) 88, 157, **181**, **268**
Romeo **75**, **181**
Rushworth 42

Santin
Aaron **204**
Alan **204**, **206**, **268**
Anna (nee Mattiazzo) 102, 108–9, **110**, 111, 148, 149, 175, 206
Clara 244
Costantina (nee Visentin) 81, 156, 205, **206**
Dean **204**
Denise (Doyban) 229, 248–9
Diana (Panazzolo) 108, 126–7, 138, 203, 232–3, 245–7
family **54**, 71n.5, 82, 107, 109, **126**, 147, **204**–7, 213, 221, 227, 229, **239**, 251
Giovanni 38, **54**, 81–2, 205
Lui 213, 250
Romildo **100**, **204**, 205, 244–6, 250
Rosina (nee Tonellato) 75, 102, **212**, 213
Sandra (Conci) 75, 108, 165, 249
Vito 109, **110**, 148, **149**, 250
Santin Avenue 233, **234**
Sbrissa family 149
Scalabrinians 165
Seaton **268**, **277**
Semola
Arturo **124**
Bruna (nee Zampin) 29, **30**, 120, 222, **253**
Sandra (nee Zampin) 122–3, **124**, 218, **253**
Shaw, Amelia (Zampin) **30**, **63**–4, 94, **253**
Sicilians 76, 131, 262n.7
Simeoni, Ermenegilda **21**
Skuse, Thomas 74
South Australian Investigation Branch 182
South Australian Italian Association (SAIA) 250, 251, 252
South Australian Railways 75
St James Park **11**, 43, 48, 79

St Kilda Beach **146**
Supreme Court of South Australia 192–3
Sydney 31, 39, 151

Tieppo
    Celso **93**
    Cesira (Ballestrin) 55, **56**, 92, **93**, **136**
Tonellato
    Adrian **1**, 148, 173–4, 219, **220**, 221
    Albert 37, 90–1, 103, 104, 194, 211, **212**, 214, 235, 250
    Angelina **70**
    Assunta (Giovannini) 108, 129, **130**, 131, 138, 151, **212**, 214
    Elisabetta (nee Gatto) 34, 36, **76**, **139**, 194, 211, **212**, 214
    family 33, **54**, **70**, 74, **76**, 77, 90, 161, 211, **212**, **213**, 214, 227, 229, 233, **234**, 235, **264**
    Italia 148, **220**
    Lino 34, 35, 67, **68**, 91, 99, 161, 178–9, 208n.24, **212**, 241–2
    Luciana **220**
    Luigi (Lui) 145, **212**, **220**, 250
    Mary (nee Zoanetti) **14**, 90, 91, 104, 190, 192, 193–4, 235
    Orlando (Nano) 91, **212**, 250
    Rosina (Santin) 75, 102, **212**, 213
    Secondo 19, 34, 36, 54, **70**, 75, 90, 91, 104, **130**, **139**, 194, 211, **212**, 213, 214
Tormena
    family **172**, 276
    Galliano **172**
    Johnny 171, **172**, 175, 176
    Maria Rosa 117, **118**, 145, **172**
    Severina **172**
Torrens River, *see* River Torrens
Torresan, John **147**
Trentino-Alto Adige (South Tyrol) 190
Trevisani nel Mondo 254, 255

Treviso Province 3, 31n.5, **32**, 67, 254, 269, **272**

Urbani, Monica 259n.2, **260**

Valdobbiadene 31n.5
Valentini, Aida (nee Recchi) 236
Valetta Road 50, **78**, 81, 82, **100**, **143**, 145, 205, **228**, 240, 249
Vallà 31n.5, 55, 71
Veneto Club 10, 229, 251, 252, **253**–4, 257
Venice 156
Vicenza 31n.5, **32**, 39, 60, 230, 259n.2
Victoria 10, 30, 42, 76, 142, 160, 162, **198**, 231, 261n.5, 262n.7
Virginia 204
Visentin, Costantina (Santin) 81, 156, 205, **206**

Waymouth Street (City of Adelaide) 52, 171
Werribee 262n.7
West Lakes **155**
White Australia policy 6n.5, 8, 26, 37, 133, 157, 169
Wollongong 259
World War I 2, 6, 16, 35, 36, 74, 85
World War II 6, 7, 18, 20, 24, 25, 26, 29, 57, 63, **65**, 79–80, 82, 84, 85, 86, 88–9, 117, 133, 162, 169, 171–6, **177**, 178–92, 194, 195–6, 211, 237, 261, 262
    interwar migration 4, 6, 32, 35, 47–8, 133, 157, 228, 252, 277, 279
    interwar period 2, 5–7, 9, 13, 16, 24, 30, 54, 66, 71, 76, 98, 129, 131, 142, 162, 231, 241, 261
    postwar migration 6, 15, 17, 20, 26, 132, 135, 140, 149, 164, 165, 166, 196, 222, 228, 229, 236, 237–8, 250, 251, 252, 253, 262

postwar period 8, 9, 10, 26, 45, 46, 58, 89, 91, 107–8, 126, 146, 148, 163, 196, 200, 208, 214, 237–8, 262–3, 266
pre-war migration 6, 7, 8, 9, 35, 175
pre-war period 10, 46, 71, 79, 148, 201
Wyatt, Albert 125

York, Duke and Duchess of 75

Zalunardo
    Eugenio 43, 64, **65**, 77, **159**, **219**, 250
    family 235
    Luigia (Luigina) (nee Ballestrin) 64, **65**, **105**
    Noemi (Campagnolo) 102, **105**, 121, 124, **159**, 218, **219**
    Renato **219**
Zampin
    Amelia (nee Shaw) **30**, **63**–4, 94, **253**
    Angela **253**
    Bruna (Semola) 29, **30**, 120, 222, **253**
    Christine 95, **139**, 236, **253**
    Cynthia **253**
    Delia **274**
    Dennis **274**
    family 33, 94, **95**–6, **168**, 195
    Irene 273, **274**, 275
    Lui **274**
    Milva (Rebuli) 94–5, 236, **253**
    Nico **274**
    Peter **95**, 96, **139**
    Roma (Bordignon) **253**
    Sandra (Semola) 122, **124**, 218, **253**
    Silvano 30, **63**–4, 94, **95**, 96, **139**, **243**, **253**
    Teresa (Mazzarolo) 165, 273, **274**, 275–6
    Virginia (Rodato) **139**, 242, 244, **253**
Zanatta, Rosalia (Piovesan) 59, 215
Zoanetti
    family 190
    Giosue 190, **191**–3, 196
    Mary (Tonellato) **14**, 90, 91, 104, 190, 192, 193–4, 235
    Metilde 190, 192–3, 194
Zolin, Father Paul 162–3

www.ingramcontent.com/pod-product-compliance
Lightning Source LLC
Chambersburg PA
CBHW051600230426
43668CB00013B/1926